OUR NATIONAL WETLAND HERITAGE
A PROTECTION GUIDEBOOK

Dr. Jon A. Kusler

assisted by
Corbin C. Harwood
Richard B. Newton

published under the supervision of
Timothy R. Henderson

An Environmental Law Institute Publication

First Printing: April 1983
Second Printing: May 1984
Third Printing: April 1985
Library of Congress Catalog Card Number: 83-80869
ISBN: O-911937-11-0

Manufactured in the United States of America

THE ENVIRONMENTAL LAW INSTITUTE

The Environmental Law Institute is a nonprofit national center for research on environmental law and policy. Founded in 1969, the Institute specializes in multi-disciplinary analyses of issues concerning the design, implementation and effectiveness of environmental quality management programs. The Institute's research is complemented by an extensive publications program and a variety of educational activities that include conferences and continued legal education courses. The Institute's flagship publication, the **Environmental Law Reporter,** is a monthly looseleaf reporting service that describes and comments on developments in environmental law. Other Institute publications include the **Environmental Forum** and the **National Wetlands Newsletter.**

The views expressed in this study are those of the author and do not necessarily reflect those of the staff or Board of Directors of the Environmental Law Institute.

Copies of this study may be purchased from:

The Environmental Law Institute
Suite 600
1346 Connecticut Avenue, N.W.
Washington, D.C. 20036

ACKNOWLEDGEMENTS

This guidebook is based upon an earlier technical report prepared with funding from the Fish and Wildlife Service, U.S. Department of the Interior. Publication of the guidebook would not have been possible without this assistance and encouragement. The Service should be applauded for its many fine efforts to further understanding of wetlands values. The funding support for this earlier report is gratefully acknowledged as well as the cooperation and guidance of Service staff.

Many individuals contributed to the present efforts. Corbin Harwood of the Environmental Law Institute was responsible for the general coordination of the study and a portion of the research. Richard Newton of the University of Massachusetts Institute for Man and Environment surveyed local wetland protection efforts and provided able research on many points. He also produced many of the graphics and photos. John Clark of the Conservation Foundation, Barbara Bedford of the University of Wisconsin, and Professor Joseph Larson of the University of Massachusetts contributed expert advice. Timothy R. Henderson, Staff Attorney at the Environmental Law Institute, orchestrated the production of the final camera ready copy, provided editorial assistance, and updated portions of the final manuscript. Karla Heiman and Janice Goldman, researchers at the Environmental Law Institute, investigated key topics. Editorial support was provided by William Toner, Carl Nelson, M.J. Marvin, and Tara Gallagher. Jean Holland assisted in the technical production of the draft and Scott Custin mocked up the final copy. Office space and research facilities were provided by the Environmmental Law Institute and by the University of Massachusetts Institute for Man and Environment. The effort of John Montanari, Bill Wilen, Porter Reed, and Marge Kolar and the many program personnel and researchers at the levels of government who supplied information and reviewed project drafts are greatly appreciated. The help and comments of Dr. Allan Hirsch, Dr. Hank Sather and Joseph Towsend were also invaluable.

To all contributors, a hearty thanks. The study would not have been possible without your help.

Dr. Jon A. Kusler
Attorney at Law

FOREWORD

This report was prepared by the Environmental Law Institute's Wetlands Program to assist local governments in developing and strengthening wetland protection programs. This work is a companion volume to Strengthening State Wetland Regulations published in 1980. Both reports were funded by the Fish and Wildlife Service, U.S. Department of the Interior, in conjunction with a broader effort to prepare and conduct a national wetlands inventory and provide technical services to states. State and local efforts are needed to reinforce the federal legal framework provided by the Clean Water Act of 1977, the National Coastal Zone Management Program, the National Flood Insurance Program, and initiatives of the U.S. Soil Conservation Service and other agencies.

Our Wetland Heritage represents a unique contribution to the literature on wetlands values and management techniques. Readers will find information on why wetlands are valuable, and ways different local governments manage their wetland areas. Regulations from a number of states and localities are reviewed, as are examples of court decisions from jurisdictions throughout the nation. Recognizing that long-term protection of these areas will require private as well as government commitment, the guidebook describes examples of private wetland management and protection efforts. Few wetlands studies offer such a comprehensive review.

Publication of Our Wetland Heritage is particularly timely. It will aid local governments and states in assuming the larger protection and management role being thrust upon them under the New Federalism. Regulations have been proposed by both the Army Corps of Engineers and the Environmental Protection Agency to reduce their jurisdiction under Section 404 of the Clean Water Act over dredge and fill activities in wetlands. Federal funds for aiding state and local acquisition programs have been cut, including those from the Coastal Zone Management Program, and the Heritage Conservation and Recreation Service. More than ever before, state and local governments and the private sector will have to actively participate in land use decisions if the nation's remaining wetlands are to be managed properly. Our Wetland Heritage offers the state, local and private wetland manager a valuable tool to use in accepting the added responsibility.

The guidebook represents the culmination of a six-year effort by the Institute and Dr. Jon Kusler. We hope that you find the materials interesting and useful not only for the purpose of preparing local ordinances which comply with the commands of state and federal law, but also for providing technically sound and politically acceptable wetland management efforts which will result in increased protection of this important resource. The Environmental Law Institute has designed the report to serve this broader goal.

J. William Futrell
President
Environmental Law Institute

SUMMARY AND RECOMMENDATIONS

This guidebook is for local governments, conservation organizations, landowners and others interested in the protection of wetlands through local action. It reflects a careful literature review, an examination of State wetland statutes and programs, a survey of local wetland protection programs, an examination of all reported wetland cases, the papers presented at the first National Wetland Symposium in 1977, and many interviews with scientists, lawyers, engineers and others.

Chapters 1 and 2 discuss the need to protect and manage wetlands, threats to wetlands, and wetland origins and characteristics. Chapters 3, 4 and 5 identify management principles and standards, wetland protection techniques, and procedures for evaluation of development proposals. Chapters 6, 7, and 8 consider Federal, State and local regulatory efforts. Chapter 9 addresses legal issues in wetland regulation. Chapters 10 and 11 consider nonregulatory management techniques and the role of the private sector in wetland protection. The Appendices include a draft wetland protection ordinance, examples of wetland protection ordinances, a guide to federal programs which affect wetlands, a list of endangered animal species dependant on wetlands, and examples of deed restrictions.

It is recommended local government protect wetlands by:

1. Adopting a general wetland protection policy. Community leaders should by ordinance or by-laws, adopt a wetland protection and management policy for public and private uses. This policy can serve as a guide for comprehensive land and water use planning, public faciltiies planning and construction, the issuance of grants-in-aid, public land use management, regulation, land acquisition, tax assessment, and other implementation efforts. This policy may be designed to:

   (a) Protect public safety from hazards such as increased flooding, water pollution, fill, septic tanks, and chemical storage in wetlands;
   (b) Prevent nuisances from incompatible uses in wetlands and adjacent lands (e.g., industries next to residences);
   (c) Prevent extraordinary costs for municipal services such as roads, water supply and sewage systems in wetland areas subject to repeated flood damages;
   (d) Protect important wetland natural values;
   (e) Ensure that wetland activities are consistent with broader planning and regulatory efforts.

Such a policy may, in some instances, be effective standing alone but can often best be integrated into a comprehensive resource management and planning program that addresses multipurpose needs and goals. Such a policy should be designed to protect wetland functions important to the community including:

   (a) Flood conveyance and flood storage;
   (b) Sediment, erosion, and pollution control;
   (c) Fish, waterfowl, and wildlife habitat;
   (d) Water supply, groundwater recharge;
   (e) Recreation, scientific research and education.

Such a policy should require that those wishing to alter or develop wetland areas should demonstrate that proposed activities cannot be located at upland sites. If activities are conducted in wetlands, measures should be taken to minimize the impact upon wetland functions.

2. <u>Educating the public</u>. The local government should promote public awareness of wetland values and hazards and threats to such areas through citizen workshops, discussions with landowners, lectures, presentations at city council meetings, slide shows, manuals, newspaper articles, pamphlets, films and other techniques. Local conservation commissions or conservation organizations can often take the lead or assist in such educational efforts. Technical assistance and educational materials are available from many sources including state agencies, national conservation organizations, and federal gencies. Wetland, floodplain and soil maps are often helpful in educational efforts.

Local governments should encourage private landowners and conservation organizations (e.g., local chapters of the Nature Conservancy) to adopt wetland protection measures such as deed restrictions, donation of easements, and buffer zones adjacent to wetlands.

3. <u>Identifying and mapping wetland areas</u>. In many instances wetland maps are already available from state wetland programs, the National Wetland Inventory or other sources. If wetland maps are not available or existing maps are at insufficient scale or accuracy, the community should remap wetland areas. Criteria for mapping should reflect the intended uses of the maps. Wetlands maps at a minimum scale of 1 inch equal to 200 to 2,000 feet (depending upon the circumstances) are usually needed for regulatory purposes. It may be unnecessary to map some wetland areas where boundaries may otherwise be defined by easily recognizable vegetation types, tidal action, or elevation.

Map criteria and scale depend upon the intended use for the maps (regulation, acquisition, public information), the nature of the wetlands, and whether refinements are to be made on a case-by-case basis as individual developments are proposed. Large-scale maps are often desirable for urban areas, but are very expensive and may give a false impression that wetland boundaries are unchangeable and can be located with mathematical precision. Where small-scale maps are developed (1 inch equals 2,000 to 4,000 feet), written wetland definition criteria based upon predominant vegetation, soil type, elevation, etc. should be provided in policy statements and regulations. These criteria can be applied through field surveys to resolve boundary disputes. Interim regulations may be adopted based upon existing information sources although relatively accurate maps are more desirable.

Where acquisition is desirable, a community may wish to evaluate and rank wetlands based upon the relative importance of their values and hazards. Ranking may be used to define acquisition priorities and help evaluate development permits. However, ranking should be approached with care. First, ranking may require large quantities of data to evaluate all relevant factors. Second, a determination that a particular wetland is of lesser importance than another may imply that the lower ranked wetland should be developed, but a low ranked wetland may be less environmentally desirable for development than virtually all upland areas. Evaluation of relative importance (if it is to be undertaken) should take into account: wetland values and hazards; the accessibility of areas for public use; sensitivity of areas; and threats from development.

4. <u>Acquiring wetlands requiring total protection</u>. Acquisition in fee simple is appropriate where active public use is planned for recreation, scientific research, or educational purposes. Public purchase is expensive but provides a high degree of protection and permits public use. Community acquisiton may be assisted in part by Federal and State open space, recreation, and wilflife grant-in-aid programs. Easement acquisition is most appropriate where development control is necessary and intensive public use of land is not contemplated.

Private donation of wetlands to the community or to conservation organizations such as the Nature Conservancy or Audubon Society may be encouraged through public education and by publicizing tax advantages. Donations often qualify landowners for substantial income, gift, estate, or real estate tax benefits.

5. <u>Regulated wetlands activities</u>. The community should regulate wetland activities which increase damages from natural hazards, threaten wetland values, cause water pollution, cause nuisances or otherwise threaten the public welfare. Regulations require an accurate data base, continuing political support, and expertise in administration and enforcement.

Regulations may, in some instances, take the form of ordinances or resolutions endorsing and adopting as a matter of community policy state wetland regulations and federal 404 permit procedures. Performance standards related to wildlife, recreation and other wetland values can be added to the flood standards for a community with floodplain or agricultural zoning. For rural areas with little development pressure, partial protection may be afforded wetlands through sanitary codes prohibiting on-side waste disposal in high groundwater areas and subdivision of flood prone lands. Regulations may also take the form of special permit requirements, zoning, subdivision regulations, regulating for filling, dredging, or grading, tree-cutting regulations, pollution controls, special wetland regulations, or other special codes.

Where zoning boards and governmental bodies such as city councils lack the biological and engineering expertise needed to develop regulations and evaluate permits, special expert local boards or agencies such as conservation commissions may be created. Citizen advisory boards may also be created to make recommendations to boards of adjustment, planning commissions, or other responsible bodies. State and federal agencies may provide technical assistance in wetland evaluation. Technical assistance may also be sought from universities, citizens, environmental organizations, and consulting firms.

Two principal regulatory approaches may be taken; (1) prohibition of all fills, dredging, and structural uses while permitting most open space uses; and (2) performance standards for wetland uses that require the valuation of each proposed use on its merits through special permit procedures. Often regulations may best prohibit a small number of uses with serious impact; permit a substantial number of open space uses that have minimal impact; establish special permit requirements for uses that may or may not have acceptable impact, depending upon the project design and site conditions.

Performance standards for wetland activities should:

- Protect wetland water supply and water regime;
- Protect wetland topographic features (depth, shoreline configuration, etc.) and flora and fauna;
- Provide a buffer between the wetland and upland activities;

- Prevent wetland activities which will increase flooding or other hazards at upland sites;
- Ensure that wetland activities are consistent with broader community, state, and regional land use planning and regulatory standards;
- Ensure that, if wetland activities are to occur, measures be taken to minimize their impact upon wetland functions;

Wetland regulations should take into account the cumulative impact of proposed uses in evaluating individual development applications.

After regulations are adopted, aggressive prosecution of wetland violations is needed to prevent and remedy unauthorized wetland alterations and to deter further violations. Sanctions may include fines, jail sentences, injunctions preventing violations and requiring restoration of the wetland. Where violations are not remedied, the regulatory agency (assuming adequate statutory authority) should remove the violating materials, restore the wetland, and charge landowners.

To avoid legal problems, the community should carefully comply with statutory procedures in adopting regulations. Where detailed wetland maps are not available, site-specific data gathering and relatively precise wetland definition criteria can resolve boundary disputes. The application of performance standards can help avoid claims of taking of private property without compensation.

6. Reduce property tax assessments. Local governments should ensure that property tax assessments reflect wetland use restrictions. Reductions in local property tax assessment may be accomplished in some instances by requiring that assessors consider regulations in their assessment. Landowners may also be encouraged to enroll their lands in special open space preferential tax assessment programs adopted in at least 42 states. Landowners may also qualify for tax reductions by executing deed restrictions or granting easements for wetland protection.

7. Undertaking rehabilitation efforts. In some instances, communities may initiate wetland rehabilitation efforts for damaged or destroyed areas to reestablish natural wetland vegetation and hydrologic regimes. If rehabilitation is infeasible, new wetlands areas may be created at other sites. The possibility of wetland destruction should not be used as a justification for wetland destruction, however, because artificial wetlands may not serve all natural wetland functions and the costs of creating and maintaining them can be high.

SUMMARY OF CONTENTS

APPENDICES

LIST OF TABLES

LIST OF FIGURES

CHAPTER 1: WHY PROTECT WETLANDS?

1.1 A Vanishing Resource

Early settlers found vast coastal and inland wetlands among the eastern and Gulf coasts, in the northern glaciated States, and along the floodplains of rivers and streams throughout the nation. (See Figure 1.) These areas were viewed as wastelands, sources of mosquitoes and impediments to development and travel. Their importance to fish and game, clear water and the beauty of the land was unappreciated. Draining and filling were applied without concern or knowledge of their impact on broader water resource systems. By 1954, drainage, fill, and construction had destroyed almost 40 percent of the nation's wetlands.[1]

In the last two decades, coastal and inland wetland values and the hazards that accompany their destruction have been well documented.

Some of these values and hazards and the activities which threaten them are outlined below and in Figure 2 and Table 1.

1.2 Wetland Values

Important natural wetland functions include:

Flood Conveyance. Riverine wetlands and adjacent floodplain lands often form natural floodways that convey flood waters from upstream to downstream points. Floodplains have been created by flood flows and provide a natural flood conveyance configuration. Fills or structures located within floodway areas block flood flows, causing increased flood heights on adjacent and upstream lands and increased downstream velocities.

Barriers to Waves and Erosion. Coastal wetlands and those inland wetlands adjoining larger lakes and rivers reduce impact of storm tides and waves before they reach upland areas. Waves break on beach and wetland areas, dissipating much of their energy. Mats of wetland vegetation, with their complicated root systems, bind and protect soil against erosion. Mangrove forests are particularly resistant.

A study of coral islands off the coast of British Honduras dramatically demonstrated the importance of mangroves. After Hurricane Hattie struck in 1961 with 200 mile-per-hour winds and tides 15 feet above normal, islands covered with natural vegetation suffered little damage and actually accumulated new material left by the storm. Islands cleared of natural vegetation were severely eroded. Since 1830, at least 20 of the cleared and farmed islands have totally disappeared due to the erosive force of tropical storms.[2]

Flood Storage. Inland wetlands may store water during times of flood and slowly release it to downstream areas, lowering flood peaks. (See Figure 3.) When severe floods struck eastern Pennsylvania sweeping out hundreds of bridges, two bridges of the type destroyed elsewhere were left standing below Cranberry Bog, a natural area protected by The Nature Conservancy.[3] The importance of wetlands in flood storage can be grasped when it is recognized that a one-acre wetland will hold 330,000 gallons of water if flooded to a depth of one foot.

A flood study of the Connecticut River indicated that wetlands reduced peak flows.[4] A study by the Massachusetts Water Resources Commission on the Neponsit River indicated that the loss of 10 percent of the wetlands along the river would result in flood stage increases of one and a half feet and that a loss of 50 percent would increase flood stage by three feet.[5] A 1965 study of the Charles River by the U.S. Army Corps of Engineers determined that if 40 percent of the Charles River wetlands were lost, flood stages in the middle and upper river would increase two to four feet, increasing annual losses by $800,000. Reversing an earlier recommendation for construction of a dam, the Corps recommended protection of 17 wetland parcels constituting 8,500 acres.[6]

Sediment Control. Wetlands reduce flood flows and the velocity of flood waters, reducing erosion and causing flood waters to release their sediment. Wetland vegetation filters and holds sediment which would otherwise enter lakes and streams. Unretarded, sediment may result in rapid filling of lakes and reservoirs, and the destruction of fish habitats.

Pollution Control. Wetlands protect water bodies from sediments, nutrients, and other natural and man-made pollutants. Wetland vegetation filters sediment, organic matter, and chemicals while micro-organisms utilize dissolved nutrients and break down organic matter. (See Figure 4.) A study of Tinicum Marsh in Pennsylvania revealed significant reductions in BOD (biochemical oxygen demand), phosphorus, and nitrogen within three to five hours in samples taken from heavily polluted waters flowing through a 512-acre marsh.[7] A study on the effects of a wetland adjacent to Lake Wingra in Wisconsin indicated that 200-300 kg/yr of phosphorus now entering the lake would have been trapped, had not 300 wetland acres been destroyed by development.[8] A number of investigators are now studying the use of man-made or natural wetlands as tertiary treatment facilities for domestic, industrial, and storm water wastes.[9]

Fish and Shellfish. Coastal wetlands are important sources of nutrients for commercial fin and shellfish industries. The net primary productivity (net plant growth) of salt marshes exceeds that of all but the most intensively cultivated agricultural areas. Estimates of 10 tons per acre per year for Spartina alterniflora have been made.[10]

When wetland plants die, decay bacteria and fungi transform the tissues into minute fragments of food and vitamin rich detritus which are carried into tidal creeks, bays, and offshore waters. Many species of sport and commercial fish and shellfish are dependent upon this detritus. In addition, salt marshes provide protected nursing areas for the fingerlings of important commercial fishes such as cod, herring, and mackerel. The nearshore and continental shelf fishing of the U.S. exceeds 4.3 million pounds with a value of $520 million dollars.[11] Investigators have estimated that 90 percent of the species of commercial importance either pass their entire lives in estuarine environments or require estuaries as nursery grounds.[12]

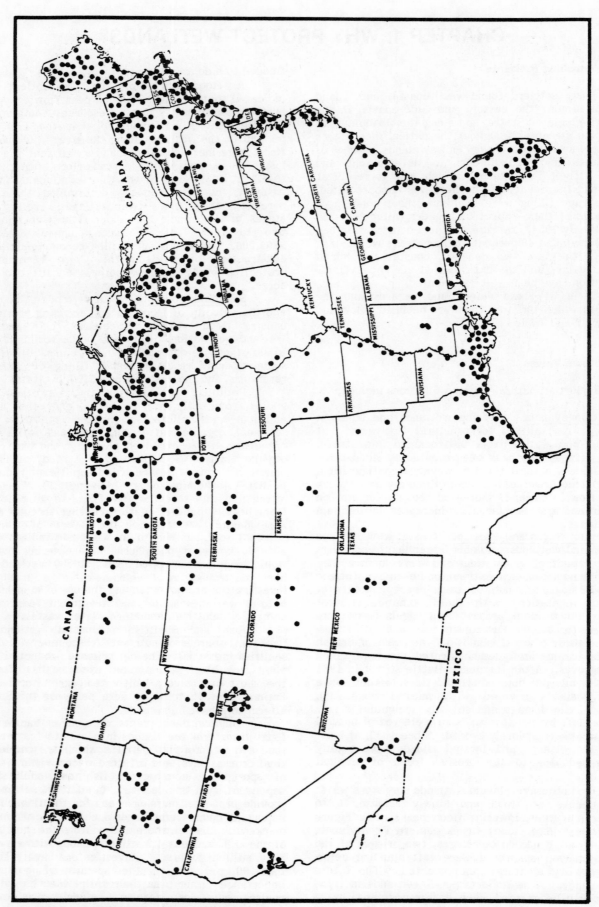

FIGURE 1. WETLANDS OF THE UNITED STATES

REAL ESTATE VALUES MAY BE ENHANCED BY ADJACENT WETLANDS. Photo source: Jon Kusler.

Inland wetlands are also important to freshwater fisheries as spawning grounds for species such as northern pike and, to a lesser extent, walleyes and muskies.

Habitat for Waterfowl and Other Wildlife. Both coastal and inland wetlands provide essential breeding, nesting, feeding, and predator escape habitats for many forms of waterfowl, mammals and reptiles.[13] The land-water interface, including upland buffer areas, is among the richest wildlife habitats in the world. This concentration of wildlife is due to the presence of: abundant water needed by all life forms; rich and diverse vegetation which serves as the basis for food chains; and adequate cover provided by both wetland and shore vegetation.

Many well known wildlife species, including ducks, geese, swans, herons, marsh hawks, egrets, muskrats, minks, beavers, otters and alligators depend upon wetlands for survival. Other species such as ospreys, marsh birds, song birds, pheasants, grouse, bobcats, raccoons and minks use wetlands for nesting, resting, or feeding areas.

The habitat value of a wetland depends upon the following factors: the diversity and arrangement of vegetation; the amount of open water; the arrangement of vegetation relative to the water; the relationship of the wetland to topographic features, lakes, streams and other wetlands; the size of the wetland and surrounding habitat; water chemistry, and permanence.[14]

Habitat for Rare and Endangered Species. The Bureau of Sport Fisheries and Wildlife in 1966 reported that 327 native vertebrate animals, including 86 different kinds of fishes, had become extinct or were in danger of becoming extinct.[15] Almost 35 percent of all rare and endangered animal species are either located in wetland areas or are dependent upon them, although wetlands constitute approximately 5 percent of the nation's lands (see Appendix E). In addition, many of the endangered plant species also require wetland habitat. A few examples of wetland dependent endangered species include the American crocodile, Everglade kite, and whooping crane.

Recreation. Twenty million Americans enjoy recreational fishing. Many sport and commercial fishes are dependent upon wetlands as sources for food or spawning. Over two million Americans hunt waterfowl which depend on wetlands for feeding, breeding and resting. Millions more use binoculars and cameras for observing wetland birds and wildlife. In 1965, the Department of the Interior estimated that over 11,000,000 people were engaged in nature study or similar activities.

Water Supply. Wetlands are increasingly important as a source of ground and surface water with the growth of urban centers and dwindling ground and surface water supplies. A study of wetlands in Massachusetts indicates that at least 60 Massachusetts cities and towns have municipal water production wells in or very near wetlands and that the number of wetlands underlain by productive groundwater supplies is large.[16] Wetlands also store and purify surface waters that may be extracted at downstream points.[17]

Food Production. Because of their high natural productivity, both tidal and inland wetlands have unrealized food production potential for harvesting of

3

VALUES

Isolated Wetlands
(Permanently high ground water levels due to discharge and drainage)

1. Waterfowl feeding and nesting habitat
2. Habitat for both upland and wetland species of wildlife
3. Flood water retention area
4. Sediment and nutrient retention area
5. Area of special scenic beauty

Lake Margin Wetlands
1. See values for permanent wetland above
2. Removal of sediment and nutrients from inflowing waters
3. Fish spawning area

Riverine Wetlands
1. See values for isolated wetlands above
2. Sediment control, stabilization of river banks
3. Flood conveyance area

Estuarine and Coastal Wetlands
1. See values for isolated wetlands above
2. Fish and shellfish habitat and spawning areas
3. Nutrient source for marine fisheries
4. Protection from erosion and storm surges

Barrier Island
1. Habitat for dune-associated plant and animal species
2. Scenic beauty

HAZARDS

Isolated Wetlands
1. Flooding and drainage problems for roads and buildings due, in some instances, to widely fluctuating surface and ground water elevations
2. Serious limitations for on-site waste disposal
3. Limited structural bearing capacity of soils for roads and buildings due to high content of organic materials

Lake Margin Wetlands
1. See hazards for isolated wetland above

Riverine Wetlands
1. See hazards for isolated wetlands above
2. Flood conveyance areas subject to deep inundation and high velocity flows
3. Sometimes erosion areas

Estuarine and Coastal Wetlands
1. See hazards for wetlands associated with rivers above
2. Often severe flood hazard due to tidal action, riverine flooding, storm surges, and wave action
3. Sometimes severe erosion area in major flood due to wave action

Barrier Island
1. Often high energy wind and wave zone
2. Often severe erosion problem
3. Protect backlying lands from high energy waves

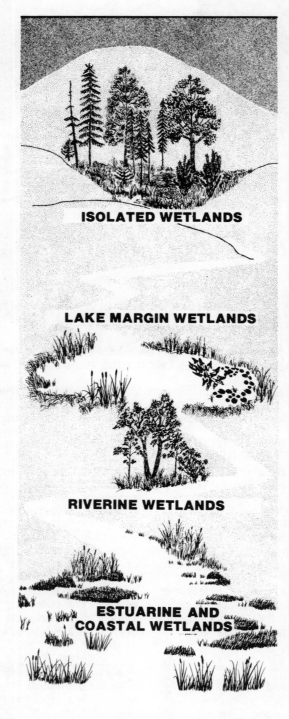

ISOLATED WETLANDS

LAKE MARGIN WETLANDS

RIVERINE WETLANDS

ESTUARINE AND COASTAL WETLANDS

BARRIER ISLAND

FIGURE 2. WETLAND VALUES AND HAZARDS

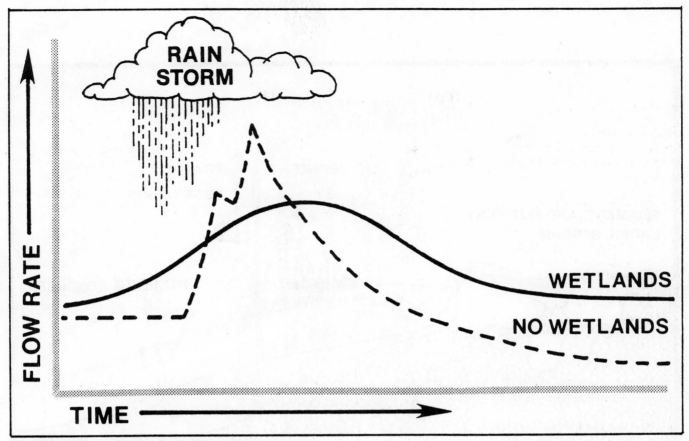

FIGURE 3. WETLANDS REDUCE PEAK FLOWS

marsh vegetation and aquaculture. With an impending world food crisis, this capability may be of international significance. In the past, coastal marshes were extensively harvested for salt hay. While this practice has declined, some harvesting continues both for feed and for use as mulch since salt hay is not subject to the weed seeds that plague inland hay.

Research indicates that cattails hold enormous potential for production of protein. One researcher suggests that cattails may yield up to 150 tons per acre and produce 35 tons of cattail flour.[18]

Coastal aquaculture, such as propagation of oysters, also has considerable potential. Oyster meats could be produced from New England grounds at the rate of 2,000 pounds per acre.[19] Inland aquaculture, such as raising carp and catfish, is even more promising. In 1954, less than 100,000 pounds of catfish were produced by fish farming. In 1973, production exceeded 50 million pounds.[20]

In some instances wetland crops may be more valuable than domestic crops. For example, a study showed that in Southampton Town, Suffolk County, New York, gross income from potato land was $520 an acre while costs of production ranged from $325 to $625 an acre. In contrast, shellfish income in the town ranged from a low of $750 an acre to $4,000 an acre with minimal production costs.[21]

Timber Production. Forested wetlands are an important source of timber despite the physical problems of timber removal. For example, timber production on 2,300 acres of the Alcovy River in Georgia was estimated to be worth $1,578,720 per year ($686 per acre per year).[22]

Historic, Archaeological Values. Some wetlands are of archaeological interest. Indian settlements are located in coastal and inland wetlands which served as sources of fish and shellfish.[23] Wetlands such as the Everglades in Florida and the Concord Marshes in Massachusetts bear important historical associations as wildlife and hunting areas, battlegrounds, and sites of early settlements.[24] Dismal Swamp in North Carolina and the cypress swamps in Louisiana were used as hiding places by runaway slaves.

Education and Research. Both tidal and coastal marshes provide educational opportunities for nature observation and scientific study. Examples include the Orono Bog used by the University of Maine, wetlands in the University of Wisconsin Arboretum, Mamacoke Island Marshes of the Connecticut Arboretum used by Connecticut College and the W.M. Walter Natural Area (a wetland area) used by Western Illinois University. At the Thames Science Center, affiliated with the Connecticut Arboretum, guided tours of wetland areas have been held for thousands of school children.

Open Space and Aesthetic Values. Both tidal and inland wetlands are areas of great diversity and beauty and provide open space for recreational and visual enjoyment. Lands adjacent to scenic salt marshes bring prices of $40,000-$60,000 an acre in Cape Cod, Massachusetts, and even higher prices in some urban areas. Visual values depend upon wetland type, size, landform, contrast, and diversity, as well as associated water body size and type, surrounding land use and other factors.

5

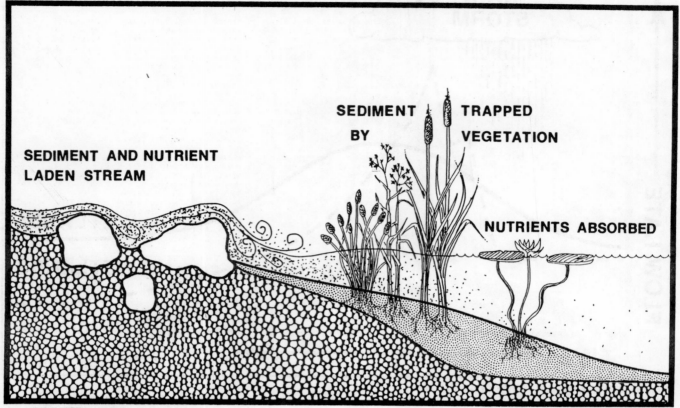

SEDIMENT AND NUTRIENT LADEN STREAM

SEDIMENT TRAPPED BY VEGETATION

NUTRIENTS ABSORBED

FIGURE 4. WETLANDS PURIFY WATER

1.3 Wetland Hazards

The importance of wetlands in conveying flood flows, storing flood waters, and acting as storm barriers was noted above. Activities in wetlands may (1) increase flood and erosion damages on other lands; and (2) be themselves subject to flood damages.

Flood Hazard. Coastal flood hazard maps prepared by the National Flood Insurance Program reveal that coastal wetlands are, with little exception, subject to serious flood hazards due to deep and frequent inundation by storm surges, and high tides. The line of wetland vegetation generally lies well within the 100 year flood line used for floodplain regulation. Coastal wetland vegetation is, in itself, evidence of low elevation and periodic inundation by salt water. During extreme flood events, such areas may be flooded to heights of 10 to 15 feet or more and buffeted by large waves.

Coastal flood problems grow more serious as the world sea level slowly rises and, in some instances, coastal land actually sinks due to compaction of peat, loss of water from aquifers, or tectonic adjustments of the earth's crust.[25] Sea level is rising at the rate of about three inches a century on a worldwide basis due to the melting of glaciers. The combined effect of sea level increase and sinking of land areas is particularly serious in areas such as the Louisiana coast and Galveston, Texas.

The filling of coastal wetlands or the construction of minor sea walls may increase flood problems. Filling often steepens the gradient of beach, causing waves to break destructively upon the newly created lands. In extreme flood events, sea walls may tear free and add to the enormous force of incoming storm waves and high velocity flood flows. The filling of inland wetlands also increases flood problems. Fills and development within these areas block the passage of flood waters, thereby increasing flood heights and velocities on other lands.

The velocity, frequency and duration of flooding depends upon the stream and wetland. Wetlands located along small, steep gradient streams in hilly and mountainous regions are often small and subject to high velocity and short duration flooding. In contrast, wetlands located along large, low gradient rivers such as the Mississippi are often large and subject to low velocity and long duration flooding. Even here, however, development near the stream channel may cumulatively block flood flows and destroy flood storage, increasing flood heights in downstream areas.

Ephemeral wetlands, which exist only in the spring or times of heavy rainfall are also flood hazard areas. Buildings located in ephemeral wetlands may be subject to basement flooding and drainage problems as well as inundation. Efforts to reduce flooding through construction of ditches or installation of drain tiles with outlets to downstream waters increase runoff and decrease groundwater recharge.

In summary, any fill or drainage of an inland wetland area may block flood flows or increase the

6

TABLE 1. WETLAND FUNCTIONS

WETLAND FUNCTION	CONCERN	HOW WETLANDS PERFORM FUNCTION	FACTORS DETERMINING IMPORTANCE OF FUNCTION	DISCIPLINE NEEDED FOR ANALYSIS
Flood Conveyance	If flood flows are blocked by fills, dikes, or other structures, increased flood heights and velocities result, causing damage to adjacent, upstream and down-stream areas.	Some wetlands (particularly those immediately adjacent to rivers and streams) serve as floodway areas by conveying flood flows from upstream to downstream points.	Stream characteristics, wetland topography and size, vegetation, location of wetland in relationship to river or stream, existing encroachment on flood-plain (dikes, dams, levees, etc.).	Engineer Hydrologist Soil Scientist Wetland Biologist
Wave Barriers	Removal of vegetation increases erosion and reduces capacity to moderate wave intensity.	Wetland vegetation, with massive root and rhizome systems, bind and protect soil. Vegetation also acts as wave barriers.	Location of wetland adjacent to coastal waters, lakes, and rivers, wave intensity, type of vegetation, and soil type.	Soil Scientist Engineer Ecologist
Flood Storage	Fill or dredging of wetlands reduces their flood storage capacity.	Some wetlands store and slowly release flood waters.	Wetland area relative to watershed, wetland position within watershed, surrounding topography, soil infiltration capacity in watershed, wetland size and depth, stream size and characteristics, outlets (size, depth), vegetation type, substrate type.	Engineer Hydrologist Soil Scientist Wetland Biologist
Sediment Control	Destruction of wetland topographic contours or vegetation decreases wetland capacity to filter surface runoff and act as sediment traps. This increases water turbidity and siltation of downstream reservoirs, storm drains, and stream channels.	Wetland vegetation binds soil particles and retards the movement of sediment in slowly flowing water.	Depth and extent of wetland, wetland vegetation (including type, condition density, growth patterns), soil texture type and structure, normal and peak flows, wetland location relative to sediment of vegetated buffer.	Soil Scientist Engineer Ecologist Range Scientist
Pollution Control	Destruction of wetland contours or vegetation decreases natural pollution capability, resulting in lowered water quality for downstream lakes, streams, and other waters.	Wetlands act as settling ponds and remove nutrients and other pollutants by filtering and causing chemical breakdown of pollutants.	Type and size of wetland, wetland vegetation (including type, condition, density, growth patterns), source and type of pollutants, water course, size, water volume, streamflow rate, microorganisms, etc.	Sanitarian Soil Scientist Geologist Hydrologist Engineer Ecologist Botanist Biologist Chemist
Fish and Wildlife Habitat	Fills, dredging, damming, and other alterations destroy and damage flora and fauna and decrease productivity. Dam construction is an impediment to fish movement.	Wetlands provide water, food supply, and nesting and resting areas. Coastal wetlands contribute nutrients needed by fish and shellfish to nearby estuarine and marine waters.	Wetland type and size, dominant wetland vegetation (including diversity of life form), edge effect, location of wetland within watershed, surrounding habitat type, juxtaposition of wetlands, water chemistry, water quality, water depth, existing uses.	Ecologist Biologist Forrester Soil Scientist Botanist Wetland Biologist Wildlife Biologist Fisheries Biologist
Recreation (water-based)	Fill, dredging or other interference with wetlands will cause loss of area for boating, swimming, bird watching, hunting, and fishing.	Wetlands provide wildlife and water for recreational uses.	Wetland vegetation, wildlife, water quality, accessibility to users, size, relative scarcity, facilities provided, surrounding land forms, vegetation, land use, degree of disturbance, availability of similar wetlands, distribution, proximity of uses, vulnerability.	Planner Sociologist Ecologist Landscape Architect Recreational Planner
Water Supply (surface)	Fills or dredging cause accelerated runoff and increase pollution.	Some wetlands store flood waters, reducing the timing and amount of surface runoff. They also filter pollutants. Some serve as sources of domestic water supply.	Precipitation, watershed runoff characteristics, wetland type, size, outlet characteristics, location of wetland in relationship to other water bodies.	Hydrologist Geologist Engineer Soil Scientist Planner
Aquifer Recharge	Fills or drainage may destroy wetland acquifer recharge capability, thereby reducing base flows to streams and groundwater supplies for domestic, commercial, or other uses.	Some wetlands store water and release it slowly to groundwater deposits. However, many other wetlands are discharge areas for a portion or all of the year.	Location of wetland relative to water table, fluctuations in water table, geology including type and depth of substrate, permeability of substrate, size of wetland, depth. Acquifer storage capacity, groundwater flow, runoff retention measures.	Geologist Engineer Hydrologist Soil Scientist Planner

Source: David Lavine et al., *Evaluation of Inland Wetland and Water Course Functions,* Connecticut Inland Wetlands Project (1974) (modified).

7

FILLING OF WETLAND. Filling for roads, solid waste disposal and construction is a major source of urban wetland loss. Photo source: Richard Newton.

amount and speed of surface runoff. The significance of wetland flood conveyance and storage differs depending upon the type of stream and its flood characteristics, watershed characteristics, the location of the wetland in the stream, the configuration and width of the floodway, and alternative flood storage areas.

Erosion. Development in coastal mangrove forests and other coastal wetland vegetation is often subject to severe flood erosion and wind damage and may increase damage to backlying lands.

Inland wetlands help prevent erosion by stabilizing easily erodible banks of lakes and streams. In addition, they reduce erosion on other lands by lowering the velocity of flood waters. Eroded material is trapped in wetland vegetation, protecting adjacent lakes and streams.

Hazards Due to Lack of Soil Support. Coastal and inland wetlands often pose structural support problems for dwellings, other structures, roads, and bridges due to the high organic and water content of wetland soils. Organic and waterlogged soils slowly compact under pressure, resulting in differential settling of construction.[26] In some instances, this may cause flooding, and, more often, cracks and shifts in building foundations and walls.

Hazards Due to Limitations for Onsite Waste Disposal. Septic tanks and solid absorption systems operate poorly in the high groundwater and organic soils found in wetlands. The plumbing and sanitary codes of many States require that the bottom of the soil absorption system be at least four feet above high groundwater.[27] Failure of a septic tank system may result in surface discharges of raw sewage, causing health hazards, odor nuisances and pollution of nearby waters.

1.4 Wetland Losses

It has been estimated that 45 million acres of an original total of 127 million acres of wetlands had been lost to commercial development, agriculture and other uses.[28] Over 17 million acres were lost in seven States alone.[29]

Much of the remaining wetland has been damaged by water pollution, timber-cutting, land drainage, and other activities. Little remains in a pristine state. One researcher estimated that salt marshes were being destroyed at the rate of one percent per year and that between 1940 and 1969 over 25 percent of the nation's remaining salt marshes were destroyed.[30] Wetland deterioration is due to loss of physical habitat (e.g., dredging), chronic stress, construction projects and pollution.[31]

The following activities have produced severe wetland losses:

o   Wetland drainage for
      -    crop production
      -    timber production
      -    mosquito control
o   Dredging and stream channelization for
      -    reservoir maintenance
      -    access channels
      -    navigation channel maintenance
      -    flood protection
      -    coastal housing developments

WETLAND DRAINAGE. Agriculture drainage is the major cause of wetland loss in the midwest, south and west.

o   Dispersion of water inflows
- irrigation
- flood control

o   Construction of dikes, dams, levees, seawalls for
- flood control
- irrigation
- storm surge protection

o   Filling for
- solid waste disposal
- roads, bridges
- commercial, residential and industrial development
- utility lines

o   Discharges of materials into waters
- herbicides, pesticides and other pollutants from industrial plants, agriculture, mosquito control efforts
- nutrient loadings from domestic sewage and agricultural runoff
- sediments from dredging and filling, agriculture, and land development

o   Surface water extraction and groundwater pumping
- for municipal water supplies and irrigation reduces water supply to wetlands

o   Mining or disturbance of wetland soils for
- sand and gravel
- coal, peat, and other minerals

In summary, most wetlands of the United States are threatened by activities within the wetland or the watershed. Piecemeal destruction and the cumulative impacts of watershed uses are particularly threatening because of their subtlety.

Not all of man's activities result in wetland loss or destruction. A variety of activities which interfere with natural drainage such as road building, irrigation and reservoir construction may increase wetland acreage. However, these new wetlands may be subject to rapid deterioration and widely-fluctuating water levels. As such, they do not perform all the functions of natural wetlands.

9

CHAPTER 2: WETLAND ORIGIN, TYPES

2.1 What is a Wetland?

A wetland is what the term implies—wet land. Questions arise, however, in the more specific application of the term to lands that are flooded infrequently and to lands that are subject to deep and constant flooding such as the littoral zone of the ocean and the beds of lakes or streams. Questions also arise as to appropriate criteria for mapping or otherwise identifying areas with wetland-related characteristics (e.g., vegetation as an indication of high groundwater). The U.S. Fish and Wildlife Service has developed a wetland definition as part of a new national wetland classification system:[1]

Wetlands are lands where saturation with water is the dominant factor determining the nature of soil development and the types of plants and animal communities living in the soil and on its surface.

Wetlands are further defined as:

Lands transitional between terrestrial and aquatic systems where the water table is usually at or near the surface or the land is covered by shallow water. For the purposes of this classification, wetlands must have one or more of the following three attributes: (1) at least periodically, the land supports predominantly hydrophytes; (2) the substrate is predominantly undrained hydric soil; and (3) the substrate is not soil and is saturated with water or covered by shallow water at some time during the growing season of each year.

Of the systems for classifying wetlands used, the best known is contained in the U.S. Fish and Wildlife Service publication Wetlands of the United States, Fish and Wildlife Service, Circular 39, published in 1956.[2] This classification uses common terms such as "fresh meadows," "shrub swamps," "wooded swamps," "bogs," "marshes," "salt marshes," and "mangrove swamps" to describe 20 types of wetlands in the nation. The problem with this approach is that many different meanings have traditionally been attached to such terms as "swamp," "bog," and "marsh." The new Fish and Wildlife Service classification, entitled, Classification of Wetland and Deepwater Habitats of the United States, meets this problem by providing a new objective set of terms which provide a common terminology for description of wetlands. The classification system progresses from fire systems at the most general level to dominance types based on plant and animal communitites at the most specific level. In addition to the hierarchy of the classification system, these are modifying terms for depth of water, water chemistry, soils and man's influences.

Whatever classification system is used, the actual physical features of the wetland, not its label, are most important from a management perspective. Wetland values, hazards, and management needs are determined by size, shape, depth, water quality, relationship to ground and surface water flow systems, vegetation, wildlife, flood hazards and soils. The following overview describes some important characteristics of wetlands, their origins, and their diversity within the United States.

2.2 Wetlands and the Water Cycle

Wetlands, as noted earlier, are lands dominated by an excess of water. At coastal locations, water comes principally from the sea through daily tidal action, storm surges, seiches, and wave action. Sea water may travel some distance inland along the surface and in the groundwater systems.

In estuarine environments, the water comes both from the sea and inland sources. In inland environments, water comes from direct precipitation on the wetland, surface runoff, and discharges from groundwater.

Most inland wetlands are closely connected with or adjacent to lakes and streams where a portion of the water comes from or is discharged to the adjacent water bodies. Many others are groundwater discharge areas where the wetland intersects the groundwater table.

Although many inland wetlands are groundwater discharge areas, some ephemeral and floodplain wetlands play important roles in groundwater recharge. In contrast, smaller wetlands are often "perched" above the water table due to the sealing effect of organics or a clay "liner" on their bottoms. The significance of wetlands to water supply, floods, and water quality becomes clear when it is understood that they are a principal conduit for precipitation flowing to the sea. Wetland complexes extend from the headwaters of lakes and streams to small stream tributaries, to the mainstream, and finally to the ocean.

Of course, not all of the water entering wetlands is discharged to surface or recharged to groundwater. At the peak of the growing season, wetland plants often use a great quantity of water in evapo-transpiration. In arid regions, a significant portion is returned directly to the atmosphere.

2.3 The Origin of Wetlands

Six principal processes creating wetlands include the following:

Glaciers. A principal group of wetlands is located in the northern tier of States including Alaska, Maine, New York, Michigan, Wisconsin, Minnesota, North Dakota, and Washington. Most of these wetlands were formed by glaciers 9-12,000 years ago. Glaciers created wetlands in several ways. First, the melting of chunks of ice left by receding glaciers created pits and depressions in glacial moraines, till, and outwash. Lakes and wetlands were formed where the depressions intersected the groundwater table or where fine clay and organics sealed their bottoms and permitted the collection of runoff waters. The majority of smaller wetlands in the northern U.S. were formed in this manner. Second, glaciers dammed rivers, often creating glacial lakes, sometimes

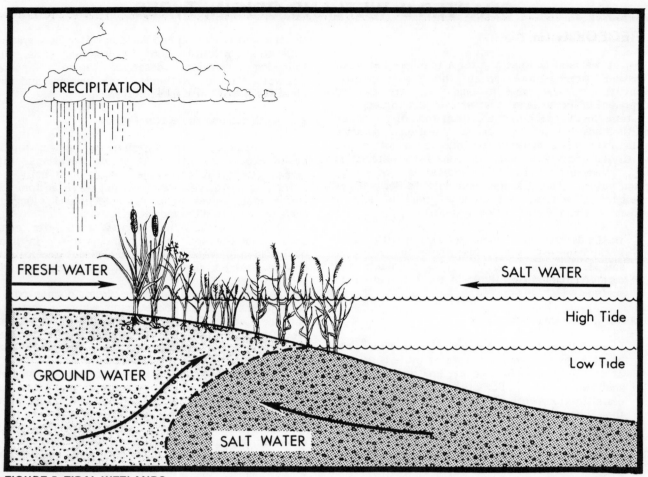

FIGURE 5. TIDAL WETLANDS

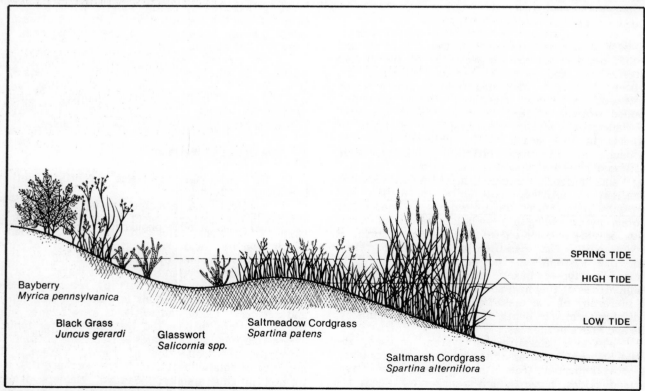

Bayberry
Myrica pennsylvanica

Black Grass
Juncus gerardi

Glasswort
Salicornia spp.

Saltmeadow Cordgrass
Spartina patens

Saltmarsh Cordgrass
Spartina alterniflora

IDEALIZED SALTMARSH SPECIES DISTRIBUTION

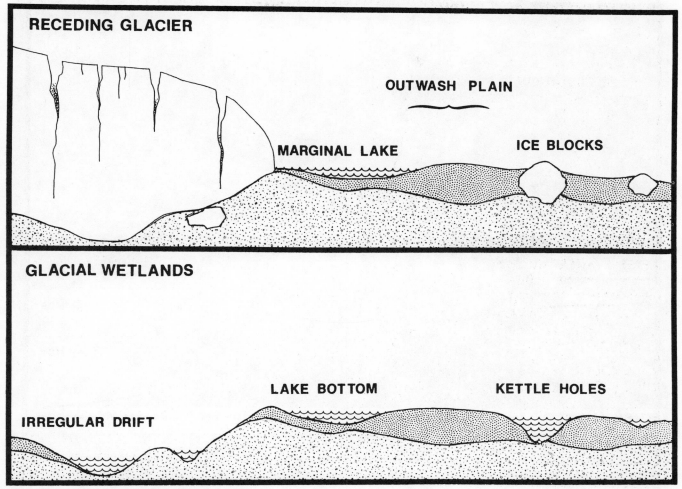

FIGURE 6. GLACIERS CREATE WETLANDS

thousands of square miles in area. Once the ice retreated, the lakes were partially drained resulting in extensive low lying areas with peat deposits. These form some of the large wetlands in the glaciated States. Third, glaciers scooped out and scoured river valleys and soft bedrock deposits creating, in some instances, large, deep lakes such as the Great Lakes and the New York Finger Lakes and, in others, shallow depressions and wetland areas including many wetlands on the Canadian Shield.

Inundation of Wave Protected Coastal Lowlands. A second principal group of wetland areas is located along the Gulf and Atlantic coasts. Coastal wetlands form wherever a gently sloping beach of sand, gravel, silt or other particulate matter is protected from wave action by a harbor, barrier island, or reef. (See Figures 5 and 6.) Wetlands are common along the mouths of rivers and streams. Wetland formation is favored by low elevation topography along the Atlantic and Gulf coasts. Wetland vegetation traps sand and other sediment, gradually building the wetland to a higher elevation. The deposit of organic matter and the formation of peat add to this process. Rising sea levels, due to the melting of glaciers, result in the gradual inland migration of coastal wetlands.

Erosion and Deposition by Rivers. The remaining major wetlands of the U.S. are located along

the floodplains of low gradient rivers such as the Mississippi. River floodplains are erosion-deposition features formed by the downcutting of streams into bedrock and glacial outwash with deposition of river alluvium on adjacent lands during times of flood. Major wetlands are found along mature streams with low gradients and large sediment loadings. These wetlands are periodically flushed and scoured by major floods. New layers of alluvium are deposited by less severe flood events.

Beaver Dams. At one time beaver dams played a major role in forming smaller inland wetlands in the forested areas of the nation. Trapping greatly reduced beaver populations, but regulations have resulted in major increases in both populations and dams during recent years.

Activities of Man. Man has created many wetland areas although the characteristics of the man-made wetlands are often quite different from those of natural wetlands. Major man-made wetlands include reservoirs and farm ponds; wetlands created by water stabilization measures on lakes; pits and depressions created by gravel pits and mines; poor drainage areas caused by roads, irrigation systems, levees, fills and buildings, and wetlands created intentionally by Federal, State, and local conservation groups. Reservoirs are often subject to severe water level

KETTLE HOLE WETLAND. The melting of an ice block created this Rhode Island wetland. Photo source: Virginia Carter.

RIVERINE WETLAND, NEW SALEM, MASSACHUSETTS. Wetlands are common in the floodplains of low gradient rivers and streams. Photo source: Jon Kusler.

WETLANDS BEHIND A BARRIER ISLAND, SAPELLO ISLAND, GEORGIA. Most coastal wetlands are located behind barrier islands and in estuaries. Photo source: Georgia Department of Natural Resources.

fluctuations. Wetlands associated with gravel pits, mines, roads, and buildings are often subject to sedimentation and pollution problems.

Miscellaneous Processes. Wetlands may be formed by other special processes. For example, wetlands in the sand hills of Nebraska were formed by wind action. The Everglades reflect a unique flow of groundwater and surface water over bedrock at and directly below the surface. Wetlands are found in "sink holes" and other areas where bedrock has been dissolved by percolating water in Kentucky, Indiana, and several other States. Reelfoot Lake in Tennessee was formed by sudden sinking of the earth due to earthquakes. Similarly, San Francisco Bay was formed by movement along the San Andreas fault.

2.4 Wetland Types

Wetlands formed by these processes include both vegetated and nonvegetated areas. Further definitions of the terms used to describe vegetated and nonvegetated wetlands can be found in the Fish and Wildlife classification system Classification of Wetlands and Deepwater Habitats of the United States. Both types have special values and are threatened by fills, dredging and development.

Vegetated Wetlands

Vegetated wetlands include water-dominated lands with trees, shrubs, grasses, sedges, mosses, lichens and aquatic beds.

Forested Wetlands. Forested wetlands are dominated by trees six meters or more in height. They are common in the glaciated regions of the Midwest and Northeast, in mountainous areas, and along low gradient meandering streams particularly in the Southeast and Gulf coast including the lower Mississippi and its tributaries. Mangroves are found in Florida.

Evergreen forested wetlands are widespread in the North where vast acreages of mineral-poor peatland are dominated by black spruce, often in association with the deciduous, needle-leaved larch. Such wetlands are commonly called "swamps." The terms "bog" or "forested bog" have also been applied to mineral-poor organic soils with tree cover and dense ground cover of mosses of the genus Sphagnum.

Along the Atlantic coast, evergreen forested wetlands are dominated by Atlantic white cedar while in the Southeast, evergreen forested wetlands are dominated by the broad-leaved bays. Mangroves are found in tropical and subtropical coastal and estuarine areas.

Deciduous forested wetlands are also widespread throughout the United States, but whereas evergreen forested wetlands tend to be dominant in the far North, the deciduous forested wetlands reach their greatest importance in the South and East. In

15

the Northeast, species such as red maple, black ash, and American elm are found on both organic and mineral soils. Deciduous forested wetlands in the South are represented by a large number of tree species. Some of the most important are the cypress, the gum, the elm-ash-maple association, and several species of oak. These southern wetlands are often referred to as "swamps" or "bottomlands", but isolated islands within emergent wetlands are also called "hammocks" and "heads".

In the central and western parts of the country, where the climate is drier, forested wetlands are much less common and are restricted to river courses. Willows and poplars are the prevalent species. Forested wetlands of the mountainous West are similar to northern forested wetlands.

One type of forested wetland, often referred to in the North as a "bog," is of particular interest. Bogs are typically glacial kettle holes with no or poorly defined outlets. They are characterized by acidic waters and a floating mat of peat formed by sphagnum moss and other vegetation. Dead plant remains accumulate due to low oxygen levels. Bogs have low nutrient levels and often contain orchids and insect eating plants such as the pitcher plant and sundew. Common tree species include the black spruce, tamarack, Atlantic white cedar, and red maple.

Forested wetlands located along streams or near marshes are valuable breeding areas for black ducks, wood ducks, and other waterfowl, particularly if surface water persists throughout the nesting period and brood areas are available nearby. They provide habitat for upland wildlife such as deer, raccoons, opossums, snowshoe hares, cottontail rabbits, ruffed grouse, and birds such as warblers, flycatchers, woodpeckers, nuthatches, grosbeaks, hawks, and owls. Forested wetlands are used for commercial timber operations, although problems with access often limit the commercial timber value or result in drainage with extensive adverse impacts.

Flood hazards vary in forested wetlands, yet serious flood hazards are common for wetlands adjacent to major rivers and for mangroves in Florida. Forested wetlands, particularly those located on peaty soils, pose several construction problems.

Scrub/Shrub Wetlands. Scrub/shrub wetlands are dominated by small trees and bushes less than six meters in height. Like forested wetlands, they are widespread throughout the United States, and much of the preceding discussion applies equally to scrub/shrub wetlands. They are found in high groundwater areas and adjacent to rivers, lakes, estuaries, and ocean shores. In estuarine areas they are dominated by plants such as buttonwood, myrtle, and marsh elder. In the North they are often called "bogs" and contain species such as leather leaf. Shrub wetlands may be dominated by either evergreen or deciduous species. A large number of deciduous shrubs occur in wetlands with species of red osier dogwood and willow most common.

Shrub wetlands offer habitat for a wide variety of upland and wetland wildlife. Game birds such as ring-necked pheasants, American woodcocks and ruffed grouse and mammals such as snowshoe hares, cottontail rabbits, and deer are common. The presence of open water enhances these areas for wood ducks and song birds.

Shrub wetlands, like forested wetlands, are often subject to flood hazards, particularly along major rivers and streams and adjacent to tidal marshes.

Emergent Wetlands. Wetlands dominated by emergent vegetation other than trees or shrubs are called "emergent wetlands". They are found throughout the United States and are particularly widespread in coastal areas, adjacent to major lakes and streams and in the arid West where desiccation prevents growth of trees. Wetlands dominated by emergent vegetation such as cattail, bulrush, arrowhead, reedgrass, cordgrass, and sawgrass are generally called "marshes". In the North, extensive areas of emergent wetlands dominated by sedges and grasses growing on peat soils are frequently called "fens". Certain types of wetlands with seasonally-flooded water are called "meadows".

Emergent wetlands dominated by cordgrass and needlerush are the major components of the estuarine systems of the Atlantic and Gulf coasts. On the Pacific coast, glasswort, seablites and saltmarsh hay are dominant.

Emergent wetlands of the "prairie pothole" region are well known as major waterfowl breeding and migration resting areas.

Emergent wetlands are important wildlife habitats. As waterfowl habitat they are used for mating, nesting, brood-rearing, and for resting and feeding during migration. They are attractive to ducks, geese, red-winged blackbirds, and wading birds like herons, egrets and bitterns. Some common mammal species include muskrats, raccoons, minks, cottontail rabbits, and deer.

In general, the absence of trees or shrubs in emergent wetlands is due to frequent flooding. These areas, are, therefore, major flood hazard areas, particularly along major rivers and streams and the coasts.

High organic content in underlying soils is often a structural problem, particularly where emergent wetlands have formed slowly due to high groundwater conditions or the gradual filling of depressions by sediment and organic matter.

Moss/Lichen Wetlands. Mosses and lichens are important components of the flora in many wetlands, especially in the North, but these plants usually form a ground cover under a dominant layer of trees, shrubs or herbs. In those cases were mosses or lichens are not overtopped by other plants for more than 30 percent of the area cover, the area is a moss/lichen wetland. Such wetlands are most common in Alaska. Mosses are of special ecological importance because of their role in peat formation.

These wetlands may be important as resting and feeding habitat for waterfowl during migration and for beavers and muskrats when located adjacent to open water areas. They pose flooding threats and structural bearing capacity problems.

Aquatic Beds. Aquatic beds are wetlands and deepwater habitats dominated by submergent plants, floating-leaved plants or floating plants. They are found in shallow bodies of inland water, at the margins

WETLAND CREATED BY A BEAVER DAM. Wetlands created by beaver dams may last more than 100 years although many are more short-lived. Photo source: Martin Weller.

of larger lakes, streams, and, in some instances, estuarine and coastal waters. They generally occur in sheltered habitats in which there is little water movement and the water depth averages 1-2 meters. The local distribution of these plants is greatly influenced by the type of substrate and the physical nature of the body of water. Typical dominants include water lily, floating-leaved pondweed, and water shield.

Floating-leaved beds are more deepwater habitats than wetlands (in the ordinary sense of the word) but they do form an important transitional habitat. These areas are important feeding and resting areas for waterfowl and spawning grounds and feeding areas for marine and inland fishes.

Nonvegetated Wetlands

In general, the term wetland has been applied to shallow-water areas and moist soil areas where vegetation is present. However, nonvegetated areas which are subject to inundation are also important habitats for certain animal species and serve many of the functions of vegetated areas such as flood storage and aquifer recharge. They are also subject to flood, erosion, and structural bearing capacity problems. Some examples of nonvegetated wetland environments described in the Department of the Interior wetland classification system and in need of protection include the following:

Rocky Shores. Rocky shores are common along the Pacific coast of California, Oregon, and Washington, the northeast Altantic in Maine, the Great Lake shores, and the shores of high gradient streams in mountainous and hilly regions throughout the nation. Rocky shores are high energy environments where bedrock surfaces or stable large rock fragments lie exposed as a result of the continuous erosion by wind-driven waves or currents. Although large boulders may be moved by storm waves or flood flows, the bottom is stable enough to permit the attachment of algae or lichens and the growth of sedentary invertebrates. Despite a lack of vascular vegetation, the areas generally support a rich assemblage of sensitive invertebrates and algae, and are thus vulnerable to walking, hiking, vehicles, and other types of uses. Rocky shores are subject to severe flood and erosion hazards and are highly undesirable sites for development.

Unconsolidated Shores. Unconsolidated shores are formed by erosion and deposition by waves and currents. They may include a number of landforms such as beaches, bars and flats.

Beaches and bars are sloping landforms composed of unconsolidated sand, gravel, or cobbles. They dominate the Gulf of Mexico, the Atlantic and southern California coastlines and are common along the margins of the larger rivers and lakes. Smaller beaches are found at other locations. These areas are

17

**WETLAND IN ABANDONED GRAVEL PIT. Wetlands commonly form where gravel pits intersect the water table.
Photo source: unknown.**

characterized by a shifting, unstable substrate with high permeability, variable surface moisture, high oxygen content in the surface layers, and low organic matter content. Beaches extend landward from the water's edge to a distinct break in the landform (cliff) or to the point of vegetation. Elongate bars, offshore ridges and banks, or mounds, are exposed at low water. The action of waves and currents builds bars, which usually run parallel to the shore.

Beaches and bars are usually sparsely vegetated, although barrier islands, a form of bar, may have substantial vegetation in upland areas. Beaches and bars are populated by a diversity of specialized, burrowing invertebrates (mollusks, crustaceans, echinoderms) and interstitial fauna and flora (including algae, diatoms and polychaetes), which are usually filter feeders. Areas with a high silt content tend to be anaerobic near the surface. They have less pore space and more organic matter and support a relatively small population of burrowing invertebrates. Areas composed of gravel and cobbles are usually nonvegetated and have extremely low animal populations.

Flats are nearly level, unconsolidated substrates and are alternatively flooded and exposed. They are usually located in areas sheltered from strong currents and wave action. They may be composed of fine or coarse mineral sediments or organic materials such as peat. Flats with a high silt content tend to be anaerobic below the surface.

Estuarine and marine flats occur in both regularly flooded and irregularly flooded intertidal zones. Regularly flooded flats support diverse populations of tube dwelling and burrowing invertebrates including worms and clams.

Irregularly flooded flats, sometimes called "salt flats", "pans" or "pannes", are typically high in salinity and are usually surrounded by, or lie on the landward side of emergent wetlands. When they occur within well established stands of emergents, the substrate is sometimes peat. These flats support burrowing crustaceans and often have an algal crust or mat.

Riverine flats are found in low gradient and tidal reaches. They are generally exposed at low water and covered at high water or flood stage. Flats associated with lakes are often uncovered at low water and may include the entire basin of an intermittent lake. In arid areas, flats may be crusted or saturated with salts and referred to as "alkali flats", "salt flats", "salt pans", or "saline seeps". Faunal diversity and abundance varies with salinity, duration of inundation and temperature.

Flats are not generally considered valuable for recreation and are, therefore, often the target for filling, dredging, and lagooning. They do, however, serve as habitat for shellfish and crabs and are important fish, waterfowl and shorebird feeding areas.

Reefs. Reefs are ridges or mound-like structures formed by colonization and growth of sedentary invertebrates, particularly corals, oysters,

18

and tubeworms in marine or estuarine environments. They are characterized by their elevation above surrounding sediments and by their interference with normal wave flow. Frequently reefs contain a great deal of skeletal material in comparison to the amount of living matter. Three principal types of reefs are found: (1) coral reefs in shallow, warm seas in Hawaii, Puerto Rico, the Virgin Islands and southern Florida; (2) mollusk reefs in the marine and estuarine environments of the Pacific, Atlantic and Gulf coasts and in Hawaii and in the Caribbean, and (3) worm reefs, constructed by colonies of serpulid worms living in individual tubes made from cemented sand grains in marine and estuarine tropical waters. Worm reefs are most common along the coasts of Florida, Puerto Rico, and the Virgin Islands.

Reefs represent deepwater habitat rather than wetland environments since they often lie below low tide. Nevertheless, worm and oyster reefs are occasionally awash at low tide. Flats may ultimately form due to deposition of sand and silt by wave action. This process is aided in Florida by the establishment of mangroves in shallow water areas.

Reefs are diverse and highly productive ecosystems which offer a substrate for sedentary and boring organisms and shelter for many others. They are commercially important as habitat for fishes, sponges, and shellfish. They also protect landforms by reducing wave energy before waves reach the coast. Major threats from man include dredging, filling, and many other forms of pollution.

Unconsolidated Bottoms. Unconsolidated bottoms are characterized by the lack of large stable surfaces for plant and animal attachment. They are usually found in low energy areas. Most animals in unconsolidated bottom areas live within the substrate. Principal unconsolidated bottom types include cobble/gravel, sand, mud, and organic matter. Exposure to wave and current action, temperature, salinity and light penetration determine the composition and distribution of organisms.

Unconsolidated bottoms are important habitats for shellfish and fish spawning. Sand and gravel bottoms may provide prime swimming and boating areas.

Principal threats include filling, dredging and extraction of sand and gravel.

Streambeds. Streambeds vary greatly in substrate and form, depending on the gradient of the channel and the velocity of the water. Streambed types, like consolidated bottoms, include bedrock, cobble/gravel, sand, mud, organic matter, and vegetated.

Streambeds may be prime swimming and boating areas as well as fish habitats. Principal threats include dredging and filling which block flood flows and destroy habitats.

Rock Bottoms. Rock bottoms include all wetlands and deepwater habitats with rock substrates and permanently flooded, intermittently exposed, and semipermanently flooded and subtidal water regimes.

The stability of rock bottoms allows a rich assemblage of plants and animals to develop. These environments share many characteristics with the rocky shores described above. Rock bottoms are usually high energy habitats with well aerated waters. Animals that live on the rocky surface are generally firmly attached by hooking or sucking devices although they may move about over the substrate in search of food. Some are permanently attached by cement. A few animals hide in rocky crevices and under rocks, some move rapidly enough to avoid being swept away and others burrow into finer substrates. Rock bottoms take two principal forms: bedrock and rubble.

Rock bottoms are important habitats for trout and other fish. They are threatened by dredging, fills and mining.

CHAPTER 3: WETLAND PROTECTION TECHNIQUES

3.1 Protection Techniques

There is no miracle technique for the protection and management of wetland areas. Efforts to apply the principles outlined in Chapter 4 often require a creative combination of public programs, such as wetland zoning and public acquisition, with private wetland protection by landowners and conservation organizations. Private approaches are discussed in Chapter 11. Public approaches that can be used individually or in combination include (see also Table 2):

o Public education efforts addressed to State and community leaders, interest groups, wetland landowners, and the public at large concerning wetland values and hazards, threats posed to wetlands by various types of development, and the relationship of wetland protection to broader water and land use goals. A high degree of public knowledge and concern is essential for successful wetland regulation and acquisition.

o Encouragement and support for private wetland protection efforts by individual landowners or conservation groups, such as The Nature Conservancy and Audubon Society. Encouragement may take the form of education, technical assistance, and, in some instances, cost sharing.

o Adoption of State and local wetland protection policies through resolutions or ordinances to guide comprehensive land use planning, public facilities planning, public land use management, regulation, land acquisition, tax assessment, and other programs. General policies can serve to coordinate public programs in wetland areas, such as the construction of public roads, dikes, and sewers, that would otherwise undermine private and public protection efforts. Tax incentive policies are also needed since tax assessment at full development value undermines wetland regulations by encouraging construction in wetlands (see Chapter 10).

o Adoption of environmental impact statement requirements for public and private projects. Environmental impact statement requirements can ensure that developers consider impacts of and alternatives to proposed developments but do not in themselves ensure wetland protection unless combined with regulations.

o Adoption of interim or long-term regulations for wetland areas to serve local management and protection goals. Goals may differ depending upon the circumstances and community preferences, but minimal goals often include floodway protection and prevention of pollution. Broader goals and standards are listed in Chapter 4.

o Tight monitoring and enforcement of Federal, State, and local land and water regulations that directly or indirectly affect the use of wetlands. For example, a community can monitor developments requiring U.S. Army Corps of Engineers permits, report violations to the Corps, and participate in hearings on proposed permits. This approach can improve existing Federal regulation without new local regulations. Other existing regulations that may help protect wetland areas, if adequately enforced, include State pollution controls, State and local sanitary codes prohibiting septic tanks in high groundwater areas, floodplain and floodway regulations, State and local subdivision regulations, State dredge and fill acts, State wetland regulations, and local comprehensive zoning regulations. Communities may influence Federal and State projects proposed for wetland areas by reviewing and commenting on environmental impact statements when these statements are required.

o Acquisition of fee or partial interest in specific wetlands. Rarely are sufficient funds available to purchase all wetlands. Therefore, acquisition efforts are generally directed to areas with development threats or special values such as sites of rare and endangered species.

o Rehabilitation of damaged wetland areas. Rehabilitation or restoration of wetland areas is sometimes needed to reduce erosion on denuded areas, recreate flood storage capability, restore and enhance wildlife habitat, and serve other objectives.

3.2 Key Issues

Although circumstances differ, States and localities nationwide face a number of key issues in establishing wetland protection programs. These issues are discussed individually below:

- How should wetlands be defined?
- Is wetland mapping necessary? If so, at what scales and levels of accuracy?
- What protection and management policies are appropriate for particular wetlands? How should these be established?
- What implementation techniques should be used?
- What sources of funds are available for program development and implementation?
- What sources of expertise are available?
- What legal restraints exist on wetland protection?
- What procedures should be followed in evaluating wetland permits?

3.3 Wetland Definition

Disagreement exists as to the most suitable wetland definition criteria. Experience with various definitions suggests that there are no right or wrong criteria—only more usable and less usable approaches. Examples of definitions applied in existing local programs are contained in Appendix A. Examples for existing State programs can be found in Strengthening State Wetland Regulations, Biological Services Program, FWS/OBS-78/98, U.S. Fish and Wildlife Service, Washington, D.C. (November 1978). The definition applied by the U.S. Fish and Wildlife

TABLE 2. SELECTED PUBLIC WETLAND PROTECTION TECHNIQUES

APPROACH	OBJECTIVE	INCIDENCE OF COSTS	ADVANTAGES	LIMITATIONS
Education of Land-owners (Films, manuals, workshops, conferences, etc.)	1. Encourage private protection of wetlands. 2. Encourage private balancing of benefits and costs.	1. Private landowners, private organizations bear costs of protection. Community may pay for education efforts.	1. Appeals to private land ethic. 2. Politically attractive. 3. Maximizes land-owner options.	1. Some landowners not responsive. 2. Time-consuming.
Environmental Impact Statement Requirements	1. Require consideration of short-term and long-term costs and benefits in decision-making.	1. Developers, public agencies.	1. Require a careful balancing of factors, by decisionmakers. 2. Expose projects to public review.	1. Impact review does not protect wetlands unless impact require-ments are combined with regulations. 2. May be costly and time-consuming.
Public or Private Acquisition in Fee or Easements, through Gift, Purchase, Devise	1. Protect wetland permanently from private development. 2. Reduce flood losses. 3. Permit scientific and educational use of wetland. 4. Permit hunting, other recreational uses.	1. Public pays for public acquisition but also receives multiple benefits. Private groups pay for private acquisition.	1. No constitutional problem of uncom-pensated "taking". 2. Can afford perma-nent protection. 3. Active public use possible. 4. B.O.R. and other Federal grants may be available for open space acquisition. 5. Particularly attrac-tive in urban areas.	1. Costly. 2. Political opposi-tion may arise to large scale land acquisition. 3. Creates public land management requirements.
Land Use Regulations	1. Protect health and safety from flooding, erosion, pollution. 2. Prevent nuisances. 3. Prevent fraud. 4. Protect wildlife, aesthetic values, other wetland values.	1. Landowner must bear cost of adjustments. Community bears cost of adoption and administration of regulations.	1. Low cost to government. 2. Promote economic social well-being. 3. Promote most suit-able use of lands. 4. Can be put into effect immediately.	1. Must not violate State and Federal constitutional provisions. 2. May not be adequately enforced. 3. Can't protect all wetlands. 4. Generally do not apply to govern-mental uses. 5. Limited applica-tion to existing uses.
Water Level Maintenance, Impoundment, Pumping, Other Management Techniques	1. Stabilize wetland water levels. 2. Increase wetland area. 3. Improve waterfowl, wildlife habitats. 4. Reestablish natural species.	1. Generally public bears the costs but may also be carried out by private individuals and organizations.	1. Enhance waterfowl, wildlife habitats. 2. Compensate for effects of prior damage.	1. Costly in some instances. 2. Maintenance required. 3. May disturb natural flora and fauna.
Conservation Restrictions (Easement or Deed Restrictions)	1. Prohibit private development while permitting continued private ownership of lands.	1. Private landowner.	1. Low cost to government. 2. Provide basis for reduction in property tax. 3. Voluntary, may be politically acceptable.	1. Expressly auth-orized in only small number of States. 2. Does not gen-erally permit public use of land. 3. Real estate tax reductions.
Real Estate Tax Incentives	1. Encourage private land owners to hold land in open state. 2. Reduce burden of restrictions.	1. Government has lowered tax revenues but also receives benefits.	1. Encourage volun-tary protection. 2. Reduce burden on landowners and threats of law suit.	1. Reduced local tax revenues. 2. Not authorized in all States. 3. May not curb speculation in some instances.

22

Service in its new wetland classification system is reproduced in Chapter 2. This definition considers vegetation, soils and inundation by surface waters.

Several approaches are taken in existing efforts:

Definition based on tidal action.[1] Usually coastal wetlands are defined with reference to tidal levels. For example, Virginia defines coastal wetlands to include all land "lying between and contiguous to mean water and an elevation above mean low water equal to the factor 1.5 times the mean tide range."[2] Tidal definitions are supplemented with vegetation criteria in most efforts.

Definition based on inundation by surface waters or flood waters. Inland wetlands are usually defined to include lands with standing water and emergent vegetation.[3] Some definitions also include areas subject to periodic flooding. However, disagreements arise as to criteria for flooding.

Definition based on vegetation. Vegetation lists are the most common test for coastal and inland wetlands. Wetlands are usually defined in terms of aquatic plants capable of growing in wet soils. Usually vegetation lists are combined with tidal or flooding criteria.

Definition based on soils. In Connecticut, inland wetland areas are defined to include poorly drained, very poorly drained, alluvial, and floodplain soils. Soils are used in other States to supplement vegetation lists. The usefulness of soil criteria is mixed. Soils do not always reflect existing conditions, particularly for drained areas. On the other hand, soils are very useful in administering programs to indicate flooding, areas inadequate for onsite waste disposal, and areas with inadequate structural support.

Definition based on horizontal distance from high water mark. Some communities define wetlands to include lands within a prescribed horizontal distance from the high water mark of streams, lakes, or the ocean. For example, the Washington shoreline program defines wetlands to include a 200-foot strip from the high water mark of specified water bodies. This approach is arbitrary, but it simplifies administration and enforcement.

All of the above approaches have advantages and disadvantages. If a wetland program is adopted pursuant to a State wetland statute, the wetland criteria incorporated in the statute or adopted by the administering agency must generally be followed.

In the absence of State statutory or administrative criteria, a State or community should carefully evaluate its intended wetland management goals and select criteria consistent with those goals. For example, a community primarily interested in regulating floodplain development may define wetlands in terms of the 100-year floodplain. A community concerned with onsite waste disposal may use soil criteria. A community primarily interested in protecting fisheries and wildlife habitats may use general vegetation criteria. A community wishing to achieve broad wetland protection and management goals may adopt a combined definition including flooding, vegetation criteria, and soils.

The availability of existing data and the cost of generating new data are often major factors in the selection of definition criteria. Communities have often selected wetland definition criteria because of the availability of particular types of maps. For example, northern Wisconsin communities used USGS topographic and planimetric maps because they were the only available data sources.

To avoid constitutional, administrative, and political problems, definition criteria should anticipate use standards and implementation techniques. For example, a broad definition of coastal wetlands, incorporating both high and low marshes, may be appropriate for planning purposes, land acquisition, or the application of regulatory performance standards that permit some private uses. However, a more restrictive definition, applying only to low marshes, may be appropriate when regulations prohibit all private uses. Courts are less likely to find that regulations "take" property where the definition applies to limited areas with particularly unique value or severe hazards. In some instances, definition criteria should distinguish subzones within defined wetland areas such as floodways within broader riverine wetlands.

3.4 Wetland Mapping

Map features, scale, and accuracy are also major issues in wetland programs. Planning boards and regulatory administrators may be uncomfortable with wetland boundaries that follow natural features and cross property lines. And yet, this is the only reasonable approach. Often arguments are made that wetlands should be mapped in urban areas at scales of one inch equals 200 feet or larger to provide certainty to landowners. However, mapping at this scale is very expensive. In addition, detailed mapping may give rise to the erroneous belief that wetland boundaries can be located with mathematical precision. In fact, boundaries must be somewhat flexible since they reflect a natural transition from water to upland and fluctuating ground or surface water levels.

Not all States and communities with wetland protection programs map their wetlands. Instead, some, like Georgia, rely upon written definitions such as vegetation criteria and tidal elevation. Such an approach is less expensive than mapping, but it creates uncertainty as to the location of wetland boundaries.

To date, most wetland mapping efforts have relied extensively on existing air photos or other existing data sources. Principal data sources differ from State to State. Some examples are listed in Table 3 and are illustrated in Figure 7.

Several mapping approaches are common, first communities often adopt existing wetland maps prepared by State or Federal agencies. This is true for communities in New York, Virginia, Massachusetts, and Connecticut where State agencies or universities have undertaken mapping efforts.

However, special wetland maps are available for only a portion of the country. An inventory of State wetland information has been compiled by the National Wetland Inventory, U.S. Fish and Wildlife Service. (Existing State and Local Wetland Surveys (1965-1975), U.S. Fish and Wildlife Service (May 1976.) Copies can be obtained from the National Technical Information Service,[4] Order Number PB-278427. The National Wetland Inventory has prepared 10,800 large scale wetland maps for the lower 48 States. In total it has mapped over 715,000 square miles in the lower 48 and 20,000 square miles in Alaska.

Existing State and Federal wetland maps are usually at scales of 1:12,000 to 1:24,000, a size that limits their application for regulatory purposes. Most State and Federal inventories have been based on air photo interpretation of vegetation with limited field surveys. Often, communities enlarge existing wetland maps for regulatory purposes. However, scale enlargement does not cure basic inaccuracies.

Second, some communities adopt as wetland maps United States Geological Survey (USGS) topographic and planimetric maps, Soil Conservation Service (SCS) soil survey maps, and flood maps prepared by the Department of Housing and Urban Development (HUD), the Army Corps of Engineers, and other agencies. As indicated by Table 3, USGS topographic and planimetric maps indicate wetland areas, but they provide little differentiation between wetland types. Map-scale is quite small (1:24,000 and smaller). Soil maps do not show wetland boundaries although certain soils (e.g., wet and flooded soils) may be designated as wetland areas. Flood maps do not ordinarily show wetland boundaries unless wetlands are defined to coincide with flood areas. However, some Corps of Engineers flood maps show wetland areas as well as floodplain boundaries.

Third, some communities and State agencies prepare new wetland maps through air photo interpretation combined with available wetland data from soil maps, topographic maps, flood maps, existing wetland inventories, field surveys, and other sources. Because of reduced costs, most efforts emphasize air photo interpretation with field sampling.

Usually, enlarged USGS topographic maps, air photos, or town tax maps are used as base maps. Information from these data sources is transferred to the base maps except in the case of air photos, which may themselves be used as base maps as well as for interpretation of wetland boundaries. Final maps take the form of printed maps, mylar overlays, or air photo reproductions. Wetland maps are often prepared at quite large scale (1:1,200 to 1:7,200), particularly if they are for regulatory purposes.

Several considerations may aid a community or State in deciding whether to map wetlands and how to develop map criteria:

o   The intended use of wetland data should be carefully evaluated. For some purposes wetland maps may need to be supplemented. For example, statistical and written data concerning the number of wetlands of a particular type, their values and hazards, uniqueness, ownership, existing uses, and threats from proposed development are important in developing wetland policies, drafting regulatory standards, establishing acquisition priorities, and processing development permits. Only a portion of this information can be presented in map form.

o   Large-scale maps (1:24,000 and larger) are usually essential for wetland regulatory efforts. Maps prepared at small scales are often of little value for regulatory purposes unless they can be enlarged with a satisfactory degree of accuracy, since correlation with ground sites is difficult. But small-scale wetland maps

(1:24,000 to 1:100,000) may serve for comprehensive land use planning, public facilities planning, and evaluation of surface and groundwater flow systems.

o   Wetland maps must reflect wetland definition criteria and statutory map requirements. New maps are required if statutes or administrative regulations specify particular vegetation or other criteria and existing maps do not incorporate these criteria. Some statutes require preparation of wetland maps, although most are silent as to the need for mapping or map specifics.

o   Available funds, expertise, and equipment must be considered. Preparation of new, large-scale maps is very expensive. Often, existing maps must be used as a matter of economic necessity.

o   Degree of urbanization and threat to wetland areas influence mapping needs. Depending on the topography of the area, smaller scale, less accurate maps may be satisfactory for rural areas with little development pressure. Legal and political challenges to the maps are less common, and individual field inspections may be used to resolve boundary disputes. In contrast, detailed, accurate maps are often needed for urban and urbanizing areas where land values are high and development pressures are severe. Large scale maps reduce political problems, legal challenges, and the need for field investigations to resolve boundary disputes but are expensive and cumbersome.

o   The development standards applied to an area are relevant to map scale and accuracy. In general, large-scale, accurate maps are needed for application of highly restrictive regulations prohibiting private uses. In contrast, small scale, less accurate maps may be acceptable where performance standards are applied since supplemental data gathering and refinement of boundary lines may be carried out on a case-by-case basis.

Too much emphasis on map scale and accuracy often interferes with the primary objective of mapping—to provide information for wetland decision-making. Communities invariably discover that maps, however accurate, provide only a portion of the data needed to evaluate the impact of a particular proposed use. Even large scale maps cannot reflect the variability in vegetation, soil types, flood hazards, wildlife, and other parameters that determine the suitability of particular sites for development. Consequently, field investigations must be undertaken to locate wetland boundaries on the ground and to evaluate the impact of each proposed development. For this reason, some communities define wetlands through both maps and written definition criteria (vegetation, soils) that can be applied on the ground through field investigations. Such an approach was approved by the Wisconsin Supreme Court in the landmark wetland case **Just v. Marinette County.**[5] There the county adopted USGS topographic maps as basic wetland maps but also provided in the ordinance that, in case of boundary dispute, field surveys would be conducted to determine whether aquatic vegetation referenced in the ordinance was actually found at the site.

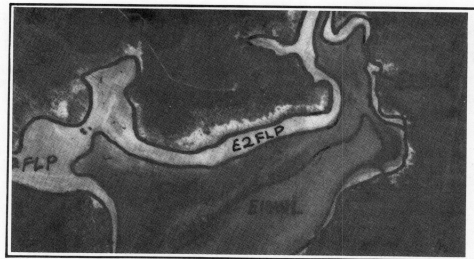

1. Air Photo. Wetland boundaries drawn on air photo. Enlarged to 1:24,000 from 1:120,000 color infrared air photo.

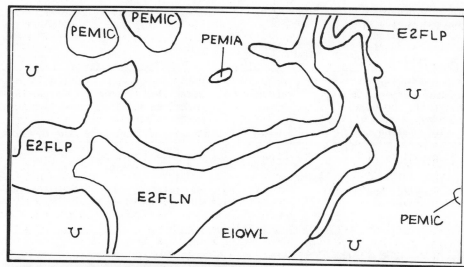

Sand and Mud Flats

2. USGS Topographic Map. U.S. Department of the Interior, Geological Survey, 7.5 minute Topographic Quadrangle at scale 1:24,000.

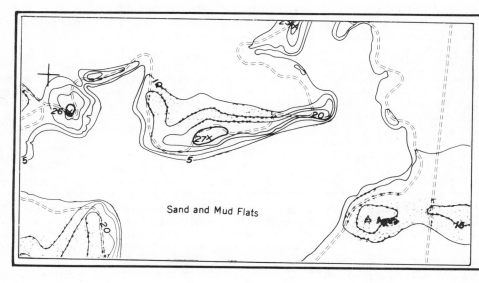

3. USFWS National Wetlands Inventory. Adapted at scale 1:24,000. Map numbers describe particular types of wetlands.

FIGURE 7. THREE APPROACHES FOR MAPPING WETLAND AREAS ARE ILLUSTRATED FOR PORT ARTHUR NORTH QUADRANGLE, TEXAS.

TABLE 3. SOME PRINCIPAL WETLAND DATA SOURCES*

TITLE OF DATA SOURCE	INFORMATION DISPLAYED	SCALE	SUGGESTED WETLAND USES	SOURCE
USGS topographic maps (7' & 15')	Topographic contours, major roads, rail-roads, utility lines, contours, water bodies, houses, town names, county and town boundaries, vegetated and non-vegetated wetlands.	1" = 2000' 1" = 24,000'	1. Enlarged for use as wetland base map. 2. Interim wetland map. 3. Watershed boundaries. 4. Source of topographic information.	U.S. Geological Survey
SCS Soil Survey Map	Soil types	1" = 2000' 1" = 1320' 4" = 1 mile	1. Interim wetland map. 2. Determination of soil suitablility for onsite waste disposal. 3. Determination of soil structural bearing capacity.	SCS USDA
State Wetland Maps	Wetland vegetation boundaries. Varied (depending on State).	1" = 24,000' to 1" = 1200'	1. Interim wetland regulation maps. 2. Permanent wetland maps (depends on scale).	State wetland programs. Consult the existing State and local wetland surveys prepared by the Fish & Wildlife Service for information concerning their program.
Flood Hazard Boundary Maps: USGS, FEMA	Flood prone areas.	Approx. 1" = 2000'	1. Interim mapping of wetlands. 2. Assess flood hazard potential at wetland sites.	HUD, USGS
Flood Plain Information Reports, Army Corps of Engineers	Standard project floodplain, 100 year flood evaluation wetland boundaries (some maps).	Range from 1" = 500' to 1" = 1000'		Army Corps of Engineers Flood Plain Management Services
USGS, Hydrologic Investigations Atlas: Hydrology & Water Resources	Each map differs and may contain: wells, test holes, bedrock, groundwater quality information.	1" = 2000' 1" = 24,000'	1. Determine ground water flow systems. 2. Determine acquifer recharge areas.	U.S. Geological Survey Distribution Office
USFWS Wetland Inventory Maps	A wide variety of information pertaining to vegetation, water regime, and other parameters.	1" = 24,000' 1" = 100,000'	1. Regulatory mapping. 2. Aid in processing permits. 3. Acquisition. 4. Siting.	U.S. Fish and Wildlife Service and U.S. Geological Survey

* Source: Massachusetts Audubon Society (Modified).

TITLE OF DATA SOURCE	INFORMATION DISPLAYED	SCALE	SUGGESTED WETLAND USES	SOURCE
Subdivision Maps	Dimensions of property, size & location of house, width of easements. Wetland and floodplain boundaries (some circumstances).	1" = 40' to 1" = 60'	1. Determine precise wetland boundaries (some instances). 2. Evaluate individual developments.	Municipal offices
Air Photos ASCS	Existing uses, vegetation, water resources, roads (black and white stereoscope).	1" = 24,000'	1. Define wetland boundaries based upon vegetation. 2. Use as base maps. 3. Evaluate individual proposed uses.	ASCS USDA
Air Photos USGS (orthophoto quadrangles)	" " " Not stereoscopic	1" = 24,000'	" " " " Are particularly useful as base maps.	USGS USDA
Air Photos (miscellaneous sources)	" " "	Varied	" " " "	USGS-National Cartographic Information
Surficial Geology USGS	Everything on USGS topographic maps plus geologic deposits, bedrock fill sites.	1" = 2,000' 1" = 24,000'	1. Determine groundwater flow. 2. Determine bedrock characteristics.	USGS Geological Division. General catalogue available: "Geologic & Water Supply Reports & Maps".
Town, City, County, Borough Zoning Maps	Each municipality has its own map information. Information can include: roads, property lines, zoning districts, wetland boundaries, floodplain boundaries.	Range from 1" = 500' to 1" = 1000'	1. Determine existing uses. 2. Determine compatibility of proposed wetland uses with zone classifications and adjacent uses. 3. Use as wetland base maps.	Municipal offices
Assessors Maps	Property lines, owners' names, easements, roads, buildings.	1" = 100' or 1" = 200'	1. Determine wetland areas. 2. Grant tax incentives to wetland areas.	Municipal, County offices (depends on State).
National Wetland Inventory Maps	Wetlands are delineated and classified and displayed on USGS topographic maps, (7 1/2' & 15') (See Figure 7)	1" = 2,0000' 1" = 24,000"	1. Display the biological limit of all wetlands. 2. Determine the extent of various types of wetlands.	U.S. Fish and Wildlife Service

TRAINING COURSE IN FIELD EVALUATION OF WETLANDS, WALLOPS ISLAND, VIRGINIA. Photo source: John Clark.

3.5 Defining Protection and Management Policies for Particular Wetlands

A community may wish to apply special policies to particular types of wetland or areas within a wetland to reflect specific land and water management goals and factual differences. For example, particularly tight protection policies may be applied to wetlands serving as habitat for a rare or endangered species or as a flood conveyance area (floodway) for rivers or streams.

Variations in protection policies may take several forms:

o In some instances localities apply protection policies to a particular type or size of wetland but not to others. For example, many States regulate only coastal wetlands. New York regulates selected inland wetlands—only those over 12 acres.

o Localities may apply more restrictive policies for some areas within a given wetland. For example, permits for activities in lower salt marsh areas may be denied while permits for activities in high marsh areas may be approved with special conditions. Permits denied for activities in the center of wetlands may be allowed at the margins.

Variations in protection policies may be established through several processes at one or more points in a program:

o Local legislative bodies may apply specific policies through written designations (e.g., all coastal marshes) or adoption of wetland regulatory maps. Quite often zoning maps apply only to larger wetland areas.

o A regulatory agency or board may establish special policies administratively through written rules or guidelines. For example, agencies in New York and Virginia have established varying policies for vegetation zones within coastal wetland areas.

o A regulatory agency or board may apply special policies administratively on a case-by-case basis as individual development permits are submitted. With this approach, the administering agency does not adopt special written policies for a particular wetland or subzone within a wetland. Rather, the board applies special policies to individual permit applications to reflect the unique characteristics of the application and the physical features of the wetland site. This approach is widely used. A careful tailoring of use restrictions to the characteristics of the use and the wetland site can minimize impact while optimizing potential uses.

With such a case-by-case approach, considerable discretion is usually afforded the regulatory agency in assessing the impact of particular development and determining whether the impact is acceptable. Once a permit application is received by

28

MAP INTERPRETATION IN WORKSHOP, ST. AUGUSTINE, FLORIDA. Photo source: Jon Kusler.

the regulatory agency, field surveys and other investigations are conducted. The regulatory agency then considers ordinance and statutory goals and criteria to determine whether the proposed action should be permitted, denied, or permitted conditionally.

In recent years a number of studies have been undertaken to develop criteria for determining the relative importance of various vegetative subzones within wetlands or determining the importance of particular wetlands. For example, the New York tidal wetlands program has divided coastal marshes into six types or zones with varying suitability for particular uses: coastal fresh marsh, intertidal marsh, high marsh or salt marsh, coastal shoals, bars and flats, littoral zone, and adjacent areas. Similarly, the State of Virginia has developed guidelines for use of particular vegetative zones in coastal marshes. The Virginia Institute of Marine Science has produced several guidebooks to assist local governments in identifying these zones, understanding the importance of each zone, and controlling development.[6]

Perhaps the most extensive and systematic community effort to map, evaluate, and rank wetlands to define specific policies for particular wetlands and subzones within wetlands was carried out for Dane County by a team from the University of Wisconsin Arboretum.[7] This team collected information for each wetland from air photos, field surveys, and other sources to evaluate wetland type, dominant vegetation, water quality, wildlife, major geologic features, acreage, upland and wetland use, extent and type of water and soil, vegetation disturbance, and existing problems. Wetland maps were prepared and each wetland was evaluated for present or possible biological value, scientific value, public use, extent of degradation, and extent of immediate or long-term threats. Wetlands were placed in five priority groupings according to use and biological value.

Several factors were considered in preparing protection and management policies for particular wetlands in Dane County:

1. <u>Knowledge of wetland characteristics.</u> The team first gained an understanding of wetland physical and biological characteristics. These characteristics determined specific wetland functions and hazards such as wildlife habitat, watershed protection, and recreational uses. A portion of this information was assembled from existing sources, but field surveys also proved essential.

2. <u>Sensitivity to disturbance, existing disturbance.</u> Sensitivities of the wetland to certain types of disturbance were evaluated by analyzing flow systems, land use within the watershed, water quality, vegetation, wildlife, and other characteristics. Impacts of previous and existing activities such as introduction of exotic species, pollution, and filling were evaluated. The susceptibility of a wetland to improvement or restoration was also analyzed.

TABLE 4. PERFORMANCE STANDARDS FOR PROTECTING WETLAND FUNCTIONS

GENERAL STANDARD	COMMON ACTIVITIES AND PROCESSES REQUIRING CONTROL	IMPACT OF UNCONTROLLED USES	APPLICATION OF STANDARD
Prevent filling of wetland by sand, gravel, solid wastes, structures, etc.	1. Land fill operations. 2. Dredge and spoil disposal. 3. Construction of roads, dikes, dams, resevoirs. 4. Activities on adjacent land or in the watershed causing sedimentation such as agriculture operations, timber cutting, road building, urban runoff, mining operations, chan-, nelization.	1. Destruction of flood storage and flood conveyance capacity. 2. Accelerated runoff. 3. Destruction of wildlife and vegetative values. 4. Reduced ground water infiltration. 5. Destruction of scenic, recreation, education, pollution control functions.	1. Prohibit or tightly control filling in all or selected types of wetland areas. 2. Prohibit activities which require fills such as dwellings, factories and roads. 3. Establish wetland buffer zones or setbacks for fills and structures to reduce sedimentation from upland sources. 4. Regulate grading, top soil removal and vegetation removal in upland areas.
Protect wetland water supply (quanlity).	1. Construction of upstream reservoirs. 2. Agricultural and other types of drainage. 3. Channelization of streams. 4. Pumping of streams, lakes, ground water supplies. 5. Establishment of dikes, levees, sea walls, blocking exchange of tidal flows, flood waters. 6. Mosquitoe control projects.	1. Destruction or deterioration of wetland vegetation. 2. Reduced acquifer recharge. 3. Disturbance or destruction of wildlife species which depend upon wetlands for breeding, feeding, and nutrients. 4. Increased salinity (in some instances) resulting in damage to wildlife, vegetation, recreation opportunities.	1. Regulate the construction of dams, drainage projects, stream channelization, water extractions. 2. Manage reservoirs and flood gates to maintain wetland water supply.

GENERAL STANDARD	COMMON ACTIVITIES AND PROCESSES REQUIRING CONTROL	IMPACT OF UNCONTROLLED USES	APPLICATION OF STANDARD
Protect wetland soils.	1. Dredging, channelization. 2. Topsoil removal. 3. Construction of reservoirs. 4. Mining.	1. Disturbance or destruction of vegetation and wildlife habitat. 2. Increased water turbidity. 3. Decreased recreation, education, wildlife values.	1. Regulate dredging, lagooning, mining, wetland soil removal.
Maintain free circulation of wetland waters.	1. Dikes, dams, levees, seawalls, roads. 2. Irrigation projects. 3. Fills, grading, buildings.	1. Deprive wetland plants and animals of nutrients from flood flows and other sources. 2. Prevent the feeding and breeding of aquatic species in wetland areas. 3. Build-up of salinity (in some instances).	1. Require that bridges and roads be constructed with minimum impediment to natural drainage. 2. Design floodgates and seawalls to maintain tidal action. 3. Regulate construction of dikes, levees. 4. Require wetland structures to be elevated on pilings.
Protect wetland vegetation from cutting, grading, etc.	1. Forestry (some instances). 2. Cranberry cultivation. 3. Agriculture. 4. Off-the-road vehicles. 5. Filling, grading. 6. Soil removal.	1. Damage to wildlife habitat. 2. Reduced pollution filtering capability. 3. Increased water velocities, erosion. 4. Destruction of scenic values.	1. Control filling, grading, soil removal, pollution sources and other activities which destroy the wetland substrate or the water quantity required for specific vegetation.

3. _Relationship of wetland to the broader hydrologic system_. Watershed boundaries and land use patterns were examined through use of topographic maps, groundwater maps, and field surveys. The source of wetland water and its quality and sources of erosion and pollution found in the watershed were evaluated. The fate of wetland waters as well as the quality of water leaving the wetlands were also studied in order to determine the watershed protection value of the wetland.

4. _Interactive wetland ecology_. The ecological importance of the wetland was evaluated in terms of plant and animal relationships within the wetlands and on adjacent lands through topographic maps, existing sources of wildlife information, and field surveys. Wetland vegetation and wildlife were evaluated to determine the extent to which adjacent habitat needed to be preserved. The role of the wetland as part of a broader complex of wetlands and open spaces was evaluated to determine wetland function with respect to animal movement, flyways for waterfowl, and niches for feeding, nesting, and breeding.

5. _Cultural parameters_. Land ownership, existing uses (public and private), archaeological sites, proposed plans, historical significance, and other parameters were evaluated through photos, field surveys, conversations with knowledgeable individuals, and other sources of information. Efforts were made to determine the current value of the wetland to the community and its historic and archaeological values. The adequacy of existing techniques and anticipated public and private uses for wetlands were also estimated. This information was important in evaluating the existing and potential value of the wetland, threats, and appropriate use standards.

This information was synthesized in The Wetlands of Dane County,[8] which provides both an overview of the size, condition, and value of wetlands in that county and proposes specific management and protection policies and techniques.

In recent years a number of studies have developed criteria and procedures for rating and ranking wetlands for protection and management purposes. One study undertaken at the University of Massachusetts under the direction of Professor Joseph S. Larson developed an evaluation model for inland wetlands of the Northeast.[9] This model suggests a three-tiered approach for evaluating wetlands. The first level identifies characteristics that are so important that wetlands with these attributes should be preserved in their natural state. The second level of evaluation applies to wetlands that do not have outstanding characteristics identified in the first level. Wetlands are given relative numerical scores based upon wildlife values, visual-cultural values, and groundwater supply. A third level of analysis translates wildlife, visual-cultural, groundwater, and flood control values into economic values.

Preliminary experience with these and other attempts to rank wetlands according to numerical ranking systems suggests that such systems are useful but have several important drawbacks:

o Any attempt to systematically rank and compare wetlands by taking into account a large number of characteristics may require large amounts of natural resource data and, to a lesser extent, cultural data. Data pertaining to site-specific soils, geology, and wildlife, including rare and endangered species, can be generated only through field surveys at considerable expense.

o Any effort to rank wetlands according to a numerical scale must deal with situations where a single value is of primary importance (e.g., a bald eagle's nest). The ranking system must permit special weighing for this characteristic, and the Massachusetts approach does so.[10]

o Any effort to rank according to numerical scale must distinguish between complementary and conflicting values. For example, value scores should not be added where a wetland is habitat for rare species and also a potential groundwater extraction site if these two uses are incompatible.

o Any effort to rank wetlands should be flexible enough to take into account all factors considered important to a particular wetland decision. For example, the University of Massachusetts model does not consider pollution control functions and flood conveyance capacity—often primary considerations in wetland regulation and management.

o If a rating system is to be used to determine the desirability of wetland development, some effort also should be made to rate upland sites. Efforts to rate only wetlands may give a false impression that wetlands with low ratings should be developed even though unrated adjacent upland areas may be more desirable development sites. For example, degree of threat to a wetland may be a primary factor in ranking wetlands for the purpose of determining acquisition priorities.[11]

3.6 Program Implementation Techniques

Wetland regulations are the most widespread wetland implementation technique, but regulations are subject to many limitations. Public acquisition of wetland areas is sometimes preferable as a means of providing permanent protection and public access. Yet acquisition is often difficult due to escalating land costs (as high as $20,000 to $50,000 an acre in urban settings) and the reluctance of communities to remove land from the tax rolls.

The advantages and disadvantages of these and other techniques are summarized in Table 3 and discussed in the chapters which follow. The selection of a particular technique or combination of techniques may depend on several factors:

Scope of local and State regulatory powers. Local units of government and State agencies possess only those powers expressly granted to them through statutes, charters, or, in the case of local governments, home rule provisions. Therefore, the power to adopt particular wetland protection or management techniques varies from one unit of government to another and from State to State.

Nevertheless, cities and villages have a wide range of regulatory and land acquisition powers under enabling statutes or home rule provisions in virtually all States.

Political acceptability. Political acceptability is a primary consideration in the selection of acquisition, regulation, rehabilitation, and other local implementation techniques. Legislative acceptance depends, in turn, on community support. In some instances, new wetland regulations have proven politically unacceptable, and protection must be achieved through nonregulatory approaches. On the other hand, many local legislative bodies are reluctant to fund expensive acquisition efforts and are opposed to condemnation. Here, regulations may be more politically acceptable.

Wetland protection and management goals. Implementation techniques must be related to community and State wetland management goals that often include some or all of the principles and standards suggested in Chapter 4. Particular goals depend on community preferences, political acceptability, wetland characteristics, land ownership, threats, and broader community land and water use plans. Many implementation techniques may serve a wide range of goals. For example, both regulation and acquisition may be used to reduce flood hazards, preserve wetland functions, and reduce water pollution. However, some techniques are needed to achieve specific goals such as adoption of regulations to control point and non-point sources of pollution throughout a watershed and the use of acquisition to permit public use of wetland areas.

Funding. Available funding is often a primary consideration. For example, public purchase of extensive wetland areas is impossible unless large sums of money are available. Regulations, public education, and environmental impact statement requirements are less expensive.

Available expertise. A community employing planners, biologists, hydrologists, and engineers is better able to adopt and administer sophisticated wetland regulations. One with less expertise may favor outright acquisition.

Rural, urbanizing, and urban conditions. Wetland acquisition is often preferable in urban and urbanizing contexts where land values and taxes are high and public use of land for recreation is needed. In contrast, regulations are often more satisfactory for low value rural wetlands with little development pressure.

3.7 Funds for Program Implementation

Typically, wetland programs must be formulated and implemented with little money although State and Federal grants-in-aid may be available. Programs often employ a variety of techniques to reduce costs:

o   Existing wetland and resource maps are used to save the cost of new map preparation. Existing air photos are often applied where new maps are needed. Small-scale mapping may be used initially with refinements through data gathering on a case-by-case basis.

o   Regulations and public education techniques are adopted in lieu of expensive public purchase of wetlands.

o   Wetland planning, data gathering, regulation, acquisition, and other management efforts are carried out on a priority basis for areas with development threats or special values.

o   Interested citizens and conservation organizations are encouraged to play major roles in public education, data gathering, formulation of policies and plans, acquisition and preservation of wetland areas, evaluation of individual developments, monitoring of development, and, in some instances, enforcement efforts.

o   Developers may be charged fees and/or required to prepare environmental impact statements to reduce program costs.

o   Wetland programs often share personnel employed by other local programs such as land use planners, municipal engineers, zoning administrators, and sanitary engineers.

3.8 Expertise

The lack of hydrological, geological, and biological expertise is a serious limitation on data gathering and permit evaluation. This problem is particularly severe for rural communities.

Communities and agencies often compensate for lack of professional staff by tapping expertise within the community or other State or Federal agencies. Communities often rely on unpaid technical assistance from local science teachers, architects, engineers, birdwatchers, and interested citizens. Communities in some eastern States have appointed local experts to conservation commissions which map wetlands, adopt regulations, and evaluate individual development permits. Conservation organizations such as The Nature Conservancy and Audubon Society often plan principal roles in providing valuable expertise in wetland protection (see Chapter 11).

Communities and agencies also rely extensively on sources of outside assistance:

Consultants are commonly used to prepare wetland maps or evaluate individual development proposals.

University staff and students may also be asked to play major technical assistance roles. For example, University of Massachusetts personnel have mapped wetlands in the entire State and have played a leadership role in State and local wetland protection programs. Similarly, the Connecticut Arboretum and the University of Connecticut have prepared guidebooks, conducted workshops, and evaluated development permits. The Virginia Institute of Marine Science has played a similar role. Wetland centers have been established at the University of Michigan, Florida State University, and Louisiana State University. In many States, university extension personnel have conducted workshops and assisted local legislative bodies in preparing and implementing regulations.

State wetland agencies, geological surveys, planning offices, coastal zone offices, shoreland and floodplain programs, scientific area programs, scenic and wild river programs, water resource agencies, and conservation agencies often play important roles in wetland mapping and program development efforts. For example, the California coastal zone management program is a major source of information for coastal wetland protection in that State; the Washington shoreline program provides a source of expertise for both coastal and inland wetlands in Washington; and the Florida State planning office has, under the critical area program, developed wetland expertise. Wetland and conservation agencies also provide technical assistance to local communities, including assistance in evaluating individual permits.

Several major Federal sources of expertise are available and have been used extensively in some efforts. U.S. Soil Conservation Service personnel have mapped Connecticut wetlands and provided technical assistance to communities in evaluating the impact of proposed development. Personnel of the U.S. Fish and Wildlife Service have also provided technical expertise, and regional staff from the Federal Emergency Management Agency have provided information concerning the National Flood Insurance Program and floodplain regulations.

3.9 Legal Restraints

Aside from money and politics, legal restraints are perhaps the greatest factor shaping wetland programs. Although legal restraints and regulations are discussed in greater depth in Chapter 9, several preliminary observations are in order.

First, communities are usually authorized by enabling statutes, home rule statutes, and constitutional provisions to exercise a wide range of regulatory, acquisition, and other powers. Basic authority usually exists, but specific statutory limitations such as zoning exemptions pertaining to agricultural uses and State constitutional prohibitions against differential taxation may present problems. In addition, statutory procedures for regulation, acquisition, and other management approaches must be carefully followed.

Second, constitutional restraints on regulations are often overestimated. Regulators and administrators should not be intimidated by the "taking" issue or by a perceived need for highly precise

boundary maps. Further, there is no need to regulate all wetlands and uses at once.

Regulations must be reasonable and nondiscriminatory. They must balance public and private needs. But community leaders should be more concerned with what is fair and sensible and less about complicated legal requirements that are not as burdensome as popularly believed. Courts are sympathetic to the administrative and budgetary needs of government and do not demand the impossible.

Programs can often avoid legal challenges through careful program design and implementation. For example, they can avoid lawsuits by educating landowners regarding wetland values and hazards and the need for public control. Public hearings can be held to explain proposed regulation or acquisition plans to landowners and permit them to express themselves in a public forum.

Negotiation is another means of avoiding litigation. Discussions between community leaders and landowners during early stages of project design can often result in project modifications which minimize adverse wetland impacts.

Subtle community pressures are often helpful in avoiding litigation. A strong community wetland protection program, backed up by community leaders and broad public support, is often a strong deterrent to litigation. Landowners who look to their neighbors for friendship and approval are reluctant to oppose community wishes.

Well conceived and executed community data gathering and planning efforts are another approach to avoid litigation. Court tests are less likely where a community can make a strong factual case for wetland protection. Accurate wetland maps, consistency in application of regulations, data demonstrating the importance of wetland hazards and value, and good record-keeping help avoid court suits.

In sum, communities may go overboard in two directions. First, they may be overly concerned with constitutional constraints and thereby be seriously restrained. Second, they may ignore private landowners and thereby invite challenge in court. Often, a creative protection approach may both protect wetlands and reduce landowner objections.

CHAPTER 4: PRINCIPLES AND STANDARDS

4.1 Shifted Burden of Proof

As suggested in Chapter 2, wetlands vary with respect to dominant vegetation, size, distribution, density, water quality, hazards and development pressures. Despite these variations, most wetlands share general characteristics with important management implications: (1) natural hazards due to flooding, erosion, and subsidence; and (2) natural values.

Because of these characteristics, wetlands are undesirable development sites with important hidden costs to landowners and the public. This does not mean that every wetland should be preserved, or that all wetland development will cause problems. But the high incidence of hazards and special values justifies the careful control of wetland activities. Activities that damage or destroy significant wetland values should be avoided. The high incidence of hazards and values warrants a shifted burden of proof to those wishing to undertake such activities.[1]

4.2 Wetland Development Control Versus Wetland Protection

An important distinction should be made between the need to control development within wetlands and the need to protect wetlands per se. A State or community may wish to control wetland uses for a variety of reasons in addition to a desire to protect natural wetland functions and reduce threats from natural hazards. These reasons may include: minimization of community expenses for public services; prevention of incompatible adjacent uses; buffer zones; open space; or allocation of lands throughout a community or region to their most appropriate uses. These objectives justify the adoption of wetland regulatory and management programs. The real issue is the appropriate use of wetlands with regard to safety and general welfare and not simply their preservation. Table 1 outlines factors determining wetland functions in specific contexts.

4.3 General Principles and Standards

Seven basic principles may be suggested for wetland use.[2] Each principle pertains to the hazards or values listed in Chapter 1 and broader objectives for protection and management of wetland areas. Each of these principles may be implemented through specific land and water use standards.

These principles and standards can serve as the basis for public education, public land use management, comprehensive land use planning, wetland acquisition, zoning ordinances, land use regulation, and/or the evaluation of proposed developments. They must be modified to reflect circumstances and preferences when applied to a specific area. They must also be balanced with broader State and community goals for water resources, land use and economic development.

Principle One: Wetland activities should not cause damaging increases in flood heights or velocities nor should the activities in themselves be seriously damaged by flooding.

A primary community objective for the control of wetland uses should be the protection of lands from increased flood damages and the requirement that damage-prone uses be protected against flooding. As noted earlier, certain wetland activities often increase flood heights and velocities on other lands. Moreover, wetland uses such as residences and commercial uses are themselves subject to flood hazards.

The adoption of regulations to reduce flood damages has sometimes been considered "protecting a man against himself." Nevertheless, broader justification is found in the protection of subsequent purchasers of property, protection of guests and family of the floodplain occupant, and the avoidance of substantial community expenses for flood relief and flood control works.

The statutes of many States require that local units of government adopt floodplain regulations meeting State standards (e.g., Washington, Wisconsin, Minnesota, Michigan, New Jersey, Kansas, California, New York). In addition, the national Flood Insurance Program requires that local units adopt floodplain and floodway regulations to qualify for national flood insurance.

Efforts to prevent increased flood heights and velocities on other lands usually emphasize the protection of one essential wetland component—wetland topography. Maintenance of natural contours is needed for the passage of flood flows, flood storage and protection of storm barriers. Standards and approaches to prevent increased flood heights and velocities and to protect flood-prone uses include the following (see also Figure 8):

o Fills, buildings, and other obstructions in wetlands which serve as floodway areas should be tightly controlled. Often floodway areas are defined at State or local levels to include stream channels and overbank areas necessary to convey the 100 year flood with no greater than one foot (or some lesser figure) of increased flood height. This standard is applied by the Federal Emergency Management Agency in the Flood Insurance Program and by most State floodplain regulatory programs.[3]

o Fills or structures in wetlands serving as flood storage areas, and should be tightly controlled. Protection of flood storage is not mandated by the National Flood Insurance Program or most State floodplain regulatory programs. However, many communities have adopted regulations to protect flood storage by controlling fills and other structures in broader floodplain areas (e.g., the 50 or 100 year floodplain). Such regulations are particularly appropriate for smaller streams in urbanizing areas where wetlands may play a critical flood storage role.

o Buildings located in wetlands forming part of the 100 year floodplain should be protected against flood through elevation on pilings or other techniques, which will allow the wetland and floodplain to function naturally. Protection to or above the elevation of the 100 year flood is required by State floodplain programs

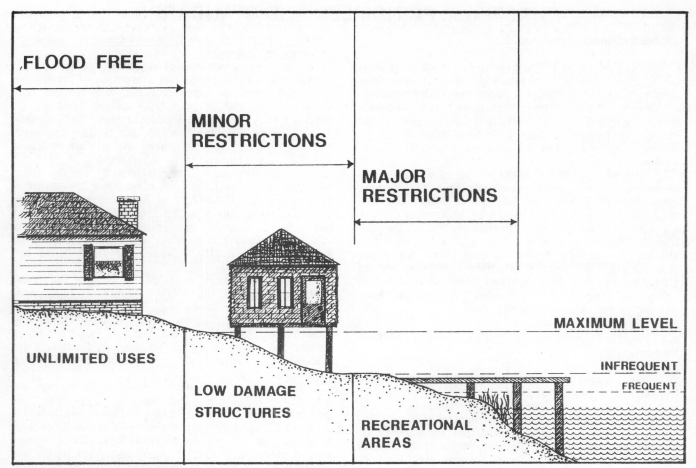

FIGURE 8. BUILDING STANDARDS FOR FLOOD HAZARD AREAS

and the National Flood Insurance Program.

o   Toxic and hazardous chemicals, wood, and other materials that threaten public safety or cause damage to other lands during flood conditions should not be stored or deposited in wetland areas.

Principle Two: Wetland activities should not cause water pollution or diminish natural pollution control functions.

Certain activities in wetlands may contribute pollutants to wetlands and downstream areas or alter the capacity of wetlands to assimilate pollutants from other sources.   Natural wetland pollution control functions may be destroyed by filling, grading, soil removal, interference with wetland water supply or circulation, and destruction of wetland vegetation.

The prevention of pollution from septic tank and soil absorption systems in high groundwater areas is often a major State and community wetland regulation objective.   Faulty septic systems may pollute nearby wells and properties as well as wetland areas.

Standards and approaches to prevent pollution from wetland activities include the following:

o   Point sources of pollution should be regulated (such as factories, houses, commercial establishments, etc.), through water quality and effluent standards. Point source pollution controls are commonly adopted at the State level although some community regulations have also been adopted.

o   Plumbing and sanitary codes, and subdivision regulations should be adopted prohibiting septic tank and soil absorption systems in high groundwater areas.   These regulations may be adopted at both State and local levels.

o   Construction of lagoons, dredging, filling, and disposal of spoil, should be regulated within wetland areas.   Discharge of dredge or fill materials into the waters of the U.S. is regulated, in part, by the U.S. Army Corps of Engineers and the Environmental Protection Agency under Section 404 of the Clean Water Act of 1977.   (See discussion in Chapter 5.) Dredging in navigable waters is regulated by the Corps of Engineers under Section 10 of the Rivers and Harbors Act of 1899.

o   Storage of chemicals, wood, fuel and other materials should be regulated in wetland and floodplain areas where the materials may be swept away by flooding.   Storage regulations are often included in State and local floodplain regulations.

o   Activities which alter wetland contours or vegetation should be regulated, especially where wetlands serve as sediment traps and nutrient filters for lakes, streams and estuaries.

Principle Three: Buildings, roads, and other structures should not be constructed in areas lacking adequate soil bearing capacity.

Buildings and other structures located on wetland soils with high water and organic content often settle differentially due to compaction of the soils. This may subject structures to flooding or damaging stresses, and could, in fact, constitute a threat to public safety particularly if the structure is a public facility (e.g., a restaurant, marina, or apartment complex).

Standards and approaches to prevent soil bearing capacity problems include:

o   Building codes, zoning and other regulations should be adopted incorporating performance standards for soil bearing capacity for buildings, roads, and other structures.

o   Performance standards should require use of pilings, hard fill or other measures to provide adequate foundation support prior to building construction.

Principle Four: Wetland activities should not destroy or seriously damage wetland functions essential to public safety and general welfare.

Efforts to protect wetland functions discussed in Chapter 1 and summarized in Table 1 must consider the topographic, hydrologic, botanical and other requirements of each function and the role each plays in maintaining the wetland area. Essential wetland features giving rise to these functions and performance standards needed to protect these are presented in Table 4. In sum:

o   A topographic depression or gradient in bedrock, glacial till, alluvium or other mineral or organic material serves as a water catchment basin, overflow area, or discharge area for ground or surface waters. Topography is the major determinant of wetland size, water depth and water flow patterns. Maintenance of topographic contours is essential to flood flows, flood storage and all other wetland functions.

o   Each wetland has a substrate of rock, sand, gravel, silt, shells, peat, etc. The suitability of a wetland for waterfowl, wildlife and vegetation (pollution control function) depends, to a considerable degree, upon the nature of the substrate.

o   Usually, wetlands derive water from several sources, such as direct precipitation, surface runoff, rivers and streams, lakes, the ocean, or groundwater. The ratio of one source to another often determines water quality. Water supply and both annual and seasonal distribution is a principal factor determining vegetation types and health of the wetland community. Wetland functions such as fish spawning, flood storage, flood conveyance and pollution control are dependent upon water supply and free circulation of waters.

o   A source of nutrients is needed from influent water, sediments, detritus and other sources. The types, diversity and quantity of wetland vegetation, waterfowl, and other forms of wildlife are determined by available nutrient supplies.

o   A source of energy is required for growth of plants and animals. Many wetland functions dependent upon vegetation (wildlife habitat, recreation, education, scientific study), require a source of energy. The principal source of energy for wetland plants and wildlife is the sun.

o   Wetland vegetation and fish and wildlife resources influence, and are influenced by, the wetland components discussed above. Vegetation is important to many wetland functions including fish reproduction, pollution control, storm damage reduction, erosion control, scientific study and recreational uses. Vegetation depends upon water depth and quality, available nutrients and the nature of the substrate. In turn, vegetation determines, over time, depth and substrate. Similarly, fish and other wildlife, such as muskrats and alligators, depend upon vegetation, yet are themselves the determinants of wetland water depth since they consume wetland vegetation and mechanically excavate channels and holes.

Maintenance of wetland functions requires not only maintaining the features but the physical and biological relationships which permit a wetland to perform those functions. For example, if a community or State wishes to maintain a wetland as a fish spawning area protection measures would be needed to maintain the entire biological system.

Principle Five: Wetland activities should be consistent with Federal, State and local land use and water planning and management programs.

Appropriate wetland uses depend upon broader land and water management goals. These are determined, in part, by existing uses, existing regulations, adjacent land uses, public facilities servicing or planned for areas, wetland values and hazards, the impact of proposed uses on wetlands, the need for development, and alternative sites for development. The compatibility of wetland activities with these factors may often be determined without comprehensive community land or water use planning. Nevertheless, such planning can help determine the compatibility of wetland uses with broader social and economic needs, including the demand for new residential, industrial and commercial development.

Standards and approaches for insuring compatibility are as follows:

o   Wetland activities should comply with existing regulations and not cause nuisances to adjacent uses by blocking flood flows, polluting waters, or by causing excessive noise, glare, dust, odors, traffic, or other impacts. Such standards may be incorporated in conservancy, residential or other zoning for wetlands and adjacent areas that separate incompatible uses (a traditional zoning function). Regulations requiring minimum separation distances between potentially incompatible uses, such as a requirement that solid waste disposal sites not be located within 1,000 feet of existing residences, are another technique for promoting compatibility of uses. Performance standards for wetland and adjacent uses provide another alternative to ensure that impacts do not exceed assigned limits.

NATURAL CONDITIONS

Precipitation

Under natural forest or prairie, hills store water for steady clean flow into wetlands, streams and lakes

Limited runoff (retarded by vegetation, soils)

Annual water-level fluctuation

Strong seeps and springs

Steady flow

Late fall high

Groundwater

Water table is high

Early fall low

Spring high

Late summer low

Glacial till

Precipitation

RURAL CONDITIONS

Trees on slope now cannot stop flow or erosion

Accelerates runoff. Agriculture and urbanization runoff carries soil and fertilizer into wetland and raises water levels temporarily. Base flows are reduced

Fast runoff

Wide erratic fluctuation

Late fall high

Groundwater

Very little flow

Spring high (flood)

Early fall low

Stable shore plants may die; few springs flow weakly

Only traces percolate down deep so water table sinks

Late summer low-low

Unstable weedy shores

Soft muddy bottom

Urban well

URBAN CONDITIONS

Urbanization further increases runoff and discharges of soil, fertilizers and pollutants into wetlands. Water tables may also be lowered through pumping

Very rapid runoff

Wide erratic fluctuation

Spring high

No springs

Only nuisance plants and animals

Late summer low-low

Cone of depression

Late fall high

Groundwater

Backward flow

Early fall low

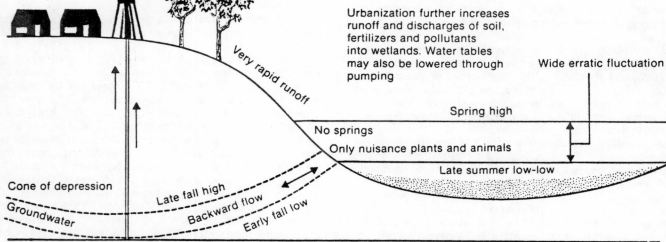

FIGURE 9. HYDROLOGY AND WETLAND HEALTH. Adapted from *Wetlands of Dane County,* Dane County Planning Committee, Madison, Wisconsin.

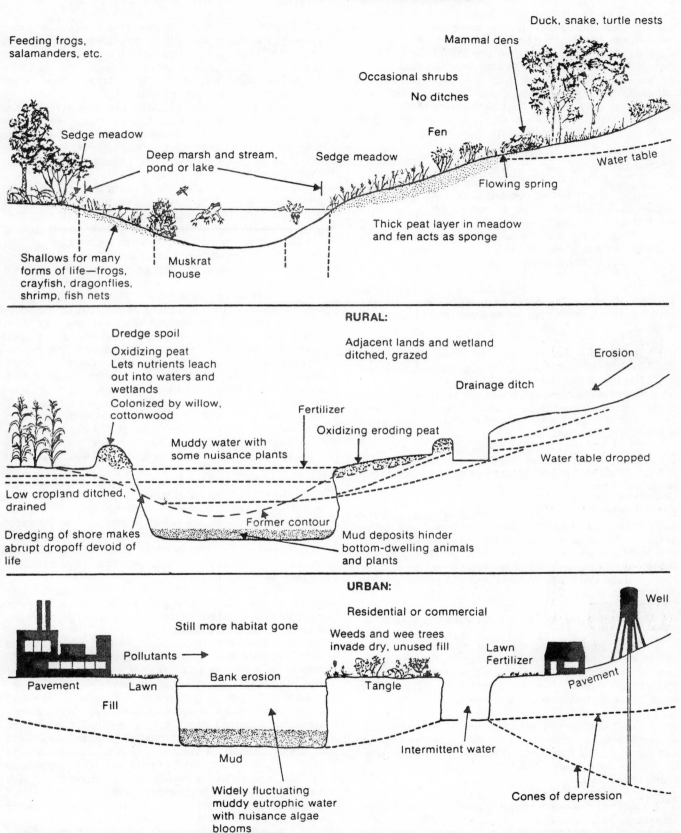

NATURAL CONDITION:

Duck, snake, turtle nests

Mammal dens

Feeding frogs, salamanders, etc.

Occasional shrubs

No ditches

Sedge meadow

Fen

Deep marsh and stream, pond or lake

Sedge meadow

Water table

Flowing spring

Thick peat layer in meadow and fen acts as sponge

Shallows for many forms of life—frogs, crayfish, dragonflies, shrimp, fish nets

Muskrat house

RURAL:

Dredge spoil

Adjacent lands and wetland ditched, grazed

Erosion

Oxidizing peat Lets nutrients leach out into waters and wetlands Colonized by willow, cottonwood

Drainage ditch

Fertilizer

Muddy water with some nuisance plants

Oxidizing eroding peat

Water table dropped

Low cropland ditched, drained

Former contour

Dredging of shore makes abrupt dropoff devoid of life

Mud deposits hinder bottom-dwelling animals and plants

URBAN:

Well

Residential or commercial

Still more habitat gone

Weeds and wee trees invade dry, unused fill

Lawn Fertilizer

Pollutants →

Bank erosion

Tangle

Pavement

Lawn

Pavement

Fill

Intermittent water

Mud

Cones of depression

Widely fluctuating muddy eutrophic water with nuisance algae blooms

FIGURE 10. SHORELINES AND WETLAND HEALTH.

o   Wetland activities should comply with community plans for sewer, water, roads, dikes, levees and other public works and not place a disproportionately heavy burden upon the community for these services. These regulations may take the form of zoning and subdivision regulations either prohibiting or carefully controlling uses in flood hazard, erosion and similar areas where roads and sewers are disproportionately expensive to construct and maintain. Subdivision regulations may require that developers at their own expense install roads, sewers, and water supply systems which meet community standards.

Principle Six: Activities should be conducted to minimize their impact upon wetlands.

Where it is not desirable or possible to locate damaging activities at upland sites, all reasonable measures should be taken to minimize impact upon natural wetland functions.

Standards and approaches for minimizing impact include many of those listed above and in Chapter 5. Additional standards are listed below.

o   Development should be located on the upland portion of lots. The total area within each lot that may be filled, paved, or otherwise altered should be limited.

o   Developers should be required to prepare environmental impact statements for larger projects.

o   Proposed activities should be required to meet performance standards for construction and operation to minimize impact upon natural drainage, vegetation, wildlife and other values.

o   Land subdivisions should be required to incorporate open space. Structures should be clustered on upland sites to preserve wetland areas.

o   Conditions should be attached to zoning, subdivision control, building, sanitary, and other permits to require replanting of denuded areas, construction of settling ponds to protect wetlands from pollutants, and, in some instances, creation of new wetland areas where development causes wetland destruction or damage.

4.4 Approaches for Applying Principles and Standards

The wetland impact of a particular activity varies according to the wetland characteristics and the type of activity, its design, location, associated uses, and other factors. Wetland regulatory efforts often separate activities into three categories:

o   Construction and maintenance of buildings such as residences, apartments, factories, farmhouses, and commercial establishments. These are often regulated by State and local building codes and zoning ordinances.

o   Construction and maintenance of non-building structures such as roads, bridges, dams, dikes, levees, tunnels, groins, and breakwaters. These are sometimes regulated at the State level through wetland or dredge and fill laws, but more often at the local level through zoning or special codes. Local land use regulations are rarely applied to governmental uses.

o   Open space uses not involving building or other construction such as agriculture, forestry, dredging, solid and liquid waste disposal, drainage, and mosquito control. Dredging and waste disposal are, in some instances, regulated at the State level. Most other open space uses are not regulated.

All three types of activities may have serious wetland impacts. For this reason, regulatory approaches that control building construction alone are only partially effective. Low density residential uses may, in many areas, have less impact upon wetlands than agriculture.

Because of the variable impact of wetland activities, two principal wetland regulatory approaches are used: (1) a broad exclusion of virtually all uses that might damage wetlands through public acquisition of land or tight regulations, and (2) application of less restrictive performance standards and guidelines incorporating many of the principles and standards discussed above.

There are advantages to complete prohibition of development. First, complete prohibition is necessary in some instances to protect vital wetland functions. Practically all uses (even carefully conducted uses) may threaten sensitive plants and animals and reduce wetland educational and scientific values. Second, complete prohibition avoids the problem of cumulative impact when individual uses are permitted on a case-by-case basis. Third, prohibition reduces the required data base since less data is needed if individual uses are not permitted within wetland areas. Fourth, prohibition requires less expertise during administrative phases of a program since no individual development permits are allowed.

On the other hand, complete prohibition through regulation is often politically unacceptable, and may result in constitutional challenges. Complete prohibition reduces the tax base and lowers the value of wetlands by preventing production of timber, marsh hay, and other natural products. Complete prohibition is, in some instances, more appropriately achieved through land acquisition.

The second approach—involving less restrictive performance standards or guidelines—has been applied widely in both State and local regulatory programs. Standards or guidelines may take the form of "performance" standards and apply to a wide range of uses, or they may take the form of more specific standards and apply to particular uses. The principles and standards suggested above and in Table 2 are examples of general performance standards that may be applied through a permit procedure. Performance standards usually employ a combination of quantified and unquantified criteria aimed at the ultimate impact of uses. Quantified standards may pertain to density of development (lot size), percentage of impermeable surface, water quality standards, and flood protection elevations (the 100 year flood). Unquantified standards pertain to wildlife protection, aesthetic values, and other functions.

Performance standards have several theoretical advantages. First, they reduce wetland protection and management to a relatively discrete and understandable set of principles that may be applied to all types of uses. Second, they permit an examination of the impact of each individual use in terms of its specific design characteristics and specific values and hazards at a site. Third, they focus data gathering efforts upon specific impacts. Fourth, they often allow a wide number of options in the private use of land, engender less political opposition, and are less vulnerable to constitutional challenges.

Performance standards are, however, subject to several limitations. First, unquantified performance standards create uncertainty regarding permissible private uses of the land. Second, regulatory agencies often have difficulty in calculating the cumulative impact of such uses. Third, performance standards require considerable time and expertise in administration and enforcement. Fourth, they lead to problems in maintaining a consistent approach.

Although the application of a performance standard approach is often desirable, performance standards may be combined with more specific standards for particular uses such as a requirement that residential uses not be located in wetland areas. These have the advantages of specificity and certainty but may lack flexibility.

4.5 Application to Specific Uses

The following discussion illustrates the application of principles and standards to particular uses.

Airports
Airports are often located in wetland areas along major lakes or the ocean where large tracts of undeveloped land are available at low price. Examples include the Washington, San Francisco, and Boston airports. The controversy over the Everglades jetport is well known. Wetland disturbance results from filling and grading for runway construction, interference with natural drainage patterns, and pollution from the runway surfaces and exhaust particles. The impact of airport construction may be reduced by:
A.   Avoiding high quality wetland sites.
B.   Providing a buffer strip of vegetation between runways and adjacent wetlands.
C.   Tightly regulating the dumping of aviation fuel and other wastes.
D.   Treating airport runoff before discharge into wetlands.
E.   Carefully designing drainage systems to maintain natural flow of waters.

Agriculture
Agricultural practices are the principal threat to wetlands in many areas. Drainage destroys wetland vegetation and wildlife. Diking interferes with wetland water and nutrient supplies. Other impacts include nutrient enrichment from agricultural runoff (fertilizers, manure), sedimentation from the erosion and discharge of soil into waterways, introduction of toxic chemicals from agricultural pesticides and herbicides, disturbance of wetland water supplies by agricultural pumping, introduction of exotic species into wetland areas, and destruction of wetland vegetation and wildlife by plowing, harvesting, and other practices.
Wetland impacts may be minimized by:
A.   Utilizing minimum tillage farming techniques.
B.   Avoiding drainage and diking.
C.   Adopting soil conservation measures to control erosion and agricultural runoff.
D.   Maintaining wetland buffer areas.
E.   Fencing streamside wetlands and influent streams to reduce erosion and direct pollution by cattle.
F.   Reducing application of manure to frozen soils during the winter.
G.   Controlling pesticide and herbicide applications.
H.   Increasing wild crop harvesting and agriculture consistent with natural wetland characteristics.

Dams
Wetlands are directly destroyed by the construction of dams and reservoirs. Fluctuating water levels in reservoirs may prevent reestablishment of wetlands at the margins of the new water bodies. Dams also destroy and damage downstream wetlands by reducing flows, altering the timing of flows, and reducing or increasing nutrient and sediment supplies.
Adverse wetland impacts may be minimized by:
A.   Avoiding major wetlands as sites for dams or reservoirs.
B.   Designing reservoirs and maintaining reservoir water levels to encourage reestablishment of wetlands at reservoir boundaries.
C.   Designing dams so that water can be withdrawn from lower levels to ensure continued conveyance of nutrients to downstream wetlands.
D.   Timing water releases to benefit downstream aquatic and animal life.

Dikes, Levees, Seawalls
Dikes, levees and seawalls are constructed as flood or erosion control measures in wetlands along streams and at coastal locations. They interfere with natural flood and drainage patterns and nutrient supplies. Interference with water circulation is a particularly serious problem at coastal locations where salt marshes must be continually exposed to tidal action if they are to provide nutrients to estuarine areas and serve as spawning and feeding areas for coastal fish and shellfish. Inland dikes and levees deprive wetlands of rich alluvial soil which is normally deposited by natural flooding. They may also deprive wetlands of water supply, ecologically separating them from nearby waters.
Wetland impacts may be reduced by:
A.   Avoiding high quality wetlands.
B.   Equipping seawalls, levees and dikes with floodgates to permit the normal circulation of waters except during times of flooding.
C.   Reestablishing vegetation on soil dikes and levees to reduce erosion.

Dredging

Dredging to deepen channel areas or create new channels is a major threat to wetland areas along rivers and streams used for water transportation, at coastal sites used for ports, marinas, and water transport, and along lakes and at ocean sites where residential boat access is desired. Deepening, widening, and straightening of natural stream channels is also undertaken along streams and rivers to reduce flood heights and lower high groundwater levels. Wetlands that are dredged are permanently destroyed. Dredging damages downstream wetlands due to increased water turbidity and sediment. Dredging may also alter circulation patterns and salinity balance. Dredge spoil is highly erodible and difficult to stabilize.

Wetland impacts may be reduced by:

A. Avoiding dredging in, adjacent to, or immediately upstream from high and medium value wetlands.
B. Avoiding stream channelization for lowering of water levels.
C. Avoiding dredging solely for the purpose of creating fill for residential or nonwater dependent development.
D. Disposing of spoil at upland sites and quickly stabilizing it.
E. Constructing channels at a minimum depth and width capable of achieving the intended purposes. Sides of channels should reflect an equilibrium shape to prevent slumping and erosion and allow revegetation.
F. Conducting dredging at times of minimum biological activity to avoid disrupting fish migration and spawning.

Power Plants

Power plants pose severe threats to both coastal and inland wetlands since they require large, low cost sites and (in some instances) water access for transport of coal or oil and for cooling purposes. Wetland areas may be displaced or damaged by filling and grading, plant construction, access roads, cooling lakes, fuel storage areas, power transmission lines, waste disposal, and by dredging to install pipelines and to maintain access channels for fuel barges. Power plants may also destroy adjacent wetland areas by interfering with natural drainage patterns, polluting air and water, and increasing water temperature by discharge of cooling waters. Fish and other organisms may be killed by impingement or entrainment in plant cooling systems.

Impacts may be reduced by:

A. Avoiding high quality wetland sites.
B. Tightly controlling air and water pollution emissions.
C. Designing plant cooling systems to prevent entrapment of fish and damaging increases in water temperature.
D. Rehabilitating damaged wetland areas through planting and other techniques.
E. Disposing of slag and other wastes at upland sites.

Industries

Industries are often constructed in coastal and riverine wetland areas due to the low cost of the land, and the availability of water for transport, cooling, manufacturing, and waste disposal. Industries destroy wetlands by filling and grading, and damage them by interfering with drainage, emitting pollutants, and extracting ground or surface water. Access roads and storage areas may also result in severe wetland impacts.

Impacts may be reduced by:

A. Avoiding high quality wetland sites.
B. Vigorous enforcement of water and air pollution laws.
C. Locating access roads, parking and storage areas, waste disposal and ancillary uses at upland sites.
D. Rehabilitating damaged wetland areas.

Marinas and Piers

Marinas and piers often displace wetlands located along rivers and coastal sites. Other impacts include wetland destruction from dredging to maintain channels, increased water turbidity and disturbance of natural vegetation and wildlife by motor boats, and pollution of waters by motor fuels. Parking and boat storage areas may destroy wildlife habitats and contribute polluted runoff.

Impacts may be reduced by:

A. Avoiding high quality wetland sites.
B. Locating marinas in naturally well flushed areas rather than in artificial channels where water circulation is often poor.
C. Locating parking and boat storage areas at upland sites.
D. Encouraging the utilization of "boatels".
E. Encouraging the use of "zonation mooring" at marinas (smaller draft boats use the shallower nearshore waters, and deeper draft boats are moored in deeper waters) thus reducing the amount of dredging necessary.

Mining

Sand and gravel operations threaten wetlands adjacent to some stream and marine habitats. Mining of shells and phosphates threatens coastal sites. Operations that remove the wetland substrate and vegetation cause direct damage and serious turbidity problems for downstream areas. Coal mining, oil and gas wells, and other extractive industries may cause water pollution, even if located far from wetland sites.

Impacts may be reduced by:

A. Avoiding high value wetland areas and immediate upstream areas.
B. Rigorous enforcement of pollution controls.
C. Avoiding coastal mining in the active surf zones.
D. Using settling ponds and other water treatment facilities to reduce sediment runoff and other pollutants from sand and gravel and other mining activities.
E. Using buffer strips between mining areas and adjacent wetlands to retard the run-

off of sediment, chemicals, oils, and other pollutants.

F. Reclaiming mine areas at upland sites to stabilize open surfaces and reduce sediment loadings.

G. Rehabilitating damaged wetland areas.

Residences

Residential development is an increasing threat to wetlands due to escalating land values that justify fill and drainage. Dredging and channelization to provide fill and boat access have been common for residential development on ocean shores and lakeshores. Other impacts of residential uses include damage to wetland wildlife from tree clearing and disturbance of wetland vegetation; sedimentation caused by grading, filling, and other construction activities; interference with wetland drainage and water supply by access roads, dikes, seawalls, and domestic wells; and increased groundwater and surface water nutrient loadings from septic tanks and lawn fertilizers.

Often wetland sites are poor residential sites even after reclamation. Low lying sites continue to be flood-prone, and basement flooding and drainage problems are common. Uneven subsidence of wetland soils causes uneven stress to structures and may result in cracks or other damage. Onsite waste disposal systems function poorly in high groundwater areas and in peaty soils where shallow fill is placed over natural wetland soils.

Impacts may be reduced by:

A. Locating buildings and access roads on upland sites.

B. Avoiding dredging and lagooning to provide fill and boat access for residential sites.

C. Grading to maintain natural topographic contours and reduce erosion.

D. Regulating tree-cutting and vegetation removal in wetlands and wetland buffers.

E. Avoiding septic tanks in high groundwater areas and peaty soils.

F. Carefully complying with flood elevation and floodway protection requirements.

G. Constructing buildings on the upland portion of lots to lower the overall density of uses.

H. Constructing access roads to maintain natural drainage.

I. Treating storm drainage before discharge into wetlands.

Roads and Bridges

Roads and bridges are constructed in wetlands in the normal course of roadbuilding and to provide access to shoreland areas for new residential, recreational, and other types of development. Damage results from roadbed fill, removal of wetland soils to provide a stable road or bridge base, interference with natural drainage, sedimentation from roadway construction, pollution by toxic chemicals from exhaust gases and road salting, oil runoff, and destruction of wetland wildlife by road traffic. In addition, roads and bridges often block flood flows, thereby increasing flood heights and velocities on other lands. Construction of roads through wetland areas encourages residential and other development.

Wetland impacts may be reduced by:

A. Locating roads at upland sites and designing them to curve around wetland areas. This will often result in a more aesthetically pleasing roadway as well as reduced wetland impacts.

B. Avoiding extension of minor roadways into wetland areas where they encourage private development.

C. Designing roadways and bridges to maintain natural flow parallel to drainage, elevation of roadway surfaces on pile supports, design of bridge openings to convey storm flows, and installation of culverts.

D. Erecting fences to protect deer, raccoons, and other wildlife from highway traffic.

E. Minimizing the impact of construction through measures to reduce erosion including the replanting of open surfaces and the construction of sediment retention facilities.

F. Rehabilitating damaged wetland areas.

G. Avoiding the use of road salt.

Septic Tanks

In rural areas, domestic waste waters are discharged into septic tanks and subsurface soil absorption systems. Soil absorption is severely limited in wetland areas by high groundwater and peaty soil conditions. Unable to flow into the soil, liquids back up into dwellings or flow out into the ground surface, causing odor nuisances, health problems, and nutrient enrichment of nearby waters.

Wetland impacts may be reduced by:

A. Avoiding the use of new and local laws prohibiting new septic tank systems in high groundwater areas including areas immediately adjacent to wetlands.

B. Inspecting existing septic systems in flood hazard and high groundwater areas to ensure proper operation.

C. Using holding tanks, gas incinerator toilets, public sewers, and other alternatives to septic tanks.

Solid Waste Disposal

Solid waste disposal sites are often located in inland and coastal wetlands due to their low cost and topographic contours. Solid waste disposal may destroy all wetland values. In addition, solid wastes may pollute downstream areas by contributing litter, nutrients, oils, and toxic chemicals to runoff. Groundwater pollution poses a severe problem, and air pollution may also result.

Wetland impacts may be reduced by:

A. Avoiding use of high value wetlands and adjacent floodplains where wastes may be dispersed by flooding. Waste disposal sites should also be located away from drainage courses.

B. Avoiding discharge of toxic materials where they may pollute runoff waters or groundwaters.

C. Recycling of materials to reduce the total

quantity of solid waste. Other techniques for reducing quantity include compaction, incineration of materials, and reduction in use.

D.   Using settling basins and other measures to reduce water pollution.

E.   Maintaining buffer strips between solid waste disposal sites and wetlands.

Storm Drains

Runoff from urban areas, residential subdivisions, marinas, and other developments may pollute wetland areas. Pollutants include, but are not limited to, trash, oils, pesticides, nutrients from lawn fertilizers and septic tanks, sediment, soap, and industrial chemicals. Natural vegetated drainage ways remove much of this material before it reaches wetland areas. However, storm drainage systems provide no filtering.

Wetland impacts may be reduced by:

A.   Maintaining natural, open, vegetated drainage ways, rather than concrete, enclosed storm sewers. If enclosed storm drain systems are necessary at a given location, place inlets in grass swales so that the storm water will be filtered prior to its entering the closed system.

B.   Treating storm runoff before it enters wetlands through settling ponds, special treatment facilities, or combined storm drainage and sewer systems.

C.   Carefully controlling the use and discharge of pesticide applications, fertilizer use, oil spills, and other sources of damaging materials in the watershed.

D.   Limiting the rate of flow of storm water from the developed site to predevelopment rates through onsite detention ponds.

CHAPTER 5: EVALUATING DEVELOPMENT PROPOSALS

As outlined in Chapter 4, two main approaches are used to protect wetlands: (1) complete prohibition of fills, dredging, and structural uses through land acquisition, agreements with landowners, or highly restrictive regulations; and (2) application of regulatory performance standards to uses to reduce flood losses, reduce impact upon wildlife, and serve a wide range of other objectives. Few local regulatory programs prohibit all public and private wetland activities. Instead, regulatory agencies evaluate individual activities on a case-by-case basis to determine their impact on wetland areas and their compliance with statutory and ordinance standards. Usually regulatory agencies exercise broad discretion in evaluating the impact of a proposed development, determining whether the development is appropriate for the proposed site, and formulating conditions for the permit that will minimize adverse impacts to wetlands.

Chapter 5 briefly outlines local procedures for evaluating development proposals. Additional analysis is provided in Chapters 6, 7, and 8 which consider Federal, State, and local wetland regulatory programs.

5.1 Steps in Evaluating Permits

Typically, six steps are followed in evaluating permits:[1]

1. Discussion prior to submission of a formal permit application. A developer often contacts the regulatory agency to discuss proposed fill, structure, or other related activities preceding the formulation of specific project plans. The developer may submit a tentative "sketch" plan. Such informal contacts are desirable before the developer invests large sums in project plans and becomes less flexible. The zoning administrator or other official may visit the proposed development site to determine whether it lies within a wetland, and, if so, the possible wetland impact. Often a developer agrees to confine his activity to the upland in order to avoid regulatory requirements and delays. Negotiations on project design may follow if all or a portion of the project lies within the wetland. All of this may take place prior to submission of a formal permit application.

2. Submission of formal application. The developer submits a formal permit application, usually on forms provided by the regulatory agency. Copies may be sent to adjacent landowners and other agencies. Usually the application must contain detailed information concerning the project design, location of the proposed activity, and the specific wetland characteristics at the site. An environmental impact statement may be required, particularly for larger projects if the proposed project is being funded or conducted by a Federal agency or State law requires one. If a field survey was not conducted at an earlier stage, regulatory agency personnel usually conduct a field investigation to evaluate the impact of the proposed use. Special studies concerning potential problems may also be required from the developer. Considerable negotiation on the project design may follow between the developer and the agency, if preliminary discussions were not carried out.

3. Public hearing. Depending on the State statute or local ordinance, a public hearing is held on the proposal.

4. Decision on the permit. The regulatory agency approves, denies, or conditionally approves the proposed activity based on information supplied by the developer, the agency, or participants in the public hearing. Often the proposed activity is permitted, subject to conditions relating to location, protection against flooding, erosion control measures, protection of natural vegetation, and other matters.

5. Appeal. If dissatisfied with the decision of the regulatory agency, the applicant or other aggrieved party may appeal the decision to a court specified in the enabling statute or, less commonly, to a State appeals board.

6. Project initiation. If the application has been approved and all necessary permits received, the developer may then initiate the proposed activity. In some instances, the developer is required to post a performance bond to ensure that the project is conducted in accordance with permit stipulations. The regulatory agency may inspect the development once it has been completed to determine compliance.

A number of key issues arises in this permitting process:

o What factors are to be considered in evaluating the impact of proposed activities?

o What minimum standards are to be applied in determining whether a proposed activity is to be approved, denied, or conditionally approved?

o What data gathering is necessary to evaluate proposed development, and who is to carry out this data gathering?

o What conditions are to be attached to permits?

5.2 Factors in Impact Assessment

The impact of a proposed activity depends upon seven major factors: (1) the type and design of the proposed activity including all ancillary uses; (2) the specific wetland characteristics, including all values and hazards at the site; (3) the location of the site in the wetland; (4) the importance of wetland functions to broader hydrological and ecological systems; (5) existing uses and adjacent land uses that may be affected by the proposed activity; (6) available and planned public services such as sewers, water, and roads; and (7) broader community land and water use plans. Tables 5 and 6 list other factors and information needs in impact assessment.

Often a quick review of a permit application will suggest factors requiring special attention. For example, a proposed industrial use may result not only in filling of the wetland but also dredging to provide for boat access and the discharge of industrial wastes.

For analytic purposes, it is important that cumulative impacts as well as impacts on specific wetland functions be evaluated. The reversibility of impact is also important. Refer back to Table 1 for a list of wetland functions that may be affected by specific development.

Various impacts accompany each of nine major steps in construction identified by Professor Rezneat

Darnell at Texas A&M University in a report prepared for the Environmental Protection Agency, Impacts of Construction Activities in Wetlands of the United States.[2] This useful report analyzes in considerable depth the impact of particular types of activities and contains an excellent 1,000 item bibliography. The report suggests "factor train analyses" for evaluating impacts, which are reproduced in Figures 11 through 16. Impacts of construction activities are analyzed in three general time-related categories: (1) direct and immediate results that take place during the construction process; (2) effects that occur during the period of stabilization following completion of the construction; and (3) long-term effects or more or less permanent change brought about by the construction itself or by subsequent human use and environmental management occasioned by the constructed facilities.

Some State and local programs evaluate not only the impacts of the immediate development proposal but potential impacts of similar proposals. Efforts to evaluate such "cumulative impact" involve the making of difficult assumptions concerning future proposals. Nevertheless, the failure to anticipate future impacts gradually undermines protection efforts.

5.3 Data Gathering for Assessment Purposes

The National Environmental Policy Act requires Federal agencies to prepare environmental impact statements for Federal or Federally funded projects with significant impacts upon the environment. Executive Orders adopted by President Carter establish criteria for projects in wetland and floodplain areas. (See Chapter 6.) In addition, at least 13 States have adopted State statutes requiring that State agencies, local units of government, and, in some instances, private developers, prepare impact statements.

These broad environmental impact laws apply to many public projects, even those not regulated through State and local wetland protection efforts. By requiring a careful analysis of project impact, they encourage informed agency decision-making.

In addition to these broad environmental impact laws, most States and local wetland regulations require that developers prepare a formal impact statement or submit detailed information concerning the specifics of the proposed activity, wetland values and hazards at the proposed site, and the impact of the activity on those values and hazards.

Some programs distinguish between activities with a high probability of impact on a wetland and those with low probability. More information is required from those with high probability.

In permit analysis, the data submitted by the developer are often supplemented by data gathering and analysis by the regulatory agency. Existing topographic maps, soil maps, flood maps, and other information sources are used to evaluate wetland values and hazards. Although these sources may not be sufficient in themselves to evaluate total impact, they are useful in determining ground and surface water flow systems, the general characteristics of wetland, watershed, and adjacent land uses, flood elevations, and the susceptibility of lands to erosion.

In addition, the regulatory agency may conduct field surveys to determine wetland vegetation, soils, erosion, existing uses, and other parameters. Some of this information can be quickly gathered by a trained observer who can spot potential problem areas such as erosion or deep organic soils. However, the gathering of other information such as subsurface geology, relationship of the site to groundwater flow systems, and the presence of specific animal life is much more difficult. Consultants are, in some instances, employed to conduct these more detailed studies, and the developer may be required to pay for them.

Additional sources of information commonly used in impact assessment include:

- Data gathering and technical assistance may be sought from Federal and State agencies. For example, local Soil Conservation Service personnel are often asked for soil evaluations. State Fish and Game personnel may be asked to conduct biological surveys.

- University personnel, conservation groups such as The Nature Conservancy and Audubon Society, and interested citizens may be asked to supply information concerning the proposed development site, wetland values and hazards, and the probable impact of the proposed development. They may also be asked to appear at public hearings concerning proposed development.

- Public hearings may be used as information generation devices to gather raw data concerning wetland characteristics and the possible impact of development and to assess public attitudes. Usually, anyone with an interest in the proposed activity is allowed to submit written evidence or testimony. While the quality of this evidence varies, it may assist the local agency in pinpointing problems and supplementing other sources of information.

5.4 Applying Regulatory Standards

Determination of project impact aids the regulatory agency in applying statutory or ordinance criteria and in determining whether a permit application should be approved. However, State and local wetland regulations do not usually establish rigid standards for evaluating permit applications. Instead, most regulations list general principles and factors that are to be applied by the regulatory agency. This approach permits maximum administrative discretion and the evaluation of each use on its merits, but it also may lead to landowner uncertainty and arbitrary issuance of permits. In addition, regulatory bodies are often reluctant to deny permit applications unless a specific minimum standard is violated. In the absence of specific minimum standards, most permits are conditionally granted.

It is desirable to have considerable certainty in regulatory standards without excessive rigidity where conditions are likely to vary greatly. Both certainty and flexibility may be provided through the simultaneous application of three general types of standards. These are as follows.

1. Minimum standards applying to certain uses or aspects of uses. Programs often establish several types of minimum standards for regulated activities. These may include:

TABLE 5. IMPACT ASSESSMENT

The following table lists key issues in assessing the impact of wetland activities. The list has been drawn from environmental impact guidelines from the Maryland wetland program and other sources.

GENERAL CRITERIA	SPECIFICS OF THE PROPOSED ACTIVITY	IMPACT ON WETLAND FUNCTIONS
1. What temporary and permanent physical changes in the wetland and the surrounding area will be caused by the proposed activity individually or in combination with existing and reasonably anticipated uses? Will these changes benefit or harm the wetland and the surrounding area? Who or what will be benefited or be harmed? What will be the magnitude of this benefit or harm? 2. What irreversible or irretrievable commitment of resources will be involved in the proposed activity? 3. What alternatives are available to the proposed action that would reduce environmental damage, including no-action alternatives? Why cannot the proposed activity be located on an upland site? Is the activity water-dependent or water-related? What measures will be taken during and after construction to reduce detrimental impacts? Will these measures be effective?	1. What type of activity is proposed (e.g., agricultural, industrial, residential)? What will be its dimensions, including width, length, height, depth? What materials will be used? What ancillary uses--such as parking lots, docks, boat channels, boat houses, roads, sewers, water supply facilities, sidewalks, loading spaces--are anticipated and what will their design specifics be? Is the proposed activity part of a broader project such as a subdivision of industrial park? If so, What are the overall characteristics of this project? 2. What is the precise location of the proposed activity in relation to wetland boundaries, flood boundaries, adjacent waters slopes, springs, existing land uses and adjacent uses? 3. How will the activity be carried out? What fill, grading, lagooning, diking, drainage or other modifications of natural topography, vegetation, and drainage will be carried out? Will water be extracted from the wetland, an influent stream, or the groundwater to serve the activity? If so, in what quantities and with what timing? Will solid or liquid wastes result from the use? What is the proposed method of water supply and waste disposal? What measures are being taken to protect the activity against flooding, erosion or other hazards? How will the proposed activity be constructed, including methods, time of the year, source of construction materials, disposal of wastes, and plants for revegetation? How will the activity be operated?	1. What impact will the activity have on specific wetland functions, including flood conveyance, flood storage, storm and erosion control, pollution control, water supply, oxygen production, recreation, fish and wildlife habitat, education and scientific study? How will the activity affect (a) the basic wetland configuration; (b) wetland water supply, including total amount, depth, rate of flow, timing, and circulation; (c) wetland water quality, including turbidity, BOD, heavy metal concentration, nutrients, toxic chemicals, temperature, salinity and other parameters; (d) wetland soils; (e) wetland nutrient sources; (f) wetland energy sources; (g) wetland vegetation, including types, dominant species, acreage, vitality and productivity; and (h) wetland fisheries, waterfowl and other wildlife, including species, dominant species, life cycles and predator-prey relationships? 2. How important are these functions? Is the wetland scarce or unique? What role does the wetland play in the broader hydrologic system? Is it a valuable water resource? Will alteration contaminate the water supplies? Will alteration harm recreation use or public rights in navigable waters? Will alteration cause increased flood damage to upstream, adjacent, or downstream properties? Will alteration destroy plant and animal life important to coastal or inland fisheries or migratory waterfowl? Will it introduce exotic species? Will it interfere with migration corridors? Will it destroy or injure threatened rare or endangered species? Will it enhance or eliminate aesthetic values with impact on adjacent property values, the integrity of the shoreline and seascape or the historical and cultural importance of the site? Will alteration affect public access to waters or the amenities of wetland areas?

IMPACT ON ADJACENT LANDS	ECONOMIC IMPACT	IMPACT ON REGULATIONS AND PLANS
1. What environment impacts will the activity have on other lands by interfering with flood conveyance, flood storage, drainage, groundwater quality and quantity, aesthetic values, fish and wildlife, storm and erosion control and water pollution control? 2. What other conflicts or damage will the activity cause to adjacent lands through dust, glare, water pollution, odor, noise, traffic, lights, smoke, storm runoff, and destruction of aesthetic values?	1. Will the activity be subject to flood, wind or erosion damages? How will these damages affect the community as a whole? Who will bear the costs? 2. Will public facilities such as roads, sewers, water, dikes, levees and sea walls be required for the activity? Will the activity destroy natural wetland water supply, pollution control, flood storage and other functions which must be re-established at other sites through construction of new public or private facilities? What will be the costs? Who will pay for them? 3. Will the activity have a beneficial or adverse effect on commercial sport fishing, hunting, biking, boating, camping, resort industry, restaurants, marine industry, agriculture and sale of land for second home or residential use? 4. How will the development affect the economy of the area, county, and State in terms of employment, tax base, public facilities and services? Are the economic benefits to the local economy of sufficient importance to justify the activity although significant alterations of the wetland would result?	1. Is the proposed activity consistent with existing Federal, State, and local regulations including zoning subdivision controls, building codes, pollution controls, dredging controls, mining controls, special wetland regulations, sanitary codes, floodplain regulations, soil and water conservation regulations, regulations pertaining to surface and ground water extraction, regulations pertaining to use of pesticides, algacides, etc., air pollution controls, and regulations for solid waste disposal? 2. Is the proposed activity consistent with local, regional, and State plans including comprehensive water and land use plans, water supply plans, recreation plans, flood control plans, sewer plans, solid waste disposal plans, road and transportation plans, and open space plans?

TABLE 6. WETLAND IMPACTS OF STEPS IN CONSTRUCTION

STEP	SPECIFIC ACTIVITIES	IMPACT	SUGGESTIONS FOR REDUCING IMPACT
1. Onsite Activities Prior to Construction (Most structural uses)	A. Surveying carried out to define terrain features, minor clearing of vegetation, placement of stakes.	A. Some destruction of natural vegetation; disturbance of wildlife due to transport of equipment to and from site, disposal of materials from drilling.	A. Use of air photo survey techniques.
	B. Engineering borings.		B. Regulation of survey methods and equipment, including time of year in which borings occur.
	C. Percolation tests.		
2. Construction of Access Roads (Most structural uses)	A. Tree cutting, vegetation removal.	A. Destruction of natural vegetation; wildlife; interference with natural drainage, sedimentation.	A. Location of roadways on upland sites, wherever possible.
	B. Excavating, filling.		B. Confinement of tree cutting and filling to immediate roadway.
			C. Requirements that natural drainage and circulation be maintained through elevation of roadway on pilings, installation of culverts; requirements that measures be taken to reduce erosion and sedimentation.
3. Establishment of Construction Camp (Larger projects such as Roads, Bridges, Dams, Reservoirs)	A. Tree-cutting, grading filling.	A. Destruction of wildlife, vegetation; interference with natural drainage; increased sedimentation.	A. Location of construction camp at upland site wherever possible, maintenance of a wetland buffer strip.
	B. Installation of electricity, water supply, telephone.		
4. Materials Storage (Most structural uses)	A. Grading, dumping, filling.	A. Interference with drainage; pollution and sedimentation from stored materials such as sand and gravel (depending upon materials).	A. Material storage on upland sites.
			B. Maintenance of wetland buffers.
			C. Installation of measures to reduce erosion from stored materials.
5. Clearing of Site (Many Structural and Nonstructural uses)	A. Vegetation removal.	A. Destruction of wildlife habitat; destruction of storm and erosion barriers; destruction of scenic beauty; increased erosion; increased runoff.	A. Vegetation removal only where absolutely necessary;
			B. Revegetation.
6. Earth Excavation and Fill (Most Structural Uses)	A. Fill of wetland area, grading of natural wetland contours, removal of peaty soils.		A. Confinement of fill to wetland margins and less sensitive wetland areas;
			B. Maintenance of natural drainage through fill and grading contours, currents, etc.;
			C. Rip-rap and revegetation to stabilize fill, reducing erosion.
7. Foundation Preparation and Construction (Most Structural Uses)	A. Dumping of crusted stone and other foundation material; installation of pilings; mixing and pouring of concrete, installation of public facilities (sewer, water).	A. Water pollution (in some instances) from mixing and pouring concrete.	A. Cofferdams, settling ponds to temporarily confine runoff from concrete mixing and pouring.
8. Disposal of Excess Excavated Materials (Most Structural Uses)		A. Erosion, water pollution, additional filling of wetland with consequential impacts.	A. Disposal of excavated sites material at upland;
			B. Rip-rap and revegetation to quickly stabilize and fill denuded areas.
9. Major Construction Activity	A. Erection of basic structure, accessory uses; roofing, siding, installation of major fixtures.	A. Pollution by sediment, debris from construction site, oil and other residuals from installation of parking areas.	A. Use construction design and practices to minimize wetland impact such as elevation of structure on pilings;
			B. Temporary settling ponds, other measures to reduce pollution.
10. Site Restoration and Cleanup	A. Removal of litter, excess materials, back filling, landscaping, planting of trees and grasses, fertilization.	A. Pollution from litter, backfilling, landscaping operations, use of fertilizers;	A. Confinement of fill to upland areas;
		B. Fill of wetland by landscaping.	B. Temporary settling ponds;
			C. Measures to reduce erosion on denuded surfaces.

SOILS TESTING, NEW ENGLAND. Field investigations are often needed to identify wetland boundaries.
Photo source: David Burke.

- Prohibition of activities that block floodway areas.
- Prohibition of activities that threaten public safety or cause nuisances to adjacent lands.
- Prohibition of activities that violate State or local pollution control standards.
- Prohibition of septic-tank and soil absorption systems in high groundwater areas.
- Prohibition of activities that destroy storm beaches or dunes which protect backlying areas from erosion.
- Prohibition of activities that threaten rare or endangered species.
- Requirements that new structures within floodplain areas be elevated or otherwise protected to the elevation of the 100-year flood.
- Requirements that land subdivisions be free from flooding and suitable for intended uses.
- Requirements that developers demonstrate that planned wetland activities cannot be located on an upland site.
- Requirements that all reasonable efforts be made to reduce the impact of development upon a wetland.
- Requirements that wetland buffers be maintained.

2.   Presumptions. Programs sometimes establish a number of presumptions that may be rebutted in a given instance. Examples include:

- Requirements that compensatory storage be provided for any loss of flood storage due to fill, diking, or other alteration of a wetland area unless it can be shown that storage is unimportant. Compensatory storage can be provided through creation of upland reservoirs or by excavation.
- Requirements that fills and other regulated activities be located at upland sites unless a showing is made that they must be located in wetland areas and that an overriding public interest is demonstrated.
- Requirements that total protection be provided certain types of wetlands while a range of activities may be conducted in other wetlands if overriding public interests are demonstrated. For example, State guidelines in North Carolina prohibit dredging and filling in coastal low salt marsh areas, but permit some activities in higher marshes.[3]
- Requirements that particular uses not be located in specific types of wetlands unless compatibility of the uses with the wetland are demonstrated.

     Table 5 lists interim guidelines promulgated by the State of New York for coastal wetlands. Presumptions of compatibility and incompatibility may be rebutted in a given instance.

3.   The weighing and balancing of broader goals, factors, and considerations. Statutes, administrative regulations, and ordinances sometimes require that the

VEGETATION ANALYSIS. Vegetation type determines wetland boundaries and values. Photo source: Jon Kusler.

regulatory agency weigh the environmental and economic costs and benefits of wetland development to determine the "public interest".[4] Often the regulatory agency is required to consider regulatory goals and other factors set forth in the regulations such as consistency with community public facility plans and broader land and water use plans. In determining the public interest, agencies often take into account public preferences expressed at public hearings as well as other sources of information.

5.5 Attachment of Conditions

Regulatory agencies usually attach conditions to permitted uses to minimize development impacts. Some conditions are attached to all permits while others are applied only to particular permits. Conditions with widespread applicability include:

- Requirements that proposed uses comply with all applicable zoning, subdivision control, sediment control and other regulations.
- Zoning, subdivision and sediment controls, plus other requirements that natural drainage be maintained through culverts, landscaping, or other measures.
- Limitations on removal of vegetation and requirements that denuded areas be quickly replanted.
- Requirements that buildings be protected to the 100-year flood elevation.

- Requirements that siltation and erosion control measures be applied to stabilize banks and other unvegetated areas.
- Requirements that as little fill as possible be used; that it be confined to the margins of the wetland area; and, that it be stabilized through plantings, riprap, and other techniques.
- Requirements that once a project has been completed, the applicant apply for a certificate of compliance.
- Requirements that all facilities and equipment be operated and maintained to comply with the regulations.

Other, more specific conditions may be attached, depending upon the specifics of the proposed use, wetland values and hazards, and other factors. Common specific conditions include:

- Time limitations for completion of the proposed activity.
- Installation of compensatory flood storage measures.
- Tight restrictions upon filling or other activities within specified areas of the wetland.
- Deed restrictions which must be recorded to ensure that the applicant and successors protect particular areas and comply with conditions specified in the permit.
- Rehabilitation of all or a portion of damaged

wetland areas through replanting of vegetation, restocking of fish or shellfish, reestablishment of drainage patterns, etc.

- Construction of vegetative screens and replanting of wetland buffer areas.

- Installation of sediment settling ponds for storm runoff and tertiary treatment facilities for sewage disposal.

- Dedication of public access easements to wetlands, installation of sewers, water, and roads (can be required in subdivision regulations).

5.6 Monitoring

Regulatory agencies may carry out site visits during project construction or at project completion to determine compliance with permit conditions. Site visits are likely for large-scale projects such as dams, dredging, or large-scale land fills. Violation of conditions may result in permit revocation or court action.

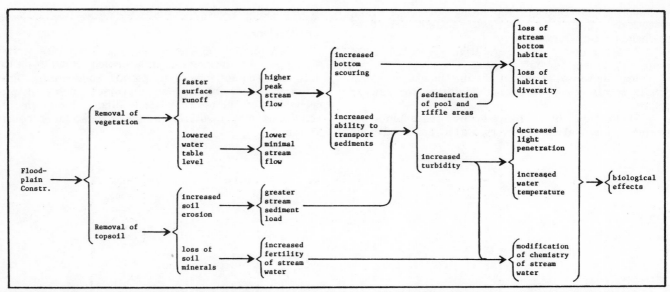

FIGURE 11. FACTOR ANALYSIS: CONSTRUCTION. Major factor train analysis of the effects of floodplain construction on wetlands. Only the major physical events are presented in detail.

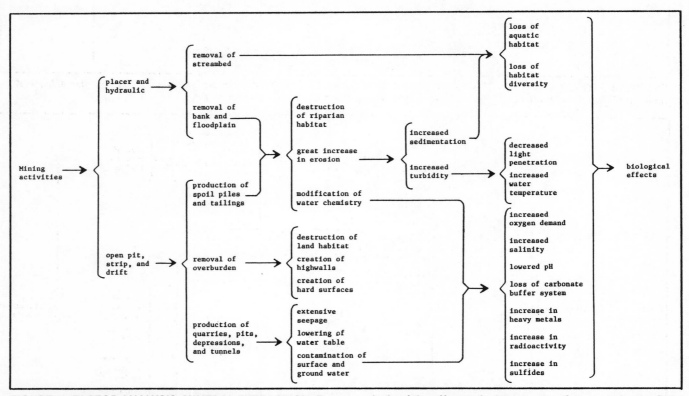

FIGURE 12. FACTOR ANALYSIS: MINERAL EXTRACTION. Factor analysis of the effects of mineral extraction on wetlands. Only the major physical and chemical events are presented.

Source: Darnell, Rezneat M. 1976. Impacts of Construction Activities on Wetlands of the U.S. U.S. Environmental Protection Agency, Office of Research and Development, Corvallis Environmental Research Laboratory, Corvallis, Oregon. EPA–600/3–76–045.

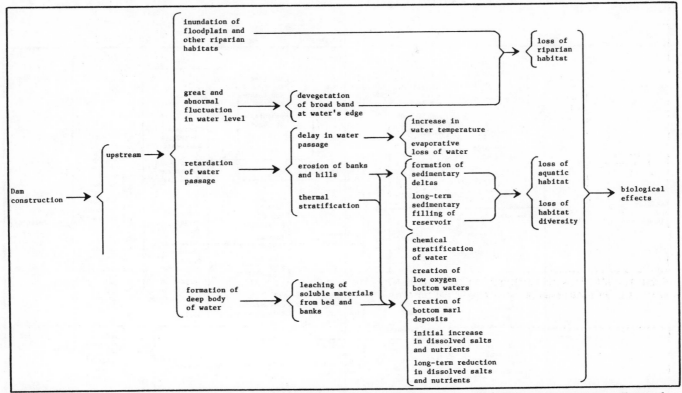

FIGURE 13. FACTOR ANALYSIS: UPSTREAM EFFECTS OF DAM CONSTRUCTION. Factor analysis of the upsteam effects of dam construction on wetlands. Only the major physical and chemical events are presented.

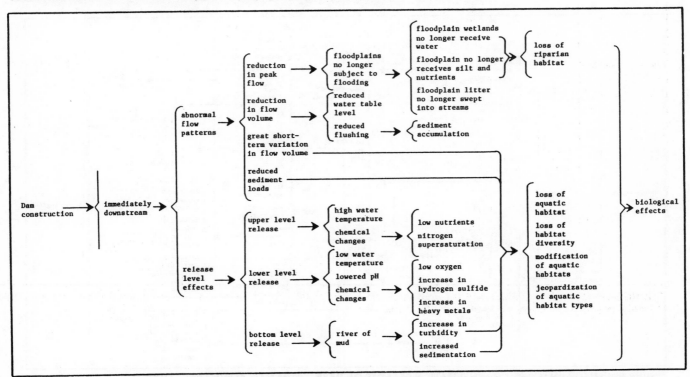

FIGURE 14. FACTOR ANALYSIS: DOWNSTREAM EFFECTS OF DAM CONSTRUCTION. Factor analysis of the immediate downstream effects of dam construction on wetlands. Only the major physical and chemical events are presented.

Source: Darnell, Rezneat M. 1976. Impacts of Construction Activities on Wetlands of the U.S. U.S. Environmental Protection Agency, Office of Research and Development, Corvallis Environmental Research Laboratory, Corvallis, Oregon. EPA–600/3–76–045.

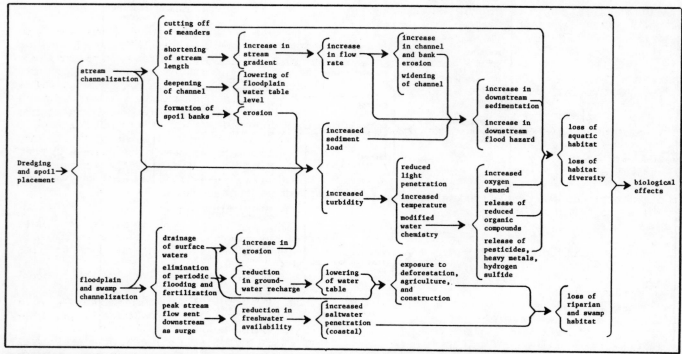

FIGURE 15. FACTOR ANALYSIS: CHANNELIZATION EFFECTS ON STREAMS. Factor analysis of the effects of channelization on streams, swamps, and floodplains. Only the major physical and chemical events are presented.

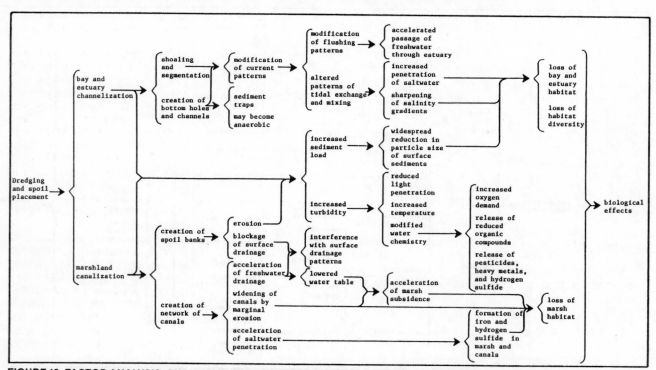

FIGURE 16. FACTOR ANALYSIS: CHANNELIZATION EFFECTS ON BAYS, ESTUARIES, AND MARSHLANDS. Factor analysis of the effect of channelization and canalization on bays, estuaries, and marshlands. Only the major physical and chemical events are presented.

Source: Darnell, Rezneat M. 1976. Impacts of Construction Activities on Wetlands of the U.S. U.S. Environmental Protection Agency, Office of Research and Development, Corvallis Environmental Research Laboratory, Corvallis, Oregon. EPA–600/3–76–045.

CHAPTER 6: FEDERAL WETLAND PROTECTION EFFORTS

6.1 Federal Policy

Communities can help protect wetlands by participating in and helping to enforce federal wetland protection efforts. In addition, they can make use of federal maps, technical assistance, and grants-in-aid.

In May 1977, President Carter issued Executive Order No. 11990, Protection of Wetlands,[1] which established wetland protection as the official policy of all Federal agencies. This Order provides:

Section 1. (a) Each agency shall provide leadership and shall take action to minimize the destruction, loss or degradation of wetlands, and to preserve and enhance the natural and beneficial values of wetlands in carrying out the agency's responsibilities for (1) acquiring, managing, and disposing of Federal lands and facilities; and (2) providing federally undertaken, financed, or assisted construction and improvement; and (3) conducting Federal activities and programs affecting land use, including but not limited to water and related land resources planning, regulating, and licensing activities.

The Order further directs that each agency shall, "to the extent permitted by law avoid undertaking or providing assistance for new construction located in wetlands unless the head of the agency finds (1) that there is no practicable alternative to such construction, and (2) that the proposed action includes all practicable measures to minimize harm to wetlands which may result from such use."

The Order directs each agency to provide early public review of plans and proposals for construction in wetlands and Section 4 provides that:

When Federally-owned wetlands or portions of wetlands are proposed for lease, easement, right-of-way or disposal to non-Federal public or private parties, the Federal agency shall (a) reference in the conveyance those uses that are restricted under identified Federal, State or local wetlands regulations; and (b) attach other appropriate restrictions to the uses of properties by the grantee or purchaser and any successor, except where prohibited by law; or (c) withhold such properties from disposal.

The Order further provides:

Section 5. In carrying out the activities described in Section 1 of this Order, each agency shall consider factors relevant to a proposal's effect on the survival and quality of wetlands. Among these factors are:

(a) public health, safety, and welfare, including water supply, quality, recharge and discharge; pollution; flood and storm hazards; and sediment and erosion;

(b) maintenance of natural systems, including conservation and long-term productivity of existing flora and fauna, species and habitat diversity and stability, hydrologic utility, fish, wildlife, timber, and food and fiber resources; and

(c) other uses of wetlands in the public interest, including recreational, scientific, and cultural uses.

Federal wetland protection efforts were also strengthened Congressionally in 1977 through adoption of the Clean Water Act. This act strengthened Corps of Engineers regulation of wetlands adjacent to navigable waters of the U.S. pursuant to Section 404 of the Federal Water Pollution Control Act Amendments of 1972. It authorized the Environmental Protection Agency to approve State wetland programs to regulate isolated wetlands and wetlands adjacent to tributary streams and lakes in lieu of Corps regulation, in some instances. However, Corps regulations continue for fill and structures in coastal wetlands and wetlands along major streams and lakes.

The Clean Water Act of 1977:

1. Established new standards for State regulation of dredge and fill pursuant to areawide water quality protection efforts (Section 208 programs).[2]

2. Authorized $6 million for the National Wetland Inventory.[3]

3. Authorized EPA to make available up to $400,000 per year for each State to assist in administration and enforcement of programs.[4]

4. Strengthened State control over Federal projects affecting navigable waters and wetlands including maintenance dredging by the Army Corps of Engineers.[5]

5. Required that a more extensive evaluation of wetland impacts be carried out for Federal projects authorized by Congress.[6]

The Wetland Protection Executive Order and these Congressional initiatives culminate a major shift in Federal policy during the last decade. Prior to this time, the Federal government pursued contradictory wetland policies. On the one hand, Congress authorized the Corps of Engineers, the Soil Conservation Service, the Bureau of Reclamation, and other agencies to carry out water resources and flood control projects that destroyed or damaged millions of acres of wetlands through dredging, drainage, and construction of reservoirs, levees, seawalls, and groins. It also offered grant-in-aid inducements to States, localities, and private landowners to drain valuable wetlands for agricultural purposes.[7]

On the other hand, it authorized the U.S. Fish and Wildlife Service to protect wetland areas through the Migratory Bird Conservation Act, the Wetland Acquisition Act, and the Land and Water Conservation Fund Act. It offered grants-in-aid and other inducements to States, localities, and private landowners to protect wetlands under the Federal Aid to Wildlife Restoration Act, Federal Aid to Fish Restoration Act, the Water Bank Program, and other programs.

Contradictions in the applications of these programs were particularly apparent in areas such as the prairie pothole region of the Midwest before 1975 where farmers on some parcels were draining wetlands with monies and technical assistance from the Soil Conservation Service, while nearby farmers (or the same farmers) were protecting their wetlands through easements from the U.S. Fish and Wildlife Service. In 1975, however, the Soil Conservation Service developed a policy to withhold technical or financial assistance for draining or altering certain types of wetlands in order to convert them to other uses.

The Executive Order and new legislation do not totally resolve policy conflicts, but they do establish a strong Federal presumption that wetlands should not be destroyed or disturbed unless overriding factors are present. This, plus the initiatives discussed below, form the basis for a major Federal effort in protecting the nation's wetlands and waters.

6.2 Federal Assistance for State and Local Protection Efforts

A variety of Federal statutes and programs, either expressly or indirectly, protect wetlands. These may be roughly divided (with some overlap) into (1) grants-in-aid, technical assistance, and other programs, to assist State, local, and private wetland protection efforts; (2) Federal land management activities; and (3) Federal regulatory programs for activities on public and private lands.

Federal incentives for State and local wetland protection efforts will be discussed first. They take the form of grants-in-aid, federally subsidized insurance, technical assistance, requirements that Federal projects conform with State and local regulations, and transfer of regulatory authority to States.

Grants-in-Aid

The Wetland Protection Executive Order described above establishes a general wetland protection policy for all Federal grants-in-aid and technical assistance to States and localities. These include not only grants-in-aid for wetland protection but grants for land and water planning, construction of roads, airports and other facilities, construction of sewage treatment facilities and open space acquisition. Grants-in-aid and technical assistance are also subject to the Flood Plain Management Executive Order (11988), which applies to most wetland areas adjacent to streams or the ocean.

Some agencies adopted wetland protection policies in providing grants-in-aid to States and localities prior to the adoption of the Wetland Protection Executive Order. For example, the Environmental Protection Agency adopted a wetland protection policy in 1973.[8] Pursuant to this policy, it has attached conditions to grants for construction of sewage treatment plants to discourage secondary residential and commercial development in wetlands in Fairfield, California and Block Island, Rhode Island.

Similarly, in 1975, the Soil Conservation Service issued a Conservation Planning Memorandum which provides that the Service is "not to provide technical and financial assistance for draining or otherwise altering wetlands. . .in order to convert them to other land uses."[9] This memorandum establishes a major shift in wetlands policy for the Service and affects all but two of the 20 types of wetlands described in the 1974 Fish and Wildlife wetland classification system (seasonally flooded basins for flats and fresh meadows).[10]

Several categories of grants-in-aid more specifically encourage and support State, local, and private wetland protection efforts:

1. Grants-in-Aid for State or Local Acquisition of Wetlands. Congress has authorized three principal grants-in-aid programs which may be used to acquire wetlands. These have been important during the last decade. However, federal funding cuts threaten their future use.

The Federal Aid to Wildlife Restoration Act (Pittman-Robertson Act) is the principal mechanism for Federal assistance to States for acquisition, restoration, and maintenance of wildlife areas including wetlands.[11] Grants for up to 75 percent of the cost of projects are available from this fund, which is derived from Federal excise taxes on the sale of firearms and ammunition.

The Land and Water Conservation Fund Act of 1968[12] (a special fund in the U.S. Treasury) has been a second major source of funds for State and local acquisition of outdoor recreation and open space areas. To qualify for funds, States must submit a comprehensive statewide outdoor recreation plan. While this program is not directed to wetland areas, some wetland acquisitions have been carried out under the broad objectives of the act.

The Coastal Zone Management Act is a third source of funds for certain types of wetland acquisition.[13] It is administered by the National Oceanic and Atmospheric Administration, U.S. Department of Commerce. This program provides grants-in-aid of up to $6 million a year to aid States, on a 50-50 basis, to acquire, develop, and operate estuarine sanctuaries which can be preserved as natural areas for scientific, cultural, or recreational uses. Wetland sanctuaries include, one of 4,100 acres in South Slough Bay in Coos Bay, Oregon and another of 6,150 acres on Sapelo Island in Georgia.

Other grants-in-aid for State or local acquisition of wetland areas include grants for fish restoration under the Federal Aid in Fish Restoration Act (Dingell-Johnson Act),[14] and for the protection of habitat for rare and endangered species under the Rare and Endangered Species Act of 1972.[15]

2. Grants-in-Aid for Land and Water Use Planning. A variety of Federal grants-in-aid have been available to States and localities for planning and managing land and water resources. Some principal programs include:

Section 701 of the Comprehensive Community Planning and Development Act authorizes the U.S. Department of Housing and Urban Development to provide grants-in-aid for comprehensive planning of land and waters.[16] Awards from this program, have been made to all 50 States and territories, and to large cities and counties. Although the program is not specifically addressed to wetland protection, an environmental assessment is required as part of land use planning. Many communities have inventoried and adopted plans for floodplains, wetlands, and other critical areas as part of Section 701 comprehensive planning efforts.

The Water Resources Planning Acts of 1972 and 1974[17] provide several sources of matching grants to States for water and related land resources planning including regional water and land assessments and special projects.

Section 208 of the Clean Water Act of 1977 provides grants-in-aid to States and regional planning agencies to develop areawide waste management plans and implementation processes.[18] These plans and processes include the identification and regulation of non-point pollutants from agriculture, silviculture, mining, construction activities, and other sources. Programs for the regulation of dredge and fill materials into the waters of the U.S. are also authorized.

3. Federal Grants-in-Aid for Regulation. Three principal sources of Federal funds are available to help States and localities adopt and administer regulatory programs, which may include wetland regulations.

A. A portion of the funds allocated to States by the Environmental Protection Agency pursuant to Section 208 of the Clean Water Act of 1977, described above, may be used to develop and administer regulatory programs to control non-point pollutants including the discharge of dredge and fill materials into the waters of the United States.[19]

B. Section 205 of the Clean Water Act of 1977 authorizes EPA to make available to each State up to $400,000 a year for administering pollution controls including dredge and fill programs which meet EPA standards.[20]

C. The Coastal Zone Management Program as amended provides up to 80-percent Federal matching grants for the development of coastal management programs.[21] Most programs give high priority to wetland protection. In addition, the program provides 80 percent Federal matching grants for the administration and enforcement of coastal management programs including land use regulatory efforts. Twenty-eight States have received approval for such program administration grants.

Most States have emphasized local and regional rather than State implementation of coastal zone policies although the State retains the power to directly regulate coastal areas in the event local units fail to adopt and administer regulations meeting State standards. States taking this approach include Maine, Oregon, Wisconsin, Minnesota, Virginia, and Washington.

4. Grants-in-Aid for Research and Training Programs. A variety of Federal sources of funds are available for State or local training in wetland protection and management. Examples follow.

A. The Environmental Protection Agency has funded the conduct of environmental systems training programs by conservation commissions in New Jersey, Connecticut, Massachusetts, New York, and Rhode Island.

B. The National Science Foundation has funded a variety of wetland-related projects including a study of the monitoring and enforcement of State wetland and shoreland programs.

Subsidized Flood Insurance

Although not a grant-in-aid program, the Federal Flood Insurance Program[22] offers federally subsidized flood insurance (up to 90 percent Federal subsidy) as an incentive for State and local regulation of flood hazard areas. This program is important since, as discussed in Chapter 2, wetlands adjacent to rivers, streams, and the ocean are flood hazard areas. Tight floodplain regulations (particularly floodway regulations) may provide a considerable degree of protection for wetland areas.[23]

The Federal Emergency Management Agency (FEMA) which administers this program, has also adopted regulations requiring that communities with mangrove forests acting as coastal flood protection barriers adopt regulations protecting the mangroves in order to qualify for subsidized flood insurance. Many communities now regulating wetland development do so through floodplain regulations designed not only to reduce flood problems but also to protect wetland functions. Combined wetland and floodplain ordinances can both qualify communities for subsidized flood insurance and meet broader water resources protection goals.

A 1973 amendment to the act establishing the program added teeth by requiring insurance purchase after FEMA has mapped floodplains in a community and made insurance available.[24] Failure of a community to adopt floodplain regulations and to purchase insurance will eventually result in the loss of Federal construction, acquisition, and disaster assistance funds to the community.

A further 1977 amendment slightly modified the requirements of the 1973 amendment so that a community failing to enter the program may nevertheless qualify for lending from federally insured banks.[25] Nevertheless, other requirements of the 1973 amendment continue in force. In addition, under the 1977 amendments, a community failing to enter the program will not be eligible for disaster assistance.

The mandatory requirements have widespread impact and may ultimately affect 20,000 communities.

Technical Assistance

Several important sources of technical assistance are available to localities to help them develop and implement wetland protection programs or broader land and water management programs with wetland components. These are listed below.

1. Section 208 of the 1977 Clean Water Act directs the U.S. Fish and Wildlife Service to provide technical assistance to States in developing regulatory programs for the discharge of dredged and fill materials into waters of the U.S. including adjacent wetlands. It also authorizes the U.S. Fish and Wildlife Service to conduct a National Wetland Inventory of the United States.[26]

As discussed in Chapter 3, this inventory is already underway, based upon a new comprehensive wetland classification system. It will create a comprehensive wetland data base in both map and computer form. This inventory is based primarily upon air photos, with the use of supplementary data when available. Wetland data will be displayed on U.S. Geological Survey base maps.

2. The Soil Conservation Service is authorized, pursuant to a number of statutes, to provide technical assistance to States, local governments, and private landowners in many aspects of resource conservation including wetland protection and management. As noted above, SCS adopted a technical assistance policy in 1975 partially protecting wetlands. Soil surveys

MANGROVES, MONROE COUNTY, FLORIDA. The National Flood Insurance Program regulations require that coastal communities protect mangroves which reduce flood damages in order to qualify for federally subsidized flood insurance. Photo source: Jon Kusler.

prepared by the Service have been used in many States to identify wetlands and apply management and protection policies. For example, the State of Connecticut has mapped inland wetlands through the use of soil maps. They are defined to include alluvial, poorly drained, and very poorly drained soils.

3. The Army Corps of Engineers provides floodplain management technical services to States and localities under its floodplain management program. This program stresses non-structural approaches such as floodplain regulations for controlling flood losses. Consequently, much of this assistance is important in wetland protection and management efforts.

In addition to these efforts, a variety of mapping and technical services, which can assist States and localities in wetland protection, are available from the U.S. Geological Survey, the U.S. Fish and Wildlife Service, the Environmental Protection Agency, and the National Oceanic and Atmospheric Administration.

6.3 Federal Land and Water Management Activities

The Federal government directly manages the one-third of the nation's lands that are in Federal ownership. In addition, it acquires additional properties for national parks and recreation areas, water resource projects, Federal buildings and works,

and wildlife refuges. Principal Federal land management agencies include the U.S. Fish and Wildlife Service, the National Park Service, the Bureau of Land Management, the U.S. Forest Service, and the U.S. Department of Defense. These agencies also carry out some activities on non-Federal lands such as construction of reservoirs and dredging of rivers and harbors.

Wetland protection is required or encouraged in the conduct of all Federal activities on both Federal and non-Federal lands by a variety of measures:

o   Wetland and Flood Plain Executive Orders. The Wetland Protection and Flood Plain Management Executive Orders establish a strong general wetland protection policy for all Federal activities including land management, dredging, fills, and construction of Federal buildings.

o   The Federal Land Policy and Management Act of 1976 requires the inventory, assessment, and planning of federal lands including the assessment of aquatic habitats.[27]

o   The Fish and Wildlife Coordination Act, as amended in 1958,[28] requires that "equal consideration" be given to wildlife conservation with other features of water resource development projects of the Army Corps of Engineers, Bureau of Reclamation, and other agencies. This Act requires that the U.S. Fish and Wildlife Service evaluate the impact on fish and

WETLAND IN ESTES NATIONAL PARK, COLORADO. Photo source: Jon Kusler.

wildlife of all new Federal projects on existing Federal lands and elsewhere (e.g., Corps of Engineers' dredging). The "equal consideration" requirement has given rise to a concept of mitigation of impacts by avoiding adverse consequences to wildlife or wetlands habitat and by replacing public wildlife conservation opportunities, destroyed by Federal projects, through public acquisition of private lands offering similar opportunities.

o   The Endangered Species Act of 1972, as amended, places restrictions on Federal agencies undertaking or funding a project that may adversely impact rare or endangered species.[29]

o   Guidelines developed by the Environmental Protection Agency pursuant to Section 404(b) of the Water Pollution Control Act Amendments of 1972 apply to most Federal discharges of dredged or fill material into the waters of the U.S. or adjacent wetlands. Federal projects require permits from the Army Corps of Engineers consistent with these guidelines unless the project has been specifically and individually authorized by Congress, and the Agency has prepared an environmental impact statement prior to authorization that complies with the guidelines.[30]

o   The National Environmental Policy Act of 1969[31] establishes a general federal policy to "fulfill the responsibilities of each generation as trustee of the environment for succeeding generations." Environmental impact statements must be prepared for Federal activities with major impacts upon the environment such as flood control projects, dredging, and land sales.

The National Environmental Policy Act does not prohibit or otherwise control Federal activities once the statement has been prepared. Nevertheless, impact statement requirements help ensure agency evaluation of the impacts of proposed projects and facilitate public review.

o   Federal activities are in some instances subject to State wetland and pollution controls. Section 404(t) of the Clean Water Act of 1977 requires that Federal projects comply with State regulations for the discharge of dredged and fill materials into the waters of the U.S., including adjacent wetlands.[32] However, a partial exemption is provided for Federal projects individually authorized by Congress.

Similarly, Section 301 of the Coastal Zone Management Act of 1972 requires that Federal agencies comply with State coastal zone programs approved by the Secretary of Commerce.[33]

6.4 Federal Regulation of Wetland Activities

Congress has adopted several laws establishing Federal or cooperative State/Federal regulations which apply in part to wetland activities on Federal and non-Federal lands:

o   Under the terms of the Rivers and Harbors Act of 1899, permits from the Army Corps of Engineers are required for any dredging, filling, or obstruction of

WETLANDS IN PLUM ISLAND NATIONAL WILDLIFE REFUGE, MASSACHUSETTS. Photo source: Jon Kusler.

navigable waters.[34]   Until the 1960's the Act was narrowly interpreted to protect waters for commercial navigation. It was not applied to wetlands above the mean high water mark.

In response to increased national concern over environmental protection, the Corps in 1968 amended its permit regulations to broaden permit criteria:

> The decision as to whether a permit will be issued must rest on evaluation of all relevant factors, including the effect of the proposed work on navigation, fish and wildlife, conservation, pollution, aesthetics, ecology and the general public interest.[35]

These broadened criteria were sustained by the U.S. Court of Appeals for the Fifth Circuit in a landmark case, **Zabel v. Tabb.**[36]   In this case, the court upheld the right of the Army to refuse a permit to fill 11 acres of mangrove wetland in Boca Ciega Bay, Florida, based solely on grounds of environmental damage.

The Corps now provides broad environmental review of wetland activities below the mean high water mark under this Act and Section 404 of the Water Pollution Control Act Amendments of 1972 and the Clean Water Act of 1977 (see discussion below).

o   The Federal Water Pollution Control Act Amendments of 1972 establish a National system for regulation of pollutants in waters of the U.S.[37] Section 404 of the Act and the Clean Water Act of 1977 require that permits be obtained from the Army Corps of Engineers or the States for discharge of dredged and fill materials into the "waters of the U.S."[38]   At first, Section 404 of the 1972 Amendments was narrowly interpreted by the Corps to apply only to traditionally navigable waters.   However, this position was challenged in **Natural Resources Defense Council v. Callaway.**[39]   In this case, the court held that Section 404 applied to all waters including wetlands, not just traditionally navigable waters.

Based upon this decision, the Corps adopted new regulations controlling activities in coastal and inland wetlands and providing a phased implementation of the Act.   Permits were required immediately for activities in Phase I waters—those commercially navigable. Permits were required after July 25, 1975 for navigable waters of the U.S. and adjacent wetlands. Permits were required after September 1, 1976 for navigable waters, adjacent wetlands, primary tributaries and their adjacent wetlands, and natural lakes greater than 5 acres in area. After July 1, 1977 discharges into all waters of the U.S. were regulated.

To simplify the administration of the Act and reduce the number of permits required for minor activities, the Corps, in regulations adopted in July 1977, also issued "nationwide" permits for certain existing uses and those uses with relatively minor impact upon wetlands.   District Engineers were also authorized to issue general permits for activities of a similar kind that would not have severe individual impact upon the environment.

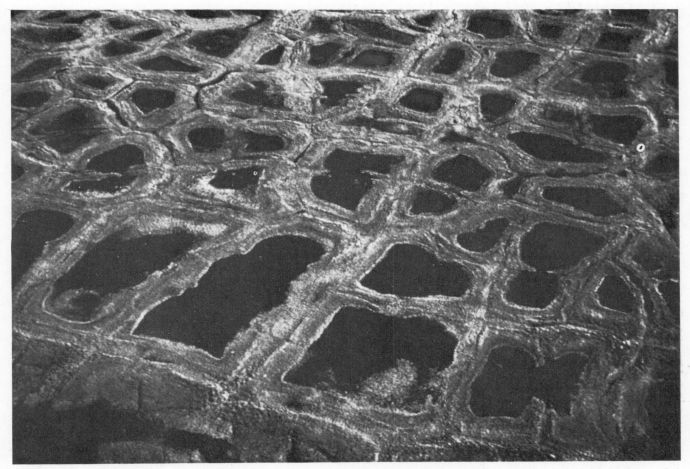

PERMAFROST WETLANDS, ALASKA. These wetlands were created by the melting of permafrost. They, like other major wetlands, are subject to federal 404 regulations. Photo source: Martin Weller.

The regulations provide that the District Engineer is not to issue an individual or general permit for wetlands, identified as important by the criteria listed below, unless he concludes that issuance is in "the public interest" considering all factors including "conservation, economics, aesthetics, general environmental concerns, historic values, fish and wildlife values, flood damage prevention, land use navigation, recreation, water supply, water quality, energy needs, safety, food production, and, in general, the needs and welfare of the people."[40] Regulations state a general policy that "wetlands are vital areas that constitute a productive and valuable public resource, the unnecessary alteration or destruction of which should be discouraged as contrary to the public interest."[41] In determining whether a proposed alteration is necessary, the District Engineer must "consider whether the proposed activity is primarily dependent on being located in, or in close proximity to, the aquatic environment and whether feasible alternative sites are available."[42] The applicant "must provide sufficient information on the need to locate the proposed activity in the wetland and must provide data on the basis of which the availability of feasible alternative sites can be evaluated."[43]

The regulations provide that:[44]

2. Wetlands considered to perform functions important to the public interest include:

i. Wetlands which serve important natural biological functions, including food chain production, general habitat, and nesting, spawning, rearing and resting sites for aquatic or land species;

ii. Wetlands set aside for study of the aquatic environment or as santuaries or refuges;

iii. Wetlands the destruction or alteration of which would affect detrimentally natural drainage characteristics, sedimentation patterns, salinity distribution, flushing characteristics, current patterns, or other environmental characteristics;

iv. Wetlands which are significant in shielding other areas from wave action, erosion, or storm damage. Such wetlands are often associated with barrier beaches, islands, reefs and bars;

v. Wetlands which serve as valuable storage areas for storm and flood waters;

vi. Wetlands which are prime natural recharge areas. Prime recharge areas are

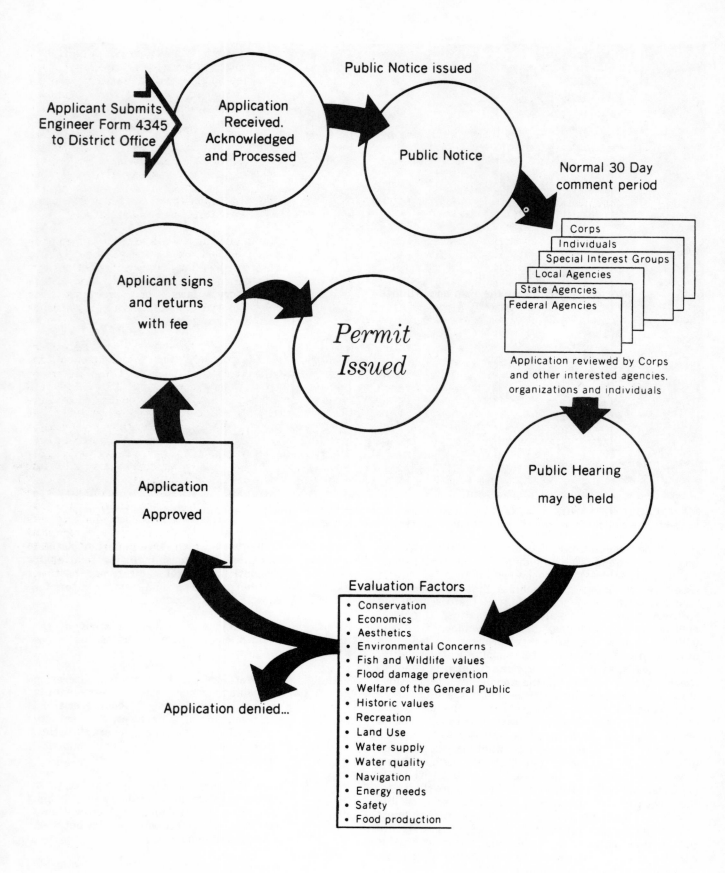

FIGURE 17. TYPICAL CORPS PERMIT REVIEW PROCESS. Source: U.S. Army Corps of Engineers.

locations where surface and groundwater are directly interconnected; and

vii. Wetlands which through natural water filtration processes serve to purify water.

3. Although a particular alteration of wetlands may constitute a minor change, the cumulative effect of such numerous piecemeal changes often results in a major impairment of the wetland resources. Thus, the particular wetland site for which an application is made will be evaluated with the recognition that it is part of a complete and interrelated wetland area. In addition, the District Engineer may undertake reviews of particular wetland areas in consultation with the appropriate Regional Director of the Fish and Wildlife Service, the Regional Director of the National Marine Fisheries Service of the National Oceanic and Atmospheric Administration, the Regional Administrator of the Environmental Protection Agency, the local representative of the Soil Conservation Service of the Department of Agriculture, and the head of the appropriate State agency to assess the cumulative effect of activities in such areas.

4. No permit will be granted to work in wetlands identified as important by subparagraph (2), above, unless the District Engineer concludes, on the basis of the analysis required in paragraph (a), above, that the benefits of the proposed alteration outweigh the damage to the wetlands resource and the proposed alteration is necessary to realize those benefits. In evaluating whether a particular alteration is necessary, the District Engineer shall consider whether the proposed activity is primarily dependent on being located in, or in close proximity to the aquatic environment and whether feasible alternative sites are available. The applicant must provide sufficient information on the need to locate the proposed activity in the wetland and must provide data on the basis of which the availability of feasible alternative sites can be evaluated.

5. In addition to the policies expressed in this subpart, the Congressional policy expressed in the Estuary Protection Act, Public Law No. 90-454, and State regulatory laws or programs for classification and protection of wetlands will be given great weight.

The Clean Water Act of 1977 also authorizes States to adopt programs for the control of the placement of dredged or fill material into waters of the U.S. including adjacent wetlands. Once a State has adopted a program meeting standards of the Environmental Protection Agency (EPA) and EPA has approved the program, the State may assume permitting authority for all waters and wetlands except those susceptible to commercial navigation. No state has applied for such approval although several have indicated a preliminary interest.

At present federal guidelines for implementation of Section 404 are under review and changes may be expected. In addition, funding cuts have affected the grant-in-aid and, technical assistance, programs. For this reason, community planning to rely on federal programs should explore their up-to-date status.

CHAPTER 7: STATE WETLAND PROGRAMS

Communities can also protect wetlands by participating in and helping to enforce State wetland regulatory and acquisition efforts. All but a few coastal States now provide some protection for coastal wetlands through wetland regulation statutes or broader coastal zone or shoreland acts with wetland components. At least seven States regulate inland wetland areas. Many other States regulate floodplain areas which contain major wetlands. Communities can help administer and enforce these regulations by informing landowners of State requirements, monitoring wetland activities and reporting violations, and participating in hearings on individual wetland permits. Communities can also supplement State regulations with their own and develop joint permit procedures.

In some States communities can also participate in State wetland acquisition programs. In some instances, State grants-in-aid are available to assist communities. State maps and technical assistance may also be available.

State wetland programs have been prompted by several considerations. First, wetlands often cross local government jurisdictions, creating problems in local definition and management. Second, wetland water supply is affected by watershed use. Watersheds often encompass several jurisdictions or even another State. Conversely, what happens to a wetland in one jurisdiction often affects flooding, water quality, and water supply in other areas. Third, local governments often lack the expertise and funds to identify and evaluate wildlife, floods, erosion, and other wetland values and hazards and to determine the impact of development. Fourth, control and protection of wetlands is closely linked with traditional State protection of wildlife and public rights in navigable waters.

A more extensive discussion of these programs can be found in a companion document available from the U.S. Fish and Wildlife Service, Strengthening State Wetland Regulations.[1] This chapter summarizes the information from that document. State wetland protection includes both regulatory and nonregulatory programs.

7.1 Regulatory Programs

State coastal wetland regulations are quite comprehensive and include the following:

o   Special coastal wetland regulation statutes Following the lead of Massachusetts in 1963, 13 States now require a permit for fill and structures in coastal wetland areas. Permits for regulated activities are evaluated on a case-by-case basis in light of statutory and administrative standards. In addition, six States authorize a State regulatory agency to adopt wetland protective orders resembling zoning regulations, require permits, and list permitted and prohibited wetland uses.

o   Coastal wetland protection as a component of broader regulatory efforts. Coastal wetland protection efforts in most of the remaining coastal

States are components of broader regulatory efforts. In some States, standards for local regulations are established in shoreland zoning programs. For example, Michigan regulates wetland areas along Lake Michigan through a shoreland zoning act. Washington requires that local governments in the coastal zone inventory and adopt regulations for natural areas and environmental areas. California provides some protection for wetland areas as part of a broader coastal zone regulatory program administered by special regional regulatory boards. Oregon has developed a coastal zone program with wetland components as part of a broader mandatory State land use program. Similarly, Florida has developed standards for the Florida Keys as part of a broader critical area program.

To date, inland wetlands have been afforded much less protection.

o   Inland wetland regulation acts. Explicit State inland wetland protection acts have been adopted only in Massachusetts, Connecticut, Rhode Island, Minnesota, Michigan, New Hampshire, and New York. Massachusetts regulates inland wetlands through two statutes. The first requires review of proposed development by a local conservation commission. The second authorizes the State Commissioner of Environmental Protection to adopt inland wetland protection orders and issue permits. New Hampshire and Rhode Island regulate both coastal and inland wetlands through State permit requirements. New York, Connecticut, and Michigan establish standards for local wetland protection and directly regulate areas only in the event of local inaction.

o   Inland wetland protection as a component of broader regulatory efforts. In several States, inland wetland regulation is a component or an indirect result of broader State regulatory efforts applying to State waters, shorelands, floodplains, wild and scenic rivers, or other areas. For example, Oregon, Wisconsin, and Michigan protect some wetlands by controlling dredging and filling in State waters. State shoreland zoning programs that apply to lake and stream shore areas have been adopted in Washington, Vermont, Maine, and Wisconsin. The Washington, Wisconsin, and Maine programs require or encourage local units to adopt special standards for wetland areas.

Direct State floodplain or floodway regulations or State standards for local regulations have been adopted in at least 30 States. Protection of ecological values is rarely an explicit objective, although a large measure of wetland protection may in fact be achieved by the very restrictive controls typically applied to floodway areas.

Scenic and wild river programs adopted in one-half of the States provide some protection for wetland areas. The Florida critical area program has adopted standards for local regulation of lands in Big Cypress Swamp. Dam permit laws in at least 30 States provide a measure of protection to wetland areas although primary emphasis is on navigation and other public rights to navigable waters and control of water pollution.

PEAT EXCAVATION IN WETLAND, ANCHORAGE, ALASKA. Alaska is helping Anchorage, Sitka and other communities develop wetland management plans. Photo source: Jon Kusler.

In addition to these acts aimed at controlling water-related uses, many States regulate onsite waste disposal systems in areas of high groundwater through plumbing and sanitary codes. These codes provide some protection for inland and coastal areas without sewers. Some protection is also provided in Vermont and Florida, through regulation of large-scale development. Additional protection is achieved through State power plant siting controls and strip mining regulations. Finally, informed decision-making is promoted through environmental impact review acts in 15 States. These acts require assessment of impact and influence wetland decisions, although they are nonregulatory devices.

7.2 Non-Regulatory Efforts

Non-regulatory wetland protection efforts provide a valuable supplement to coastal and inland regulatory programs.

o <u>Waterfowl and wildlife protection programs.</u> All States have adopted wildlife protection and conservation programs. Programs include hunting regulations, acquisition of wildlife and waterfowl protection areas, propagation and stocking of fish and waterfowl, protection of rare and endangered species, and conservation education efforts. Many programs involve the acquisition and management of wetland areas. Communities can often help establish priorities for acquisition.

o <u>Public land management programs.</u> Wetland management is often a component of State public land management programs. These include State forestry, park, trust land (beaches, lake bottoms), scientific area, and scenic and wild river programs. Communities can review and comment upon management policies for lands within their jurisdiction.

o <u>Flood control efforts.</u> Wetland acquisition is a component of a few State flood control programs. For example, the State of Massachusetts has recommended acquisition of wetlands along the Neponsit River to protect flood storage. Communities can often influence State plans or comment upon permits.

o <u>Public education.</u> Universities in several States, including the University of Wisconsin and the University of Minnesota, have acquired wetlands for educational and scientific purposes.

o <u>Tax incentive programs.</u> Some States, including California, Connecticut, Michigan, New Hampshire, Pennsylvania, Rhode Island, and Washington, authorize tax relief for wetland and open space areas (see discussion in Chapter 10).

ESTUARINE WETLANDS SUBJECT TO STATE REGULATIONS. These estuarine wetlands along the Severn Run in Maryland are subject to state regulations. Photo source: Jon Kusler.

7.3 Statutory Approaches

Coastal and inland wetland regulatory statutes often contain the following types of provisions.[2]

1. <u>Legislative findings of fact concerning wetland losses and the need for protection.</u> Most statutes stress the importance of wetlands to fisheries, waterfowl, and other forms of wildlife. Others stress pollution control, flood storage, recreation, educational and scientific values, and water supply. These findings help establish the policy basis for the statutes, educate landowners and the general public to the need for regulation, and aid the regulatory agency in interpreting the act and administering permits.

2. <u>Statement of statutory purposes and policies.</u> Statutes generally establish strong protection policies, although some balance preservation and economic or development goals.

3. <u>Wetland definitions.</u> Most statutes define wetlands with considerable specificity.[3] Coastal definitions usually combine tidal action criteria with vegetation type. Inland definitions usually combine periodic surface water inundation or high groundwater levels with vegetation type.

4. <u>Authorization for a designated agency to map</u> wetlands. Wetland regulatory statutes usually contain several types of provisions that indirectly or directly require gathering particular types and scales of data. Many acts contain explicit data gathering requirements pertaining to data scale and format such as a Connecticut Coastal Wetland Act, which requires mapping at a scale of one inch to equal 200 feet.[4] Other acts indirectly require gathering particular types of data by requiring the regulatory agency to adopt wetland maps and orders complying with statutory wetland definition criteria.

5. <u>Delegation of power to a designated agency either to directly regulate wetlands or establish standards for regulation by local governments.</u> Most statutes authorizing direct State regulation of wetlands apply to coastal wetlands although the Rhode Island and New Hampshire acts apply both to inland and coastal wetlands. The responsible agency is usually a natural resources or water resources agency. In contrast, most inland wetland statutes rely primarily upon local governments for the administration and enforcement of State minimum standards. Virtually all statutes authorize the regulatory agency to adopt administrative rules and regulations to supplement statutory standards. Some statutes authorize the agency to adopt formal orders for particular wetlands as well as general written rules for all wetlands. Many statutes authorize the

GLACIAL LAKE BOTTOM WETLANDS, MINNESOTA. Minnesota and Oregon regulate wetlands pursuant to state laws requiring permits for altering state "waters". Photo source: Martin Weller.

regulatory agency to undertake a number of additional wetland protection and management functions including acquiring wetlands in fee or easement and providing assistance to local governments.

6. <u>A requirement that landowners seek permits for specified kinds of uses in wetland areas (piers, fills, dredging, structures) from the State agency or local government.</u> The statute usually contains partial or complete exemptions for activities of State and Federal agencies, public utilities, local political subdivisions, agriculture, and mosquito control projects. The statute may also list uses permitted and prohibited uses. Statutes contain criteria for evaluating permits and procedures for applying for and issuing permits.

7. <u>Penalties for violating regulatory standards.</u> Statutes generally provide that any person violating any provision of the statute shall be liable for a fine ranging from $100 to $10,000, with each violation usually considered a separate offense. In case of continuing violations, each day of continuance is generally viewed as a separate offense. Some statutes authorize imprisonment up to one year as well as fines. Under many statutes, the regulatory agency or the court can order restoration of the wetland or assess the cost of restoration against the offending landowner.

8. <u>Appeal procedures.</u> Most statutes provide that any party with an interest in the proceedings who is dissatisfied with the action of the regulatory agency on the proposed permit may appeal to a specified court. Administrative appeals to an appeals board or regulatory agency are also provided in Massachusetts, North Carolina, Maryland, Virginia, New York, Washington, and Delaware. Appeal procedures may also establish standards for determining whether a taking of property has occurred and provide remedies.

7.4 Implementation of Wetland Statutes

Program, Budgets, Functions

Most State programs are handicapped by small budgets and limited staff. Community assistance in data gathering, monitoring, permit evaluation and other activities is welcomed. State staff typically divide their time among such tasks as mapping, adopting orders and rules, conducting workshops and maintaining liaison with local government, liaison with other agencies, discussions with landowners, processing permits, and conducting public hearings, field investigations (to determine precise wetland boundaries and evaluate permit applications), enforcement activites, and, in some instances, wetland acquisition. Wetland mapping, whether carried out by the staff or consultants, is often a principal budget item during early phases of program implementation.

68

The evaluation of wetland permits, another major staff function, varies in its demand on staff time. Because of multiple program responsibilities and limited staffs, monitoring wetland activities often receives low priority.

Data Gathering

Wetland data gathering often takes several principal forms: (1) obtain existing maps, (2) prepare new wetland maps (if necessary), and (3) conduct field surveys to evaluate the impact of proposed development.

Many State regulatory programs have prepared formal wetland maps at scales from one inch equals 200 feet to one inch equals 2,000 feet.[5] Maps are typically based upon interpretation of black and white, color, or color infrared air photos used, although other data sources such as soil surveys and tidal records are used in some efforts.

The scale of wetland mapping is often an issue. Not all programs agree with the need for large scale and accurate maps. Field surveys are needed to resolve boundary disputes and to evaluate individual development proposals even where very detailed maps are available. Large-scale mapping is very expensive and may create a false impression that wetlands can be located with mathematical certainty.

A second mapping approach advocated by some States (Wisconsin, Maryland) is to adopt wetland maps with less initial accuracy and use field surveys to apply vegetative or other criteria to resolve boundary disputes.

Most regulatory programs map wetlands on an area-by-area basis (such as one town at a time). A few States have relied solely on vegetation criteria, not mapping, in applying regulations (the Georgia marshland program and the New York interim regulations for freshwater areas). Only a small number of wetland regulatory programs have completed mapping on a Statewide basis although efforts are now underway in Michigan, New York, Wisconsin and perhaps other States in cooperation with the National Wetland Inventory.

Data gathering to calculate individual development proposals is conducted on a case-by-case basis to assess natural values and hazards and the probable impact of the particular development. Site-specific data are usually derived from two sources: (1) information supplied by the developer in his application form, environmental impact statement (if one is required), or special studies, and (2) information generated by the regulatory agency through air photos, topographic maps, field surveys and other available sources of information. Usually, a field investigation is conducted for each permit. A staff engineer or biologist determines the precise wetland boundary and evaluates the probable impact of the project on wetland soils, hydrology, water quality, vegetation, and other parameters. The specific data gathered depend on the proposed project design and the characteristics of the site. Community assistance in permit evaluation can be particularly important.

State wetland regulatory programs have rarely mapped specific subzones within wetland areas. However, New York divides tidal wetlands into more specific subzones. They include coastal fresh marsh, intertidal marsh, coastal shoals, bars and flats, littoral zones, high marsh or salt meadow, formerly connected tidal wetlands, and unclassified tidal wetlands. Virginia has adopted guidelines for coastal wetlands suggesting variations in use potential for various vegetation zones. North Carolina administrative regulations place special emphasis on protecting coastal low marshes.

Administrative Rules and Orders

Most States have adopted administrative rules and regulations to supplement standards and criteria contained in enabling statutes. Typically these regulations repeat much of the language of enabling statutes pertaining to program objectives, wetland definitions, criteria, and penalties, but they add new, more detailed definitions for basic terms, specify permit application procedures in detail, and establish specific standards and criteria for processing permits. The latter may include lists of permitted, prohibited, and special permit uses.

The administrative regulations of several States vary permit requirements depending on the type of activity and its potential impact on wetlands. For example, the New Jersey program requires "Type A" permits for projects with relatively minor potential impact and "Type B" permits for projects with major impacts. More detailed information and environmental impact statements are required for "Type B" permits.

Wetland orders are authorized by the statutes of at least eight States.[6] This approach, designed to provide "once and for all" regulatory policies for particular wetlands, has worked with varied success. Orders consist of a map and written text. The written text typically contains language from a model order designed by the agency but with modifications for specific circumstances.

Most orders adopted to date have applied to coastal wetlands. However, Massachusetts has adopted protective orders for between 5,000 and 6,000 acres of inland wetlands. Adoption of orders has been hindered by the detailed map requirements of most acts (map scales of 1:2,400 in Connecticut and Rhode Island) and the requirement that landowners be notified in writing prior to adoption. Written notification of regulations is not required by traditional zoning approaches. This special requirement has greatly increased the time and expense of order procedures. There is some evidence, however, that written notice procedures facilitate enforcement. Written notice may also strengthen regulations against legal challenge, particularly where the landowners' right to contest the constitutionality of an order is forever barred after a specified period as provided by some statutes.

Regulatory agencies typically negotiate with landowners in preparing final boundaries for the regulatory order. Lines may be shifted somewhat to accommodate private needs where the essential integrity of the wetland can still be maintained.

Processing Permits

Most statutes require case-by-case evaluation of proposals for excavations, fills, or structures in wetland areas. The vast majority of permits are conditionally approved. However, many developers are discouraged in early discussion from submitting formal permit applications. They are likely to do so only if they believe that the permits will be approved or if they wish to initiate a formal court challenge. In addition, extensive negotiation sometimes occurs on the developers' plans prior to final disapproval or approval of the permit application. Performance bonds have been required in some instances to ensure that projects are carried out as specified.

Regulatory administrators cite several major problems in processing permits. First, the cumulative impact of development from piecemeal issuance of permits may gradually destroy a wetland. It is difficult to evaluate the probable cumulative impact of development or deny a permit because of future anticipated development. Second, difficulties are encountered in the application of general performance standards that do not establish quantitative minimums. Agencies often feel uncomfortable in refusing permits when there is no violation of a minimum quantified standard (protection of structures to the 100-year flood elevation). Communities can adopt supplementary regulations to help address these problems.

Enforcement

Monitoring and enforcement of State regulations are often hindered by lack of staff. This is particularly true for inland wetlands. Enforcement is less a problem in coastal wetland programs due in part to their more limited geographical scope and more easily identified physical characteristics.

Monitoring techniques vary from State to State and range from principal reliance upon interest groups and adjacent landowners to report violations to weekly surveys of coastal wetlands through overflights with a small plane (Georgia). Experiments have also been made with monitoring through satellite imagery in New Jersey and Georgia, although the scale of the imagery is too small for most monitoring purposes.

Communities can assist States in monitoring and enforcement by periodically surveying wetland activities and reporting violations.

7.5 Relationship of State to Local Programs

Despite some misgivings, most State wetland programs have moved toward increased local involvement. For example, the Massachusetts program which originally stressed permitting at the State level, has shifted much of the task of permit evaluation to local conservation commissions. Similarly, a task force appointed by the governor of Rhode Island to review the State inland wetland law urged increased local involvement. Basic enabling statutes in Virginia, Connecticut (inland wetlands), and New York (inland wetlands) place primary responsibility for wetland regulation at the local level.

State programs have generally encouraged and assisted local government in regulating wetlands. Connecticut, Rhode Island, Massachusetts, Wisconsin, and Virginia have held workshops to train local administrators. Virginia has developed guidebooks and manuals for use by local governments. A model ordinance has been drafted by the New York State regulatory agency.

Based upon the experience of the last decade, the advisability of a strong local role in wetland regulation is now clear, particularly for inland wetlands. Wetland protection is best interrelated with broader community land and water use planning, including the protection of the quality and quantity of surface waters and groundwater.

CHAPTER 8: WETLAND ZONING AND OTHER LOCAL REGULATIONS

8.1 Introduction

Local regulation of wetland activities is required by State wetland protection acts in Virginia, Massachusetts, Connecticut, and New York. The Wisconsin and Washington shoreland zoning programs and the Florida critical area program, which has been interpreted to apply to Big Cypress and Green Swamps, also require local controls. More than 1,000 local communities have adopted wetland protection regulations in these States. A larger number of other communities have adopted land use regulations for wetland areas pursuant to coastal zone or floodplain regulatory efforts or broader land use zoning or subdivision programs.

Local adoption of wetland regulations has been encouraged not only by State wetland acts but also by the requirements of the National Flood Insurance Program, which requires local regulation of the 100-year floodplain in order to qualify for federally subsidized flood insurance. More than 17,000 communities have adopted or indicated an intent to adopt floodplain regulations to qualify for this program. Other Federal incentives for wetland protection by localities include the Coastal Zone Act of 1972 and the Corps of Engineers' "404" permit requirements. The Corps will not ordinarily issue a permit where a locality denies a permit—thereby strengthening local controls.

Local as well as State and Federal incentives exist for wetland regulation. These include the achievement of land and water use planning objectives such as reasonable minimization of natural hazards, provision for open space and recreation areas, prevention of drainage and flood problems, prohibition of septic tanks in unsuitable areas, allocation of lands throughout a community to their most appropriate uses, and protection of water supplies. Rarely are sufficient funds available at the local level to purchase more than a small portion of community wetlands to serve these objectives. In addition, it is often politically unacceptable to remove large acreages of land totally from the tax rolls. For this reason, land use regulations are adopted to restrict wetland activities while permitting some continued private use of lands.

8.2 Regulatory Approaches and Techniques

Of the two main regulatory approaches applied to wetland areas outlined in Chapter 3, application of performance standards to uses is most common to reduce flood losses, reduce impact upon wildlife, and serve a wide range of other objectives, although many communities have also adopted very restrictive controls.

Wetland protection provisions are typically adopted in several types of ordinances (see also Table 8) as follows.

o Wetland zoning. Wetland zoning regulations, the most common type of local wetland regulation, are adopted as part of a comprehensive zoning ordinance, or, alternatively, as a separate wetland ordinance.

Zoning regulations consist of a map showing wetland boundaries and a written text listing prohibited and permitted uses and establishing general standards for special permit uses. Usually a zoning board of adjustment, planning board, or special board (a conservation commission) is authorized to evaluate applications for special permits within wetland areas. Table 10 presents more information concerning wetland zoning.

o Special wetland protection bylaws and ordinances. Special bylaws or ordinances are also quite common. They may be adopted pursuant to home rule powers to special State wetland protection statutes (e.g., a Massachusetts statute authorizes local units of government to regulate directly or comment upon wetland uses), or to statutes authorizing local control of grading and filling, tree-cutting, and other activities. Special bylaws or ordinances typically contain a written text setting forth prohibited, permitted, and special permit uses. Wetlands may be defined by description or with reference to a map.

o Floodplain zoning. Floodplain zoning ordinances with wetland protection provisions are a third common approach. Floodplain zoning regulations are, like wetland regulations, adopted either as part of broader zoning efforts or as separate ordinances. Usually, floodplain regulations apply only to mapped flood zones along major streams and the ocean. Therefore, independent wetland areas not associated with rivers or streams are generally not affected. Flood maps for urban areas are often based upon engineering studies defining the 100-year floodplain, and for some riverine areas, the 100-year floodway. Flood maps may also be based upon historic flood records, soil maps, or air photos.

Where wetland protection is not an explicit regulatory objective, minor amendments could often strengthen wetland protection by adding tight control of structures, fills and dredging in wetland areas. Separate but overlapping floodplain and wetland regulations may also be applied to provide an independent factual base for evaluating development permits. Wetland regulations should also be applied to wetland areas not lying within mapped floodplain zones.

o Subdivision regulations. Subdivision regulations are usually adopted on a communitywide basis and not solely for wetland or floodplain areas. Subdivision regulations typically require that subdividers prepare detailed maps or "plats" which must be approved by the local planning board prior to division of lots for sale or construction of buildings. For approval, plats must comply with zoning and special subdivision regulations pertaining to lot size and width, access roads, the suitability of land for subdivision purposes, drainage and flooding, and the adequacy of public facilities. Subdividers must usually provide roads, sewers, drainage systems, and parks needed for subdivision residents. Although most subdivision ordinances do not specifically mention wetlands, many contain specific provisions prohibiting the subdivision

TABLE 7. LOCAL WETLAND REGULATION EFFORTS IN SELECTED STATES

The following table describes local wetland regulation in States with a large number of programs.

STATE	AREAS REGULATED	DESCRIPTION	COMMENTS
Connecticut	Inland wetlands	1. The Inland Wetland Protection Act of 1972 authorized towns to adopt Wetland regulations. A State regulatory agency is authorized to adopt regulations in the event towns do not. 2. Wetlands are mapped based upon soils (poorly drained, very poorly drained, alluvial and floodplain) delineated by the Soil Conservation Service. 3. The State has conducted data gathering efforts and workshops.	1. Some problems have been encountered with map scale, accuracy, administration, and enforcement of the act.
Florida	Tidal Wetlands	1. Local regulations of inland wetlands is required by State "Critical area" regulations adopted for Big Cypress and Green Swamp critical areas and the Florida Keys. In addition, a number of local units have independently adopted wetland regulations. 2. The State regulates fill and dredging of wetlands under a water pollution control act.	1. There is widespread interest in wetlands, particularly in coastal mangrove and barrier islands. 2. Some communities, like Sanibel, have assumed leadership roles in wetland protection.
Massachusetts	Tidal wetlands Inland wetlands	1. Permits for alteration of inland and coastal wetlands must be submitted to town conservation commissions. The State wetland regulatory agency is authorized to adopt protective orders for inland and coastal wetlands. Landowners may appeal local decisions to the State regulatory agency. 2. State has mapped both coastal and inland wetlands. State protective orders have been adopted primarily for coastal wetlands but some orders have also been adopted for inland areas. 3. Many towns have adopted their own wetland zoning or special protection bylaws.	1. There is widespread interest in wetlands throughout the State. 2. The Audubon Society has conducted a three-year study of local wetland regulation to aid local wetland protection programs. 3. Problems have arisen with administration and enforcement of the act.
New York	Inland, some coastal wetlands	1. Municipal or county regulation of inland wetlands consistent with State standards is required by the Freshwater Wetlands Act of 1975. If municipalities fail to regulate wetlands, the regulatory function is transferred to the county. If the county fails, the function is transferred to the State. 2. The State is encouraging local programs through regulations, technical assistance, wetland mapping. 3. The State has adopted a moratorium for tidal wetlands.	1. Both coastal and inland programs are in early stages of implementation. 2. Programs are seriously limited by lack of budget.
Virginia	Tidal wetlands	1. The Tidal Wetland Protection Act of 1973 establishes a cooperative state/local protection program. A model wetland ordinance is contained in the act. If municipalities do not regulate wetlands, permits for development must be obtained from the counties. If counties fail to regulate, permits must be obtained from the State. 2. The State has inventoried wetlands and developed guidelines and guidebooks for local implementation with the help of the Virginia Institute of Marine Sciences. The Institute evaluates each proposed wetland application and makes recommendations to local wetland boards.	1. Regulations have been adopted by 25 communities which contain 90% of State coastal wetlands. 2. State-University-Local cooperation is very good. 3. The trend of losing 450 acres of wetlands per year has been reversed to an estimated 20 acres per year.
Washington	Inland and coastal wetlands within "shoreline" areas	1. Washington Shoreline Zoning Act of 1971 requires that local governments adopt "master programs" for shoreline areas defined to include wetlands. 2. The State has developed guidelines for shoreland use.	1. This act defines wetlands to include not only wet-vegetated areas but other lands. 2. The State has worked closely with local units in developing master programs.
Wisconsin	Inland wetlands within "shoreland" areas	1. County regulation of shoreland areas within 1,000 feet of lakes and 300 feet of streams is required by the Shoreland Zoning Act of 1966. The State regulatory agency is authorized to adopt regulations for shoreland areas if counties fail to adopt satisfactory controls. 2. The State has adopted administrative regulations and model shoreland zoning ordinances, which encourage conservancy zoning for wetlands within shoreland areas. 3. The State has worked closely with local units and provided manuals, guidebooks, technical assistance. 4. Wetlands have been defined based upon topographic and soils maps.	1. The program has worked with fair success. However, there have been some problems with wetland definition and enforcement of regulations. 2. A new wetland mapping effort is anticipated in the near future.

of flood-prone areas and require that lots be suitable for building and onsite waste disposal if public sewers are not provided. This, combined with requirements that subdividers provide recreation and open spaces, provides communities with bargaining power for the protection of wetlands. Additional bargaining power may be provided by "cluster" subdivision provisions which encourage subdividers to group buildings together in upland areas so that other low lying areas can be maintained as open space. The overall density of the subdivision is maintained.

o   Building codes. Many communities have adopted building codes to control the design and materials used in structures. These rarely contain reference to wetlands although several provisions, such as requirements that buildings be elevated above the flood protection elevations and that buildings be located on suitable foundation material, may provide some protection for wetland areas.

o   Sanitary codes. Many communities have adopted sanitary codes regulating or prohibiting the use of septic tank and soil absorption systems in high groundwater areas and within specified distances of lakes and streams. If adequately enforced, these regulations can quite effectively control building development in rural wetlands.

o   Special codes. Communities often adopt special codes for tree-cutting, grading, mosquito control, application of pesticides, solid waste disposal, storm sewers, air and water pollution emissions, and surface and groundwater extraction. These regulations, if adequately enforced, provide some protection for wetland areas including the quality and quantity of waters entering wetlands from watershed lands.

o   Comprehensive zoning controls. Communities often adopt comprehensive zoning regulations that place wetlands, steep slopes, forestry areas, and other valuable or unique lands into conservancy or low density residential and open space zones with minimum lot sizes ranging from two to 60 acres. Lot size restrictions are typically combined with siting controls and regulation of tree-cutting, grading, filling, dredging, construction of roads, and other activities. A considerable degree of wetland protection may be achieved if each proposed use is carefully evaluated and efforts are made to shift development to upland areas. In addition, large lot zoning reduces the density of wetland development.

8.3 Steps in Wetland Regulation

Seven steps highlighted in the following discussion and Table 10 are often applied in the adoption and implementation of wetland regulations.

1. Data gathering. Wetland maps are usually prepared prior to adoption of wetland zoning ordinances and special codes. However, some ordinances rely on tidal elevations or vegetation types rather than maps to define wetlands.

Mapping is only the first step in wetland data gathering. Site investigations are typically conducted to resolve boundary disputes and evaluate the impact of individual proposed development.

2. Prior comprehensive planning. It is sometimes argued that wetland regulations must be based upon a comprehensive plan since zoning enabling acts often require prior planning. However, few efforts have been preceded by extensive planning. In traditional zoning contexts, courts have often found the required plan within the regulations themselves. In an ideal sense, wetland regulations should be linked to a broader water resources and land use plan for a community based upon hydrological, ecological, and other relationships.

3. Drafting of regulations. Often the drafting of proposed regulations is a "cut and paste" effort based upon published model regulations or regulations adopted in other communities. Modifications may be required—including exemptions for particular uses—to gain political support and to tailor the regulations to local circumstances.

4. Notice and public hearing. A public hearing must be held prior to adoption of regulations. Notice of the hearing must first be published in a local newspaper. However, written notice is not required for affected landowners.

5. Adoption of regulations. Normally, a majority vote of a quorum of the local legislative body is required for adoption of regulations. After adoption, regulations must be published in a local newspaper and filed in the city hall or another public office for public inspection. Communities often print and make available copies.

6. Administration. Typically, proposed uses are evaluated on a case-by-case basis by a local regulatory board to determine wetland impact. Regulations usually require that developers provide a portion of the required information. The regulatory board has broad discretion in permitting and denying uses.

7. Enforcement. Enforcement, the final phase of wetland regulation, is often quite weak unless there is strong local support for regulations.

8.4 Principal Wetland Zoning and Special Bylaw Provisions

Wetland zoning and special bylaw regulations often contain the following elements. These are either set out as a separate ordinance or integrated into a broader zoning or other code: (1) purposes; (2) wetland definition criteria and maps; (3) prohibited, permitted, and special permit uses, and (4) penalties.

Purposes
Local wetland ordinances typically list objectives for control of wetland development related to both natural hazards and values. A strong statement of public purpose establishes public intent and may be helpful in later court suits. For example, a Lexington, Massachusetts ordinance provides:[1]

Purpose of District. The purposes of the Wetland Protection District are to preserve and maintain the groundwater table; to protect the public health and safety by protecting persons and property against the hazards of flood water inundation; and to protect the community against the costs which may be incurred when unsuitable development occurs in swamps, marshes, along water courses or in areas subject to floods.

More detailed standards are provided in an Orono, Minnesota ordinance which provides in part:[2]

In addition to (other) general purposes, the specific intent of this ordinance is to:
(a) Reduce danger to health by protecting surface and groundwater supplies from the impairment which results from incompatible land uses by providing safe and sanitary drainage.
(b) Reduce the financial burdens imposed both on this community and on communities within the Minnehaha Creek Watershed District and the individuals therein by frequent floods and overflow of water on lands.
(c) Permit and encourage planned development land uses which will not impede the flow of flood water or cause danger to life or property.
(d) Permit and encourage land uses compatible with the preservation of the natural vegetation and marshes which are a principal factor in the maintenance of constant rates of water flow through the year and which sustain many species of wildlife and plant growth.
(e) Avoid fast runoff of surface waters from development areas to prevent pollutional materials such as animal feces, motor oils, paper, sand, salt and other debris, garbage, and foreign materials from being carried directly into the nearest natural stream, lake, or other public waters.
(f) Encourage a suitable system of ponding areas to permit the temporary withholding of rapid water runoff which presently contributes to downstream flooding and general water pollution giving preference to areas which contribute to groundwater infiltration and recharge, thereby reducing the need for public projects to contain, store, and control such runoff.
(g) Provide sufficient land area to carry abnormal flows of storm water in periods of heavy precipitation, and to prevent needless expenditures of public funds for storm sewers and flood protection devices which proper planning could have avoided.
(h) Prevent the development of structures in areas unfit for human usage by reason of danger from flooding, unsanitary conditions, or other hazards.
(i) Prevent the placement of artificial obstructions which restrict the right of public passage and use of the bed, bank and water of any creeks, marshes, or watercourses within the Village.

Wetland Definition Criteria
Most local wetland ordinances include general written wetland definitions and rely on wetland maps to specifically define wetlands subject to the ordinance. Wetland maps, discussed earlier in this report, include air photos with wetland boundary delineations, soil maps, USGS topographic maps, and special maps. Wetland maps and regulations often "overlay" and supplement other zoning and mapping

efforts. For example, a Lincoln, Massachusetts ordinance provides:[3]
Wetland and Watershed Protection District. 1. Overlay District. The W-Wetland and Watershed Protection District is an overlay district and shall be superimposed on the other districts established by this By-Law. Any land lying with the W-Wetland and Watershed Protection District shall also be subject to the development and use regulations of the underlying district in which such land is situated but only to the extent not inconsistent with the regulations for the W-Wetland and Watershed Protection District.

Where a State statute has defined wetland areas for regulatory purposes, local units generally incorporate this definition. For example, a Glastonbury, Connecticut, ordinance incorporates a State wetland definition based upon soils:[4]
"Wetlands" means land, including submerged land, not regulated as tidal wetlands pursuant to Sections...which consists of any of the soil types designated as poorly drained, very poorly drained, alluvial, and flood plain by the National Cooperative Soil Survey (as may be amended from time to time) by the United States Department of Agriculture, Soil Conservation Service.

In some instances, ordinances incorporate several definition approaches. For example, a Worburn, Massachusetts ordinance provides in part:[5]

Definition
1) All lands within the elevations shown on the zoning map and designated as wetlands. These include lakes, ponds, swamps, and marshes.
2) All lands designated on the zoning map as having a shallow depth to water table. These lands are the poorly and very poorly drained mineral soils, and very poorly drained soils formed in organic deposits. Poorly drained mineral soils have a water table at or near the surface for 7 to 9 months during the year. The water table remains at or close to the surface of very poorly drained mineral and organic soils throughout most of the year.
3) All land area along all rivers, brooks, and streams for a horizontal distance of 25 feet from the center line thereof are included in the Inland Wetland and Watershed Protection District.
A model shoreland zoning ordinance promulgated by the Wisconsin Department of Natural Resources and adopted by many counties for wetland areas suggests two alternative approaches for mapping wetland conservancy districts:[6]
Designation. This district includes all shorelands designated as swamps or marshes on the United States Geological Survey Quadrangle map sheets which have been designated the Shoreland Zoning Map of _____ County, Wisconsin or on the detailed Insert Shoreland Zoning Maps.

Or in the Alternative

This district shall include all lands within the jurisdiction of this Ordinance which are

TABLE 8. A COMPARISON OF COMMON REGULATORY TOOLS

TOOL	DISTINGUISHING FEATURES	APPLICATION TO NEW USES	APPLICATION TO EXISTING USES	WHO ADMINISTERS	EXTRATERRITORIAL APPLICATION
Zoning	1. Map and text. Regulates type of use and provides minimum specifications for uses in each zone. 2. A tool of comprehensive planning. 3. Does not regulate land division or provide detailed standards for building design or materials.	1. Wide potential in regulating construction, land alteration, tree cutting, many other aspects of land use.	1. Some potential for eliminating existing wetland uses, particularly nuisance flood way or flood fringe uses. 2. Often requires that existing uses be brought into conformity upon their abandonment, destruction, or need for substantial repair.	1. Zoning administrator issues permits. 2. Board of Adjustment issues variances and special exceptions.	1. Authorized in 40 percent of States.
Subdivision	1. Text only. Applies to sale and division or land. Approval of "plat" required. 2. Does not in itself regulate type of land use. Regulations apply uniformly.	1. Wide potential in requiring disclosure of flood hazards, ensuring that lands are suitable for intended purposes, and requiring installation of public facilities by subdivider.	1. None.	1. Planning Commission.	1. Authorized in 60 percent of States. Particularly useful tool for urbanizing areas.
Building Code	1. Text only. Applies to building design and materials. Building permit required. 2. Does not regulate type of use of land or subdivision of land.	1. Wide potential in establishing detailed construction standards including structural flood proofing measures.	1. Usually none; however, housing codes (a variety of building codes) apply to existing as well as new uses.	1. Building Inspector.	1. Authorized in 4 States.
Special Wetland Regulation Bylaw	1. Text only (usually) but may incorporate a map. Typically adopted pursuant to special wetland regulation statute or home rule powers.	1. Wide potential in regulating construction, land alteration, tree-cutting, many other aspects of land use.	1. Usually none.	1. Local legislative body, conservation commissions, building Inspector.	1. Usually none.

TABLE 9. OVERVIEW OF WETLAND ZONING

PURPOSES	REGULATORY STANDARDS	ADVANTAGES	LIMITATIONS
1. Protect wildlife habitat, scenic beauty, and provide flood storage wetland recreation by control of grading, filling, dredging, tree-cutting, type and density of wetland uses, buffer area uses. 2. Protect public safety and prevent nuisances by prohibiting dangerous uses (chemical factories in flood heights due to floodway encroachments), threats to safety by location of quasi-public uses such as motels in flash-flood areas, water pollution from location of onsite waste disposal and solid waste disposal in wetland areas. 3. Promote most suitable and economic use of community lands as a whole by implementing comprehensive land use plans allocating wetland areas to uses consistent with values and hazards 4. Reduce the cost of public facilities and assist in the implementation of facility plans for roads, sewer, water, schools, etc. by preventing or limiting the type and density of development in wetland areas.	1. Delineate wetland areas, prohibit destructive uses, and apply performance standards to other uses. 2. Delineate floodway areas and prohibit new structural uses and land alterations that will individually or cumulatively increase flood heights or velocities beyond defined levels. 3. Establish flood protection elevations and protection standards for floodway and flood fringe areas and uses. 4. In some instances, abate existing wetland uses of a nuisance nature and require flood-proofing with major alteration of flood fringe uses.	1. Can incorporate wide range of provisions relating to wetland management and other objectives. 2. Can separate wetlands into zones depending upon flood hazard and other factors and apply varying standards to the zones. 3. Most common tool in preserving wetland areas. 4. Can be applied (in some areas) to existing uses with a nuisance character.	1. May "take" private property if too restrictive. 2. Does not regulate sale or transfer of lands. 3. Often weakened by irrational variances and exceptions. 4. Is largely prospective in nature (applies only to new uses and usually unsuccessful when applied to high-value, non-nuisance existing uses.

TABLE 10. STEPS IN LOCAL WETLAND REGULATION

STEP	COMMENTARY	ZONING	SUBDIVISION
1. Data Gathering	Often the most expensive and time-consuming step in the adoption of legally sound and politically acceptable regulations. A variety of data may be needed to identify wetland boundaries. All data need not be gathered at once. The ultimate data used for regulation will determine the rationality of the regulation. Two approaches are often combined: (1) initial data gathering to identify wetland limits gathered in advance of adoption of regulations and (2) case-by-case gathering of more specific data when building permit applications are submitted.	Zoning may require wetland maps.	Mapping of wetland boundaries is desirable prior to adoption of regulations but such boundaries may be determined on a case-by-case basis.
2. Planning	Planning can help form wetland policies reflecting not only environmental values but transportation, housing, and other needs. Planning is usually the responsibility of consultant or in-house land-use planners acting under the direction of a local planning commission.	While zoning enabling acts often require adoption of a "comprehensive plan," prior to preparing zoning maps this has not been strictly enforced by the courts.	Some enabling acts require adoption of a "master plan" prior to adoption of subdivision regulations, though often this is not strictly enforced. Master plans showing proposed community public works are important if the subdivider is required to install sewer, water, roads, and drainage facilities consistent with overall community needs.
3. Drafting of Regulation	Drafting is often the responsibility of a consultant, a resident land-use planner, or a member of the local conservation commission cooperating with the city attorney, planning commission, city council, or conservation commission.	Both a text and map are generally required.	Usually drafted by the planning commission cooperating with the city or county officials.
4. Notice of Public Hearings	At least one hearing must be held prior to adoption of regulations. Often several hearings are held on proposed regulations. Regulations and maps are often modified based upon the hearings.	Required prior to adoption of regulations. A zoning map which determines where particular regulations will apply is often the most controversial subject at the hearing.	Required prior to adoption of regulations.
5. Adoption of Regulations	Adoption usually requires a majority of the local legislative body (city, county, town, village, borough council). Regulations must be published in the local newspaper. Regulations must be available at a public place (zoning office, etc.) for inspection by interested individuals.	Generally adoption is the responsibility of the local governing body.	Generally adoption is the responsibility of the local municipal governing body or the planning commission.
6. Administration	Administration of ordinances requires engineering and biological expertise to ensure that proposed development meets ordinance standards. Widespread issuance of exceptions and variances undermines ordinance policies.	Building permits are generally issued by the zoning administration or the conservation commission. Enabling acts typically authorize the issuance of variances and special exceptions by the zoning board of appeals.	Enabling acts typically designate planning commissions as "plat review" agencies. Preliminary and final plat procedures and specifications may be defined in some detail.
7. Enforcement	Ordinances establish fines and other penalties, including jail sentences, for violations. Courts enforce fines and wetland restoration requirements (in some instances) but rarely require jail sentences.	Penalties vary.	Penalties vary.

designated on map sheets 1 through inclusive of the Soil Survey _____ County, Wisconsin. (USDA SCS Series ___ . No. _____) by the following letter symbols....

Brockton, Massachusetts separates wetlands into three subdistricts for regulatory purposes:[7]

Scope

The Flood Plain, Watershed, and Wetlands Protection Zone overlies the basic zoning in an area and its provisions apply in addition to those of the basic zone, and of any other City regulations and ordinances, and any State laws.

The District is divided into three subdistricts reflecting the sensitivities and limitations of the wetlands involved. These are the : (1) Major Importance, (2) Moderate Importance and (3) Minor Importance subdistricts.

In Major Importance subdistricts the complete Flood Plain, Watershed, and Wetlands land use regulations and special permit procedures apply to all actions. In addition, all proposed actions must be submitted to the City Engineer and the Highway Division of the Department of Public Works for engineering plan review, and to the Conservation Commission as required under Chapter 131, Section 40 of the General Laws.

In Moderate Importance subdistricts, the complete land use regulations and special permit procedures apply to all actions in which combined building coverage and paving and filling of land exceeds five thousand square feet (5000 sq. ft.) or thirty-five percent (35%) of the site area. In addition, all actions must be submitted to the City Engineer and the Highway Division of the Department of Public Works for engineering plan review, and to the Conservation Commission as required under Chapter 131, Section 40 of the General Laws.

In areas of Minor Importance, all actions must be submitted to the Conservation Commission as required by Chapter 131, Section 40 of the General Laws.

Interpretation of boundaries of zones.

The Flood Plain, Watershed, and Wetland Protection Zone.

This zone (which is divided into three subdistricts) covers all property so identified on the map entitled "The City of Brockton, Massachusetts Zoning District Map". To simplify interpretation, small partially affected parcels have been included in their entirety.

Distinctions between areas of Major, Moderate, and Minor wetlands importance reflect their relative hydrological and ecological significance and the extent and duration of their high water tables.

The Major Importance subdistrict includes surface water bodies and their banks to the contour or distance noted below, areas subject to flooding, as described below, and areas where the water table is at or near the surface most of the year.

The Moderate Importance subdistrict includes areas with the water table at or near the surface seven months of the year.

The Minor Importance subdistrict includes areas where the water table is within 18 inches of the surface in winter and early spring.

Prohibited, Permitted, and Special Permit Uses

Local ordinances typically specify "prohibited", "permitted", and "special permit" uses. Ordinances generally prohibit all uses which are not permitted as of right or issued individual permits after case-by-case evaluation. Some ordinances list prohibited uses. A Lexington, Massachusetts ordinance mandates:[8]

No landfill or dumping or excavation of any kind.

No drainage work other than by an authorized public agency.

No damming or relocation of any watercourse except as part of an overall drainage basin plan.

No building or structure.

No permanent storage of materials or equipment.

Sometimes qualifications are placed on the prohibited uses. For example, a Wayland, Massachusetts ordinance provides:[9]
a) No building, wall, dam, or other structure shall be erected, constructed, altered, enlarged or otherwise created or moved for any living or other purpose, provided that noncommercial signs not exceeding four feet square in size, tents, fences, wildlife management shelters, foot paths, bicycle paths, horse paths, and foot bridges are permitted if:
(i)   they are necessary to lawful primary uses in a single residence district and
(ii)   they do not affect the natural flow pattern of any watercourse.
b) Dumping, filling, excavating or transferring of any material which will reduce the natural flood-water storage capacity or interfere with the natural flow patterns of any watercourse within the District are prohibited.

Most ordinances also contain a list of "permitted uses" (no permit is required or one is issued automatically). This list is similar for most coastal and inland wetland protection ordinances. A list from Lincoln, Massachusetts is typical:[10]

Uses Permitted. The following uses are permitted provided that any and all necessary permits, orders, or approvals required by local, State, or Federal law shall be obtained:
A.   Conservation of soil, water, plants, and wildlife.

B.   Outdoor recreation, including play and sporting areas, nature study, boating, fishing and hunting where otherwise legally permitted.

C.   Flower or vegetable gardens, lawns, pastures, forestry, grazing and farming, including nurseries, truck gardening, and harvesting of crops.

D.   Duck-walks, landings, foot, bicycle and/or horse paths, and bridges; and small structures for non-commercial recreational uses.

Ordinances also establish a list of "special permit" uses which the ordinances neither prohibit nor permit outright. These uses must be evaluated on a case-by-case basis. Special permit uses (also termed special exceptions or conditional uses) are generally those that may or may not have serious wetland impact, depending upon circumstances. A board of adjustment, planning commission, conservation commission, or other local board is authorized to issue special permits. Usually ordinances establish standards and procedures for the evaluation of special permits. A Wayland, Massachusetts ordinance contains a typical list of special permit uses:[11]

Upon the issuance of a special permit for an exception by the Board of Appeals, and subject to the conditions hereinafter specified and such other special conditions and safeguards as the Board of Appeals deems necessary to fulfill the purposes set forth in paragraph 1, the following uses, structures and actions, as permitted in single residence districts are permitted.

(1) Duck-walks and boat landings;
(2) Appropriate municipal use, such as waterworks pumping stations and parks;
(3) Temporary storage of materials or equipment;
(4) Dams, excavations, or grading, consistent with the purposes of this section to create ponds, pools, or other changes in watercourses, for swimming, fishing, or other recreational uses, agricultural uses, scenic features or drainage improvements;
(5) Driveways and roads;
(6) Any other filling, excavating, or transferring of any material, or erection, construction, alteration, enlargement, or removal or demolition of any structure, upon the condition that with respect to each such action and structure the Board of Appeals determines that granting a special permit therefore would not result in any substantial risk of pollution or contamination of any waterway or pond, substantial reduction of seasonal high water storage areas, substantial reduction of groundwater absorption areas, which serve the public water supply or other derogation from the intent and purpose of this Section X-C.

A Lexington, Massachusetts ordinance illustrates general standards for such permits:[12]

Special Permits for Uses in Harmony With General Purposes of the District. The Board of Appeals may issue a special permit for any use of land which would otherwise be permitted if such land were not, by operation of this section, in the Wetland Protection District if the Board finds (1) that such land within the District is ... not subject to flooding or is not unsuitable because of drainage conditions for such use, and (2) that the use of such land for any such use will not interfere with the general purposes for which Wetland Protection Districts have been established, and (3) that such use will not be detrimental to the public health, safety, or welfare.

Ordinances usually do not establish detailed standards for special permits and instead apply general performance guidelines. However, some ordinances list factors to be considered by the regulatory board. A Clearwater, Florida ordinance applicable to aquatic districts provides:[13]

...Such requests (for special exceptions) shall be accompanied by evidence that the proposed use of any waters and submerged lands will:

(1) Protect the right of the public to use and enjoy for recreational purposes any of the waters or submerged lands affected;
(2) Preserve grass flats and mud flats for breeding and spawning grounds for fish;
(3) Not cause or contribute to erosion of waterfront properties;
(4) Not create any alteration of waterflow, accumulation of debris, or creation of water pockets for incubation of "red tide";
(5) Demonstrate that adequate precautions are taken to prevent salt water intrusions into surface water tables; and
(6) Display that there are proper provisions to be taken for protection of an access to existing or proposed navigable channels or basins.

An inland wetland protection ordinance from Ledyard, Connecticut directs the regulatory agency to consider the following factors in evaluating the importance of the wetland at the site of a proposed activity:[14]

The existing or potential use of the area as a surface or groundwater supply.

The extent to which the area serves as a recharge area or purifier of surface or ground waters.

The function of the area as part of the natural drainage system for the watershed.

The importance of the area as a natural wildlife feeding or breeding area.

The existence of rare or unusual concentrations of botanical species.

The existing and potential use of the area for recreation purposes.

The availability of other open space in the surrounding area.

The size of the wetland and its relationship to other wetlands or water courses which may be affected by the proposed activity.

The importance of the area in preventing leaching or siltation or otherwise affecting water quality.

The ordinance also directs the regulatory agency to consider the following environmental impacts of the proposed activity:
The ability of the regulated area to continue to absorb, store, or purify water or prevent flooding.

Increased erosion problems resulting from changes in grades, ground cover, or drainage features.

The extent of additional siltation or leaching and its affect on water quality and aquatic life.

The influence of toxic materials on water supplies, aquatic organisms, or wildlife.

Changes in the volume, velocity, temperature, or course of a waterway and their resulting affects on plant, animal, or aquatic life.

Some wetland ordinances establish minimum lot size requirements of one to 15 acres for structural uses. In other instances, zoning ordinances place restrictions upon the use of wetland areas to meet traditional lot area restrictions (e.g., 20,000 square feet in residential areas). This, in effect, requires larger lot sizes in wetland areas. For example, a Brockton, Massachusetts wetland overlay ordinance permits a landowner to use wetland areas to meet "up to 60% of the lot area requirements for uses allowed in the underlying zone. The actual development must be confined to the portion of the site (a minimum of 40% of the total required area) which is outside the Flood Plain, Watershed, and Wetlands Protection District."[15]

Often the applicant is required to submit detailed information to help the regulatory board apply special permit criteria. For example, a model local wetland protection ordinance promulgated by the State of New York provides:[16]

An application for a permit shall be filed by the applicant on a form prescribed by the Agency. Such application shall set forth the purpose, character and extent of the proposed regulated activity. The application shall include a detailed description of the regulated activity, a map showing the area of freshwater wetland or adjacent area directly affected, with the location of the proposed regulated activity thereon, a deed or other legal description describing the subject property and such additional information as the Agency deems sufficient to enable it to make the findings and determinations required under this law.

The application shall be accompanied by a list of the names of the owners of record of lands adjacent to the freshwater wetland or adjacent area upon which the project is to be undertaken and the names of known claimants of water rights, of whom the applicant has notice, which related to any land within, or within one hundred feet of the boundary of, the property on which the proposed regulated activity will be located.

An application shall not be deemed to be completed or received until the Agency determines that all such information, including any additional information requested, has been supplied in a complete and satisfactory form.

Generally, the regulatory agency is authorized to attach conditions to permits to minimize development impact such as restrictions on the amount and location of fill.

Some ordinances authorize the regulatory agency to require a permit processing fee and to require a performance bond from an applicant to ensure that conditions are carried out. For example, an Easton, Connecticut ordinance provides:[17]

The applicant, upon approval of the permit, in the discretion of the Commission, may be required to file a performance bond in an amount and with sureties and in a form approved by the Commission.

The bond and sureties shall be conditioned on compliance with all provisions of these regulations and conditions imposed on license approval.

The applicant may be required to certify that he has public liability insurance against liability which might result from proposed operation or use covering any and all damage which might occur within three years of completion of such operations, in an amount to be determined by the Commission commensurate with the projected operation.

Penalties

Most ordinances provide a combination of fines and possible jail sentences for violation of ordinance provisions. Many require that the affected wetland area be restored. For example, a Ledyard, Connecticut ordinance provides:[18]

Any person who commits, takes part in, or assists in any violation of any provision of these Regulations shall be fined not more than One Thousand ($1,000.00) Dollars for each offense. Each violation shall be a separate and distinct offense, and in the case of a continuing violation each day's continuance thereof shall be deemed to be a separate and distinct offense. The Superior Court, in any action brought by the Commission, the Town of Ledyard or any person shall have jurisdiction to restrain a continuing violation of these Regulations or to issue orders directing that the violation be corrected or removed. All costs, fees and expenses in connection with such action shall be assessed as damages against the violator. The moneys collected pursuant to this Section shall be used to restore the affected wetland and/or watercourse to its condition prior to the violation, where possible.

MANGROVES SUBJECT TO LOCAL REGULATION, SANIBEL, FLORIDA. Many Florida coastal communities protect mangroves. Photo source: Jon Kusler.

8.5 The Implementation of Local Programs

Some of the key issues in local implementation include the following.

Wetland Maps

The adequacy of the wetland maps is a widespread issue for several reasons. First, detailed wetland maps are rarely available except for some coastal wetland areas where detailed State mapping has occurred (New Jersey, Maryland). Often soil maps, topographic maps, and generalized wetland maps are used for regulatory purposes in the absence of more detailed data. These maps may be outdated, too small scale for regulation, or do not cover the community as a whole.

The accuracy of maps and map scale has been more of a problem for inland than coastal wetlands since coastal wetlands are more readily identifiable, even without maps, due to tidal actions and a relatively small number of characteristic plant species. Some communities have adopted both maps and written definition criteria for wetland areas and have required that field surveys be conducted to apply the written definition criteria in case of boundary disputes.

Second, local zoning administrators and government officials are often uncomfortable with wetland zone boundaries that lack mathematical certainty and do not coincide with property lines.

There is a general belief that the zoning ordinance should contain precise boundary locations so that by inspecting the map, any boundary question could be settled. Wetland boundaries are, of course, not precise since saturated soils and wetland vegetation types grade into upland soils and vegetation. Fluctuating water levels over a period of years complicate the problem. Any attempt to define boundaries with mathematical precision is, therefore, bound to fail. Landowners are often able to exploit feelings of uneasiness on the part of zoning administrators and local legislative bodies by claiming that they will challenge the sufficiency of maps in court.

Problems with boundary location are minimized, in some instances by mapping wetland boundaries directly on large-scale air photos and incorporating the photos in official zoning maps. If a landowner wishes to develop a particular site, the precise location of the site and its relationship to wetland boundaries can usually be located with reference to trees, roads, buildings, and other features visible on the photo.

Only a small number of communities have conducted data gathering efforts sufficient to rank wetlands for regulatory purposes although informal ranking based upon size, threats, landownership, and special values and hazards is quite common for acquisition. A ranking procedure based upon wetland values alone may be of relatively limited value for regulations based primarily upon flood or other

BULKHEADING IN COASTAL WETLANDS, WELLFLEET, MASSACHUSETTS. New fills or structures require a permit from the behind local conservation commission as well as the state. Photo source: Jon Kusler.

hazards. In addition, a ranking procedure may encourage development of wetlands with a low ranking.

Many communities in Wisconsin and New York have applied regulations only to larger and readily mappable wetlands. This approach has proven politically expedient and minimizes administrative problems while preserving the more important wetlands.

Communities have universally found that wetland maps provide only a portion of the data required for evaluating proposed development. Field investigations are usually required to evaluate the seriousness of flood hazards at a site, suitability for on-site waste disposal, hydrologic characteristics, and other factors. Flood hazard maps, soil maps, and detailed air photos are widely used to make these additional determinations.

Budget Restrictions

Most local programs are faced with limited funds and personnel for wetland mapping, site investigations, and enforcement actions. A variety of approaches may be taken to reduce program costs. First, developers are often required to file environmental impact statements or undertake other data gathering to help evaluate proposed development. Second, a fee may be charged to help defray the costs of field inspections and the processing

of permits. Third, interest groups are often encouraged to testify at public hearings on proposed permits in order to generate free information on the permits. Fourth, local regulatory programs "make do" with existing wetland maps rather than produce their own. Finally, volunteer groups, such as The Nature Conservancy and Audubon Society, may be used to monitor development and report violations of regulations.

Public Education

The success of local wetland programs has depended upon public and landowner education and community support. Some communities such as Concord Massachusetts and Sanibel, Florida have met with all individual wetland landowners to discuss the law and the need for wetland protection. Other communities and interest groups have conducted public education efforts through lectures, slide shows, workshops, and lobbying. For example, the Massachusetts Audubon Society completed a three-year project, funded by the Rockefeller Foundation, to assist local conservation commissions in wetland protection. Universities have played major educational roles in assisting communities in Wisconsin, Washington, Massachusetts, and other states.

The Evaluation of Permit Applications

Careful evaluation of permits is essential to a

strong local program. However, evaluation may be handicapped by limited budgets and data base and lack of expertise in the local regulatory agency. As a result, local governments rely upon environmental impact statements provided by developers and seek help from nearby universities, State agencies with hydrological and biological expertise, and Federal employees such as Soil Conservation Service soil scientists. The success of local programs often depends upon outside assistance.

Permit applications submitted to local units of government are typically approved but usually with conditions attached to minimize development impact. Developers with unacceptable projects are often discouraged from applying for permits. In addition, stringent conditions are often attached to permits.

Evaluation of the cumulative impact of development is often a serious problem in processing permits. Two approaches may be taken. First, all new uses may be prohibited based upon arguments of cumulative impact. Second, the density of new uses may be limited through lot size restrictions or restrictions on the percentage of wetland areas that may be altered within a parcel. In this way, the total impact of uses may be held within acceptable limits.

Legal Issues

Concern that regulations will "take" property is often an impediment to adoption and tight enforcement of wetland regulations.

A variety of approaches have been taken to achieve wetland protection while avoiding the taking issues. First, performance standards rather than outright prohibition of all structural uses can be applied. Second, negotiation can occur between the governmental body and the landowner in the processing of individual development permits. For example, the local regulatory body may agree upon wetland boundaries that preserve most but not all of a wetland. In return the landowner may agree to minimize impact upon the wetland by locating most if not all of a regulated activity in upland areas. Issues subject to nego-

tiation commonly include the size, design, and precise location of the proposed project. Communities can also carefully coordinate tax policies with regulations to alleviate the burden of restrictive land use controls.

Wetland Protection Through Regulations Other Than Wetland Controls

The advisability of regulating land solely to protect wetlands is sometimes questioned in contrast with broader regulation to reduce flood hazards, prevent septic tank systems in high groundwater areas, control filling and grading, and control tree-cutting. Often a considerable degree of wetland protection can be achieved through the vigorous enforcement of regulations applying to these broader objectives without clearly confronting the political issue of wetland regulations. Nevertheless, such a broader approach may result in fragmentation of regulatory activities and lack of clear focus.

The applicability of a particular approach depends upon the physical circumstances and the political climate. Considerable wetland protection is achieved in some areas through vigorous enforcement of sanitary codes prohibiting septic tanks in high groundwater areas and subdivision regulations prohibiting the division of flood prone areas. Wetland in urbanizing and urban areas may be effectively protected through vigorous enforcement of floodway and coastal high-hazard restrictions that prohibit all fills and structures in these areas.

Enforcement

Enforcement is, of course, the key to wetland protection. Strong public education programs and watchdog interest groups who report violations and appear at public hearings can facilitate local enforcement. Periodic surveys of wetland areas and consistent prosecutional violations of not only wetland regulations but floodplain zoning, septic tank permit requirements, and other regulations will discourage violations.

CHAPTER 9: WETLAND REGULATIONS AND THE COURTS

9.1 Introduction

Wetland regulations raise the same constitutional issues faced by broader planning and regulatory programs, but with several special features. Public rights and interests in waters are involved. Scientific determinations form the basis for restrictions. Issues of special interest are summarized below.

The issue in successful regulation is not simply what regulations courts will uphold, but also the political acceptability of specific wetland regulations as applied to private landowners. As legislative acts, wetland regulations depend upon the will of the legislators, and ultimately the voting public.

Often, arguments are made that regulations are unreasonable, discriminatory, or "take" private property without payment of just compensation. As will be discussed shortly, courts have found some wetlands regulations invalid because they violate property rights protected by the Federal Constitution under the 5th and 14th Amendments or State constitutions. But most regulations have been sustained, particularly in the last five years. The spectre of legal challenge is overdone.

9.2 Approaches to Determination of Constitutionality

State and local regulations enjoy a strong presumption of constitutionality and the burden of proving unconstitutionality is upon the attacking party.[1] In determining constitutionality, courts first look to the general validity of regulations and then to their validity as applied to particular lands. Courts in all 50 States have sustained the general validity of regulations substantially reducing private property values. Courts in approximately twenty States have considered the validity of wetland regulations. All have endorsed the general validity of such regulations.

The majority of attacks upon land use controls and, more specifically, upon wetland regulations are upon the application of regulations to particular properties. This "pinpoint" approach to the determination of constitutionality originated with two United States Supreme Court decisions in the 1920's.

In the first of these cases, **Euclid v. Village of Ambler**,[2] the Court upheld the basic concept of zoning—the division of a community into districts and the application of differing land use standards to each district. Two years later, the Court in **Nectow v. City of Cambridge**[3] faced a dilemma when it considered the validity of a zoning ordinance that made sense as applied to community lands as a whole but was unreasonable as applied to a particular parcel. To have struck down the ordinance as a whole would have left the community without zoning and would have invalidated the good elements of zoning. Taking a compromise position, the Court held that the zoning regulations were valid in general, but invalid as applied to the particular property.

This pinpoint approach to determination of constitutionality has been followed by State courts. In other words, a landowner may concede the general validity of a wetlands or floodplain regulation but argue its unconstitutionality as applied to specific property. A court decision invalidating regulations as applied to that property does not invalidate regulations as applied to other lands. Understandably, this case-by-case approach has led to a great deal of litigation.

Despite some early adverse decisions, courts have sustained wetlands regulations as applied to particular lands in a broad range of contexts. Examples follow:

o Inland Wetlands. In a 1972 decision, **Just v. Marinette County**,[4] the Wisconsin Supreme Court upheld, against claims of "taking", a county shoreland zoning ordinance for a wetland area despite the restrictive nature of the controls. This ordinance had been adopted to satisfy state shoreland zoning requirements. The court stressed the importance of the wetlands to the adjacent lake and the need to protect wetlands as part of government's role as trustee of public waters. The courts of Rhode Island,[5] New York[6], Connecticut[7] and Massachusetts[8] have also strongly endorsed inland wetland protection regulations. In the most recent of these decisions, **Moskow v. Commissioner of Department of Environmental Management**,[9] the Supreme Court of Massachusetts held that a highly restrictive State regulation adopted for an inland wetland area was not a taking of private property. The court observed that the entire property, not just the wetland area, must be considered in determining whether regulations take property and that "(a)s long as the restrictions (are) reasonably related to the implementations of a policy...expected to produce a widespread public benefit and applicable to all similarly situated property, they need not produce a reciprocal benefit (to the owner)...."[10]

o Coastal Wetlands. Courts have also strongly endorsed coastal wetland regulations. Strong endorsement began in 1970 with **Zabel v. Tabb**[11] in which the Fifth Circuit, U.S. Court of Appeals upheld the denial by the U.S. Army Corps of Engineers of a permit to dredge and fill a mangrove wetland near St. Petersburg, Florida. Many Federal court decisions have upheld denial of permits for mangrove[12] and other coastal wetlands[13] since then.

State permit requirements were upheld for a mangrove wetland by the Florida Supreme Court in 1981 in **Graham v. Estuary Properties**,[14]. The court upheld denial of a permit to destroy 1,800 acres of mangrove for a housing project through dredging a 7.5 mile "interceptor waterway." The court stated that it agreed with the Wisconsin court's statement in **Just v. Marinette County** that "(a)n owner of land has no absolute and unlimited right to change the essential nature of his land so as to use it for a purpose for which it is unsuited in its natural state and which injures the rights of others."[15] Coastal wetlands regulations have also been endorsed by the Supreme Courts of New Jersey,[16] New Hampshire,[17] Maryland,[18] Connecticut,[19] California,[20] New York,[21] and North Carolina.[22]

9.3 Constitutional Tests

In determining the validity of wetland regula-

tions, courts make several preliminary inquiries:
1. Does the State agency or local unit possess the power to adopt regulations? In general, courts hold that agencies and local units of government can exercise only those land use powers specifically delegated to them by State legislatures or derived from home rule statutes or constitutional provisions. Regulations that exceed this authority are invalid.
2. Do the regulations comply with statutory procedures? Courts demand that agencies and local units carefully follow statutory procedures established in enabling regulations. These procedures often pertain to notice and hearing, voting, publication of regulations, issuance of special permits, amendment, penalties, and other matters. Regulations that are not in compliance with statutory procedures are almost always held invalid as exceeding the scope of statutory authority.
3. If regulations delegate responsibility for issuance of permits of a regulatory board, do the regulations establish sufficiently specific standards for issuance of those permits? Courts require that legislative bodies establish relatively specific policies for delegating policy-making powers to non-legislative boards and officials.
4. Do regulations serve valid police power objectives? Courts require that regulations meet valid public goals such as protection of public safety or prevention of nuisances.

Having determined the general sufficiency of regulatory powers, courts may apply one or more additional tests as applied to specific property.

o   Are the regulations reasonable?
o   Do the regulations afford equal treatment to similarly situated landowners?
o   Do the regulations take private property without payment of just compensation?

Both general and more specific tests are discussed below.

Sufficiency of Enabling Authority
Arguments are sometimes made that local zoning, subdivision control, building code, and other land use control enabling statutes do not authorize adoption of wetland regulations, since only a small portion of these statutes specifically address wetland protection. No court has invalidated regulations on this basis. Authorization for adoption of wetland regulations may be found in the broad language of zoning enabling acts which authorize cities, towns, villages, and, in many instances, counties to regulate lands to "promote health" and the "public welfare."[23] Most zoning enabling acts also authorize regulations to encourage the "most appropriate use of land throughout such municipality."[24] A significant number of acts specifically authorize regulations to protect natural resources.[25] The Massachusetts Supreme Court in **Turnpike Realty Co. v. Town of Dedham**[26] observed that the broad zoning enabling language similar to that in most States authorized the adoption of floodplain regulations which are analogous to wetland regulations. The court noted that the legislature had expressly amended the general zoning enabling act to authorize floodplain zoning, but that such an

amendment was unnecessary. The court held:

> Even before the last sentence (pertaining to floods) became part of the enabling act, we believe that a municipality could validly have enacted a floodplain zoning by-law under the general grant of authority in G.L. c.40A, 32 (to promote the "health, safety, convenience, morals or welfare"), and for the reasons set forth in G.L. c.40A S3 ("to secure safety from fire, panic and other dangers").[27]

Although the zoning and subdivision control enabling acts do not specifically mention wetlands, zoning enabling acts in 32 States and subdivision enabling acts in 34 States authorize local flood hazard regulations.[28] This explicit flood language may also serve as the basis for wetland regulation. For example, the Massachusetts court in **MacGibbon v. Board of Appeals of Duxbury**[29] held that a town ordinance adopted "for the purpose of protecting and preserving from despoilation the natural features and resources of the town, such as salt marshes, wetlands, brooks and ponds" was authorized under an amendment to the general zoning enabling act which stated that zoning "may provide that lands deemed subject to seasonal or periodic flooding shall not be used for residence or other purposes in such a manner as to endanger the health or safety of the occupants thereof."[30]

In many States, local units of government need not rely upon general land use control enabling authority or home rule powers. State wetland acts in Massachusetts, New York, Connecticut and Virginia specifically authorize local wetland controls. In addition, coastal zone or shoreland zoning acts of many States authorize special local ordinances for coastal, lake, and stream shore areas which include wetlands. Some of the better known programs include those of California, Washington, Minnesota, Wisconsin, Michigan, Vermont, Maine, and North Carolina. Finally, statutory or constitutional home rule provisions for municipalities or counties in 35 States provide a possible additional source of wetland powers.[31] The Massachusetts Supreme Court in **Loveguist v. Conservation Commission**[32] held that town wetland regulations could be adopted pursuant to home rule powers in that State.

Although most communities possess sufficient general power to adopt wetland regulations, these powers may be limited by exemptions. The zoning enabling acts of 20 States exempt agricultural uses[33] and the acts of 26 States partially or wholly exempt existing uses.[34]

The sufficiency of local enabling authority has also been an issue in some States that authorize direct State regulation of wetland areas while remaining silent as to local regulations. Courts in Connecticut[35] and New York[36] have held that acts authorizing direct State regulation of coastal wetland areas preempt local regulation. This is not a problem in most States with State wetland controls since statutes typically authorize local as well as State control or provide that more restrictive local regulations will prevail if both State and local regulations apply to an area.[37] Cases from Massachusetts,[38] New York,[39] and Rhode Island[40] have upheld local regulation of inland wetlands where a State agency was also authorized to regulate such wetland areas.

Compliance with Statutory Procedures

Courts generally require that local governments carefully follow statutory procedures for adoption, administration and amendment of regulations. For example, the Maryland Supreme Court held that State coastal wetland maps were invalid as applied to a specific property because statutory procedures for filing the maps in local recorder's office had not been met. However, courts sometimes permit minor irregularities in statutory procedures and may make exceptions in emergencies. In **Ramsey v. Stevens,**[41] the Minnesota Supreme Court sustained floodplain regulations adopted by the City of Lilydale in order to qualify the city despite the failure of the city to provide public notice of the regulations as required by State zoning laws. The regulations had been adopted pursuant to a court order from a lower court directing adoption within 72 hours due to an impending flood. Courts have ignored other minor omissions that do not seriously prejudice landowners.[42] They have also refused, in some instances, to enforce vague or ambiguous statutory requirements found in many local zoning enabling acts. In other contexts, courts have often found comprehensive plans within the regulations themselves.[43] No court has invalidated floodplain or wetland regulations for failure to prepare a prior comprehensive plan, although only a few of the present regulatory efforts are preceded by such planning.

The Sufficiency of Standards in Delegating Discretionary Powers to Regulatory Boards

The sufficiency of statutory or ordinance standards delegating discretionary power to State agencies, conservation commissions or zoning boards of adjustment to evaluate permits for proposed wetland uses is sometimes at issue. As noted in Chapter 8, most wetland ordinances authorize a regulatory board to issue permits for a wide range of uses, providing the uses are consistent with ordinance goals or meet unquantified wetland protection standards. Ordinances often list factors that are to be considered in evaluating permit applications, but quantified minimum standards are rarely provided for issuance or denial of permits.

In broader zoning contexts, courts have sometimes held invalid general standards such as requirements that regulatory boards determine whether permits are in the "public welfare" without more specific guidelines.[44] Such broad standards are not a problem for those wetland regulations with much more specific determinations. Wetland regulations often contain "nuisance" and "public safety" standards that have been endorsed by courts.[45] Nuisance or public safety standards require that regulatory boards determine whether permits will have nuisance impact upon adjacent uses, threaten public safety, or threaten water quality.

The sufficiency of standards for issuance of wetland permits was considered in **J.M. Mills, Inc. v. Murphy.**[46] Here the Rhode Island Supreme Court upheld a statute that authorized the director of the Rhode Island Department of Natural Resources to deny permits for inland wetlands "if in the opinion of the director granting of such approval would not be the best public interest" or "if the city council or town council within whose borders the project lies has disapproved the project." The court held that the section of the statute that detailed wetland functions and the need for protection sufficiently defined the "public interest" to justify delegating regulatory powers to the director and establishing a policy for evaluation of permits by local units of government. Similarly, in **MacGibbon v. Board of Appeals of Duxbury**[47] the Massachusetts court upheld the delegation of powers to a zoning board of adjustment to issue special exceptions in harmony with the "general purposes and intent" of the ordinance. Although the ordinance did not contain very specific standards, the court noted that "(t)he manifest objects and purposes of the enabling act and the by-law furnish a large measure of guidance for the board." The Massachusetts court also upheld broad standards for local issuance of special exceptions in **Turnpike Realty Company v. Town of Dedham.**[48]

Validity of Regulatory Objectives

Courts afford legislatures broad discretion in the selection of regulatory objectives.[49] Nevertheless, in traditional zoning or wetland regulations contexts, they have sometimes invalidated regulations designed to serve several objectives, as follows.

1. _Protection of aesthetics._ Protection of aesthetics has not traditionally been considered a proper sole objective for exercise of police powers. This position is slowly changing.[50] Aesthetics are now recognized as a valid primary objective in some States and a valid secondary objective in all States, adding weight to primary goals such as flood damage reduction and wildlife protection.

The traditional unwillingness to uphold regulations designed solely to protect aesthetic values was based, in part, upon a conviction that beauty is purely subjective and not capable of objective evaluation. However, some courts have upheld regulations designed primarily to protect aesthetic values and the tax base dependent upon them.[51] Even as a valid police power objective, the question remains: "How tightly may private property be controlled in the name of beauty?" Courts have sustained some restriction of private uses but disapproved prohibition of all private uses.[52]

2. _Maintenance of land in an open condition until public purchase is possible._ Courts have often held invalid attempts to zone lands to hold them in an open condition until public purchase is possible,[53] but official mapping to preserve sites for future roadways until purchase is possible have been sustained.[54] In addition, the California court in **Turner v. County of Del Norte**[55] upheld a highly restrictive floodplain regulation for an area subject to extreme flood hazards that the public contemplated for future purchase. Plans for long-term public purchase of property should not undermine the validity of present regulation based upon valid objectives such as protection of floodway conveyance capacity.

Courts have strongly endorsed other wetland protection objectives:

1. _Protection of health and safety._ Without

exception, courts have upheld regulations to protect public health and safety. As noted by the U.S. Supreme Court in **Queenside Hills Realty Co. v. Saxl,** when threats to human life are involved, a legislature may adopt "the most conservative course which science and engineering offer."[56] Regulations to protect health and safety are sustained even where they regulate existing uses[57] or prevent new ones.

2. Prevention of nuisances. Courts have also strongly endorsed regulations to prevent nuisances[58] or control uses with nuisance characteristics such as commercial or industrial uses in residential areas. Several cases relating to flood or wetland areas are of interest. For example, the California Supreme Court in **Consolidated Rock Products Company v. City of Los Angeles**[59] sustained an ordinance prohibiting sand and gravel operations in a dry stream bed where no other economic use could be made of the land because nearby residential areas would be affected by the dust and noise of the mining operation. The court observed that the primary purpose of zoning was to prevent land uses that would threaten other landowners or the public.

Applying a similar analysis, the Minnesota Supreme Court in **Filister v. City of Minneapolis**[60] sustained a single family residential classification for a swampy area surrounded by residences in part because proposed apartments would have been nuisance-like in the low density surroundings.

3. Prevention of fraud. Courts have strongly endorsed regulations for lands subject to flooding and other hazards to prevent their sale to innocent purchasers.[61] In **America Land Company v. Keene,**[62] a Federal court sustained an ordinance that prohibited construction or residences in a flood-prone area. A dissenting judge who agreed with the validity of the ordinance but disagreed with other aspects of the case, noted that:[63]

It (a zoning ordinance) furnished a legal prohibition to selling the land, for a purpose which it was not in fact fit. This was an eminently proper exercise of the city's police powers in order to protect possible purchasers from being victimized....

4. Protection of wildlife and fisheries. Many wetland cases have given strong support to the protection of wildlife and fisheries. The Fifth Circuit Court of Appeals in **Zabel v. Tabb**[64] upheld the denial by the U.S. Army Corps of Engineers of a permit to fill in Boca Ciega Bay in St. Petersburg-Tampa, Florida. In its opinion, the court strongly emphasized protection of fish and wildlife:[65]

In this time of awakening to the reality that we cannot continue to despoil our environment and yet exist, the nation knows, if the Courts do not, that the destruction of fish and wildlife in our estuarine waters does have a substantial, and in some areas a devastating effect on interstate commerce. Landholders do not contend otherwise. Nor is it challenged that dredge and fill projects are activities which may tend to destroy the ecological balance and thereby affect commerce substantially.

Similarly, the Maryland Supreme Court in **Potomac Sand & Gravel Co. v. Governor of Maryland**[66] endorsed a statute prohibiting dredging of tidal waters or marshlands of Charles County because of the impact upon fisheries and wildlife. The language of the court is of special note:[67]

It has already been noted that the sites in question support such species of fish as herring, American shad, hickory shad, striped bass, white perch and eel perch, among others. These fish are sources for commercial fishing and sport fishing throughout Maryland. The testimony is undisputed that dredging would irreparably destroy the immediate marsh habitat, converting it into a deep-water habitat. Consequently, those anadromous fish which spawn in shallow waters and which instinctively return each year to the same spawning areas would be deprived of such spawning areas with a concomitant loss of the benefits of their reproductive process.

There was testimony that rare native vegetation at Mattawoman Creek would be destroyed by these particular dredging operations. Dredging increases the water's turbidity. Turbidity is the suspension of dirt particles in the water. A high turbidity reduces the amount of sunlight which reaches aquatic plants, which, through photosynthesis, produce oxygen for fish. The plants themselves are a food source for fish which would be reduced both due to the failure of plants to reproduce and by the smothering of plants by dirt particles.

Testimony also showed the Mattawoman Creek supports declining but still substantial wildlife which would be frightened away by dredging noises as well as driven away by a loss of an accessible food supply. At Craney Island the diving ducks would be unable to readily retrieve their food fifty feet below the surface.

The court endorsed a broad resource protection goal:[68]

Chapter 792 has an ecological purpose. As has been shown, the protection of exhaustible natural resources is a valid exercise of the police powers. The prohibition of anyone from dredging sand, gravel or other aggregates or minerals in the wetlands of Charles County is a rational regulation in light of the potential and real harm caused by dredging as testified to by experts for both parties.

Support for protection of fish and wildlife may also be found in cases from such States as Massachusetts,[69] New Hampshire,[70] and Wisconsin.[71]

5. Prevention of flood damages. Many cases have endorsed regulations prohibiting structures and fills in coastal and inland areas that would be subject to flood damage or would block flood flows, thereby increasing flood damages on other lands. For example, a California court in **Turner v. County of Del Norte**[72] endorsed a county zoning ordinance that limited an area of extreme flooding to parks, recreation, and agricultural uses. Similarly, the Massachusetts Supreme Court in **Turnpike Realty Co. v. Town of Dedham**[73] endorsed local floodplain zoning and observed, that the "general necessity of floodplain zoning to reduce the damage to life and property caused by flooding is unquestionable."[74]

In **Subaru of New England, Inc. v. Board of Appeals of Canton,**[75] a Massachusetts Court of Appeals upheld the denial of a permit to fill a wetland area where there was testimony that filling would deprive the town of 23.8 acre feet of water storage or 7.77 million gallons. Although there was testimony that this loss would have resulted in a small increase in flood heights (perhaps 1/2 of an inch) the court held that seriousness of the problem was for the local regulatory board not the court to determine.

6. Control of water pollution. Several wetland cases strongly link the regulation of wetland areas to the maintenance of water quality. In one case, **Reuter v. Department of Natural Resources,**[76] the Wisconsin Supreme Court specifically required the Wisconsin Department of Natural Resources to evaluate the impact on water quality of a proposed project to dredge a two acre floating bog along the margin of a lake. In a second Wisconsin case, **Just v. Marinette County,**[77] the court emphasized the interrelationships between wetlands and water quality in sustaining wetland regulations:[78]

> We start with the premise that lakes and rivers in their natural state are unpolluted and the pollution which now exists is manmade. The State of Wisconsin under the trust doctrine has a duty to eradicate the present pollution and to prevent further pollution in its navigable waters. This is not, in a legal sense, a gain or a securing of a benefit by the maintaining of the natural status quo of the environment. What makes this case different from most condemnation or police power zoning cases is the interrelationship of the wetlands, the swamps and the natural environment of shorelands to the purity of the water and to such natural resources as navigation, fishing, and scenic beauty. Swamps and wetlands were once considered wasteland, undesirable, and not picturesque. But as the people became more sophisticated, an appreciation was acquired that swamps and wetlands serve a vital role in nature, are part of the balance of nature and are essential to the purity of the water in our lakes and streams. Swamps and wetlands are a necessary part of the ecological creation and now, even to the uninitiated, possess their own beauty in nature.

Cases from other States and Federal courts determining the validity of section 404 regulations have also noted the relationship between regulation of wetlands uses and control of pollution.[79] The Maine Supreme Court in **State v. Johnson**[80] held invalid a restriction on fill in a coastal wetland but noted that additional considerations of health and pollution which are "separable from and independent of" the "fill" restriction may well support validity of the Act in those areas of concern.[81]

7. Protection of public rights in navigable waters and adjacent lands. Courts have in many cases sustained wetland regulations to protect public rights in navigable waters. (See the discussion of the taking issue below.[82])

8. Protection of the natural suitability of the land. The Wisconsin Supreme Court in the landmark wetland protection case, **Just v. Marinette County,**[83] upheld highly restrictive county wetland regulations adopted as part of a State supervised shoreland zoning program. The court emphasized the importance of wetlands to public waters and held that the landowner had no right to destroy the natural suitability of the wetland where such destruction harmed public interest. This language was endorsed by the New Hampshire Supreme Court in **Sibson v. State**[84] and by the Florida Supreme Court in **Graham v. Estuary Properties.**[85]

9. Protection of waters used for water supply. A number of cases have upheld regulations designed to control water or watershed activities that would affect public water supplies.[86] For example, the U.S. Supreme Court in **Perley v. North Carolina**[87] upheld a State statute regulating private forestry operations within 400 feet of watersheds held by cities or towns for water supply purposes. The Massachusetts Supreme Court in **Lovequist v. Conservation Commission of the Town of Dennis,**[88] upheld wetland regulations adopted, in part, to protect groundwater supplies. It held that proposed excavation of 6,000 cubic yards of peat for a road and its replacement by 9,000 to 12,000 cubic yards of sand and gravel might have significant impact on local groundwater supplies; the permit was validly denied. The court observed:

> All parties agreed that the water source on the plaintiffs' property is part of a much larger and important groundwater supply located in underground reservoirs throughout the adjoining area. Thus, the effect of the excavation could be aptly analogized as one of the witnesses before the Commission so stated, to "taking the plug out of a bathtub." Having held that the protection of groundwater is a valid public interest, **Turnpike Realty Co. v. Dedham,** 362 Mass. 221, 227-229, 284 N.E. 2d 891 (1972), we think the Commission did not act improperly in denying the plaintiffs permission for the proposed road construction.[89]

Discrimination

Courts have held, as a general principle, that regulations must afford equal treatment to "similarly situated" landowners to comply with prohibitions against discrimination and guarantees of due process found in the 14th Amendment of the U.S. Constitution. But questions arise concerning whether landowners are similarly situated. In a broader land use control context, courts have recognized that lands with identical or similar natural resource characteristics need not be treated alike in all circumstances,[90] since planning differences often exist with regard to existing uses, location, traffic, adjacent districts, and other factors. Courts have also held that regulations need not apply equally to new and existing uses[91] and have not generally demanded that all areas (e.g., all wetlands in a municipality) be regulated at the same time.[92]

A number of wetland cases have involved regulations contested on the ground of discrimination. In one case, the New Jersey Supreme Court upheld the establishment of Hackensack Meadowlands Special Protection District despite claims that this statute singled out some wetlands in the Hackensack area for special treatment.[93] In a second New Jersey case, **Sands Point Harbor, Inc. v. Sullivan,**[94] the court held that the Wetland Act of 1970, applying to some coastal wetland areas but excluding areas characterized by heavy industrial, commercial and residential

WETLANDS LOCATED IN A COASTAL FLOOD HAZARD AREA, SHELTER ISLAND, NEW YORK. Courts have strongly supported regulations with flood loss reduction goals. Photo source: Jon Kusler.

development, was not discriminatory since differing conditions afforded "reasonable grounds for the differing treatment of lands."[95]

In a Maryland case, **Potomac Sand and Gravel Co. v. Governor of Maryland,**[96] the court upheld prohibition of dredging of sand, gravel, or their aggregates or minerals in the coastal area of Charles County. The Sand and Gravel Company claimed that the law was discriminatory because it did not regulate inland areas. The court observed that coastal wetlands were particularly important as fish spawning areas and as sites of rare native vegetation and held that the distinction between coastal and inland wetlands was valid.

In **J.M. Mills, Inc. v. Murphy,**[97] the Rhode Island Supreme Court upheld an inland wetland protection statute despite somewhat similar arguments. The plaintiff charged that the inland wetland law failed to provide public hearings on permits like a similar coastal wetland law and that the inland law made no provision for payment of compensation like the coastal act. The court held that the legislature had a logical basis for applying different approaches to inland and coastal wetlands and that there was no discrimination.

However, courts have considered some floodplain and wetland regulations discriminatory. In **City of Welch v. Mitchell,**[98] a West Virginia court held that a local floodplain regulation that regulated one side of a stream and not the other was discriminatory. The

New Jersey Supreme Court in **Morris County Land Improvement Co. v. Parsippany-Troy Hills Township**[99] held that a conservancy zone designed to preserve wetlands and flood storage was invalid in part because it discriminated between upstream and downstream landowners.

Reasonableness

Courts require that regulations (the means) be reasonably related to the regulatory objectives (the ends) to satisfy due process requirements.[100] Wetland regulations have not generally been contested as unreasonable, although reasonableness is a common issue for broader land and water use controls. For example, courts have held floodplain regulations invalid for areas with no evidence of floodings;[101] drainage regulations invalid requiring an enclosed drainage system where open drainage systems were more appropriate;[102] and pollution controls invalid where there was little threat of pollution.[103]

Courts demand a strong relationship between ends and means where regulations restrict private uses, reducing property values. A Connecticut court in **Strain v. Mims** observed:[104]

(W)here the value of property of an individual is seriously affected by a zoning regulation especially applicable to it, this fact imposes an obligation to consider carefully the questions whether the regulation does in fact tend to serve the public welfare and the recognized purposes of zoning.

A number of questions commonly arise concerning the reasonableness of wetland regulations.

1. What data must be used for wetland mapping? Regulations based upon inadequate data may lack the necessary relationship to regulatory goals. There are few cases addressing this issue. Nevertheless, several observations may be made, based upon general legal principles. At a minimum, statutory data gathering and mapping requirements must be followed. If there are no statutory requirements, the issue of reasonableness depends not only upon the quality and quantity of data, but also upon the specific nature of the regulations based upon these data, the impact of the regulations upon private property owners, and the data refinement procedures available during administration of regulations. Soil maps may be sufficient for wetland definition in rural environments where property values are relatively low and the impact of regulations upon landowners is minimal, but soil maps may be less acceptable for high value urban areas. Soil maps may also be insufficient if used alone, but satisfactory if a special permit regulatory approach is used which employs case-by-case refinement of boundary lines through supplementary data gathering.

Several cases have considered the reasonableness of wetland maps. In the **Just**[105] case, the Wisconsin Supreme Court upheld the use of U.S. Geological Survey topographic maps for wetland mapping combined with written wetland definition criteria which were applied on a case-by-case basis through field surveys in the case of boundary disputes. The regulations in that case defined wetlands to include:[106]

> (A)reas where groundwater is at or near the surface much of the year or where any segment of plant cover is deemed an aquatic according to N.C. Fassett's "Manual of Aquatic Plants."

A landowner contested the regulations arguing, in part, that the wetland maps were not sufficiently specific and that his land was not a wetland. The court did not specifically discuss the validity of the maps, but sustained the regulations, noting that, by the written test, the land was clearly wetland.

In a second case, **Loveladies Property Owners Ass'n., Inc. v. Raab,**[107] the New Jersey Supreme Court upheld the position of the New Jersey Department of Environmental Protection that mapping of wetlands and adoption of restrictive orders were prerequisites to requiring permits from landowners for regulated wetland activities. In a Rhode Island case, **State v. Capuano Bros., Inc.**[108] the Rhode Island Supreme Court upheld the use of air photos to indicate wetland boundaries where wetlands were defined to include the 50-year floodplain.

Several floodplain zoning cases have considered the validity of floodplain mapping (or the absence thereof). In **Iowa Natural Resources Council v. Van Zee,**[109] the Iowa Supreme Court upheld a State floodplain zoning law which required permits for floodplain uses whether or not floodplains had been mapped by the State. In other words, landowners were required to determine whether proposed uses were or were not located in floodplain areas. However, the landowner contesting the regulations in this case was in no position to claim ignorance of flooding problems—he had built a levee at the site.

In **Sturdy Homes, Inc. v. Township of Redford,**[110] a Michigan court held that floodplain maps were invalid as applied to particular property where there was no evidence of flooding. This case suggests that courts will not tolerate gross inaccuracy. However, some inaccuracy may be acceptable if procedures are available to correct errors during program administration. For example, in **Turnpike Realty v. Dedham,**[111] the Massachusetts Supreme Court upheld floodplain zoning with strong wetland protection elements for an area where floodplain maps contained some upland areas. The court noted that "special exceptions" were available under the terms of the ordinance to correct errors.

Finally, in **A.H. Smith Sand & Gravel Co. v. Department of Water Resources,**[112] the Maryland Supreme Court upheld State pollution control for floodplain areas but required that floodplain maps be modified to reflect recent data concerning flooding. This case is interesting since it suggests that courts may require better wetland and flood maps as improved data gathering approaches become available.

2. Should most subzones, such as floodways and areas of special value for habitat, be defined within wetland areas? Apparently no court has considered this issue.[113] However, the courts of New Jersey and Connecticut[114] have held invalid, as a taking, the application of highly restrictive wetland regulations to entire wetland or floodplain areas. Definition of subzones may be advisable in some circumstances to permit varying degrees of restriction where property values are high and substantial differences do exist in the flood hazards, pollution potential, wildlife value, or other wetland features.

3. Should regulations take into account the cumulative impact of uses? Cases have upheld regulations that consider the cumulative impact of fills or other uses upon navigable waters. For example in **Hixon v. Public Service Commission,**[115] the Supreme Court of Wisconsin affirmed a denial of a permit to maintain a breakwater on the grounds that the breakwater was an unnecessary obstruction to navigation, did not allow for free flow of water, and was detrimental to the public interest. The court observed:[116]

> There are over 9,000 navigable lakes in Wisconsin covering an area of over 54,000 square miles. A little fill here and there may seem to be nothing to become excited about. But one fill, though comparatively inconsequential, may lead to another, and before long a great body of water may be eaten away until it may no longer exist. Our navigable waters are a precious natural heritage; once gone, they disappear forever.

Similarly, the California Supreme Court sustained regulations controlling filling within San Francisco Bay based in part upon arguments of cumulative impact.[117]

A Federal district court in **Corsa v. Tawes**[118] sustained a Maryland law prohibiting the use of certain nets for fishing in tidal waters. While not a wetland case, the analysis of the court is interesting in terms of future impacts:[119]

> We think...that the protective hand of the State may be extended before danger is unmistakably imminent. Conditions may go unnoticed so long that when the threat is demonstrated it is too late to avert the harm. One witness for the plaintiffs testified that no matter how much a supply may be reduced by over-fishing, provided that the stock is not completely annihilated, it may in time replenish itself. We need not quarrel with this statement of scientific opinion, but in the practical management of its resources, the State may conclude that the time for action is long before the destruction has gone that far. The State is interested not merely in the preservation of specimens for museums but in conserving and perpetuating a constant supply.

Despite these cases, apparently no court has held that regulations must consider cumulative impact. Courts have warned in other contexts that assumptions concerning cumulative impact must be reasonable.[120]

The Taking Issue

The "taking" issue continues to be the most volatile and controversial issue in wetland regulation. The Fifth and Fourteenth Amendments of the Federal Constitution and similar provisions in State constitutions prohibit the "taking" of private property without payment of just compensation. Wetland regulations which permanently restrict fills, dredging and other development have been attacked as a taking and some decisions have invalidated regulations on this basis. However, few successful challenges have been made in the last five years.

Courts have broadly agreed that some reduction in property values is not a taking. For example in **Deltona Corporation v. The United States**,[121] the U.S. Court of Claims held that the Corp's denial of a permit for filling mangroves in Florida was not a taking. It concluded that:[122]

> (W)e have rejected plaintiff's argument that the denial of highest and best use can constitute a taking. We have found that subsequent to Deltona's purchase of the land in question, a significant change occurred in the statutes and regulations affecting its land use, and this development did have a significant impact upon the values incident to Deltona's Marco Island property. However, in view of the many remaining economically viable uses for plaintiff's property, and the substantial public benefits which the new statutes and regulations serve to bring about, we have concluded that no taking occurred.

Courts have upheld highly restrictive, interim regulations which do not permanently prevent all private economic uses for both inland and tidal wetlands. For example, in **New York Housing Authority v. Commissioner of Environmental Conservation**,[123] a New York court upheld a moratorium on alteration of tidal wetlands in New York. Similarly, a New Jersey court sustained a moratorium on construction in the Hackensack Meadowlands in **Meadowland Regional Development Agency v. Hackensack Meadowlands Development Commission.**[124]

Whether a taking has occurred is a more difficult issue for permanent, highly restrictive regulations.

A variety of tests have been used by the courts to determine whether regulations take property.[125] A determination of taking is often closely related to determinations concerning the reasonableness of regulations and compliance with other constitutional requirements. Regulations that lack sufficient factual basis are often considered both unreasonable and a taking since unreasonable restrictions, however slight, are unjustified. Similarly, regulations that do not serve valid police power objectives impose an undue restraint on private property. Finally, regulations that discriminate may be held a taking, based on the rationale that tight restrictions are acceptable if they affect all in like circumstances but unacceptable if they single out a few.

Regulations may validly reduce land values if practical uses remain for the land. For example, the New Jersey court in **Sands Point v. Sullivan**[126] upheld a State coastal wetland protection order that prohibited dumping of solid wastes, discharging of sewage, and the storage or application of pesticides in an area. The court observed that the order did not prevent other practical uses. Similarly, the Maryland Supreme Court in **Potomac Sand and Gravel Co. v. Governor of Maryland**[127] upheld complete prohibition of dredging sand, gravel, or other aggregates or minerals in State wetlands in Charles County but did not prohibit other uses.

Almost all cases invalidating regulations have involved regulations that prevented all development in wetland areas regardless of whether hazards or nuisances were a serious problem or whether practical uses were possible for the lands. As discussed below, less restrictive regulations have, in most contexts, been sustained. Very tight regulations have been sustained for severe hazard areas and where all practical uses for lands were nuisance-like. In addition, a number of important cases have sustained very tight wetland regulations in special circumstances despite lack of hazards or nuisance impact.

Courts typically balance the public need for regulation with the impact of the regulation upon private property owners in determining whether regulations take property. In addition, courts apply several specific tests which qualify the balancing process:

1. Physical invasion. Courts hold that public entry and use of private property is a taking. For example, the U.S. Supreme Court in **Pumpelly v. Green Bay Company**[128] held that a taking occurred when the Federal government constructed a dam which flooded private property. Similarly, the New Jersey Supreme Court held invalid as a taking the construction of a large sand dune by the Army Corps of Engineers on private property to protect the surrounding area against hurricane damage.[129] The test of physical invasion has limited application to wetland regulations since regulations do not require the physical use of private property for public purposes. Borderline situations exist, however, such as the zoning of private beaches for public recreational uses.

ROAD ROUTED TO AVOID WETLAND. Construction costs are often much higher when a road is routed through rather than around a wetland. Photo source: Carl Carlozzi.

2. Diminution in value. The classic "diminution in value" test for taking was formulated by Supreme Court Justice Holmes in **Pennsylvania Coal Co. v. Mahon,**[130] when he stated that in determining the limits of police power:[131]

> One fact for consideration...is the extent of the diminution. When it reaches a certain magnitude, in most if not all cases there must be an exercise of eminent domain and compensation to sustain the act. So the question depends upon the particular facts.

In a second case, the Supreme Court held that "(t)here is no set formula to determine where regulation ends and taking begins. Although a comparison of values before and after is relevant...it is by no means conclusive."[132] The diminution in value test has been cited in wetland cases but not widely applied as a final measure of taking.

3. Prevention of a harm versus conferring a benefit. A third test for taking has also been cited in several wetland cases but not widely applied. The test asks the question: "Do regulations prevent landowners from harming the public or require landowners to confer an uncompensated public benefit? A "taking" will be found if the regulations require landowners to confer an uncompensated benefit on the public.[133] For example, a taking may be found if regulations require that private land be used as a public park. A

taking will not be found if regulations merely prevent a public harm. For example, the New Hampshire Supreme Court upheld regulations denying a permit to fill a four acre tract of salt marsh in **Sibson v. State,**[134] because such a permit would injure public rights in adjacent waters. The court proposed a rule for taking:[135]

> Under the proposed rule, if the action of the state is a valid exercise of the police power prescribing activities which would harm the public, then there is no taking under the eminent domain clause.

The **Just v. Marinette County** case discussed below also applied a version of this test.

4. Denial of all reasonable or practical use of land. The most common test applied in wetland cases for determining whether regulations take property focuses upon the practicability and reasonableness of uses that remain for the land, not the speculative loss to the landowner. It is generally stated that restrictions which deny all "practical" or "reasonable" uses of land take property. The test for taking in terms of "practical" use was stated by the Massachusetts court in **Commissioner of Natural Resources v. S. Volpe & County,**[136] where the court concluded:[137]

> A crucial issue is whether, notwithstanding the meritorious character of the regulation, there

91

has been such a deprivation of the practical uses of a landowner's property as to be the equivalent of a taking without compensation.

The test for taking in terms of "reasonable use" was stated by the Maryland court in **Walker v. Board of County Commissioners,**[138] where the court observed:[139]

> To sustain an attack upon the validity of the ordinance, an aggrieved property owner must show that if the ordinance is enforced the consequent restrictions upon his property preclude its use for any purpose to which it is reasonably adapted.

A distinction between denial of all "practical" use and all "reasonable" use may be important in some instances. For example, highly restrictive regulations for a coastal wetland subject to severe flood hazards may prevent all practical (profitable) uses of the land for marinas or other buildings. However, if these uses are considered unreasonable due to flood hazards or incompatibility with adjacent uses, the regulations do not necessarily prevent all reasonable use of the land.

Courts have usually not defined the terms "practical" or "reasonable". However, the Massachusetts Supreme Court in **Commissioner of Natural Resources v. S. Volpe & Co.**[140] directed a lower court to take further evidence on a number of points relevant to a determination of "practical" use:[141]

o The uses which can be made of the locus in its natural state (a) independently of other land of the owner in the area; (b) in conjunction with other land of the owner.

o The assessed value of the locus.

o The cost of the locus to the defendant.

o The present fair market value of the locus (a) subject to the limitations imposed by the Commissioner; (b) free of such limitations.

o The estimated cost of the improvements proposed by the defendant.

The rule pertaining to denial of all reasonable or practical uses has eight important qualifications. Because of their importance, each will be discussed separately.

Exception One: Where all profitable uses threaten safety or conflict with adjacent uses. Courts uphold regulations required to protect public safety or prevent nuisances even where such regulations prevent all or essentially all practical uses of land. Regulations for the protection of safety are afforded a special presumption of constitutionality.[142] For example, the U.S. Supreme Court in **Goldblatt v. Town of Hempstead**[143] upheld a local ordinance which indirectly prevented all economic use of an area by prohibiting sand and gravel extraction below the water table, in part because of possible threats to safety from open excavations.

Several cases have upheld tight control of residential and apartment uses in flood hazard areas due to flooding threats. In **McCarthy v. City of Manhattan Beach,**[144] the California Supreme Court sustained a zoning ordinance restricting ocean-front property to beach recreation purposes, although there was little evidence that open space uses were

practical. The court attached significance to the erosion and wave damage and the "safety of the proposed construction of houses thereon was 'a question upon which reasonable minds might differ.'"[145]

Similarly, in **Spiegle v. Borough of Beach Haven**[146] the New Jersey Supreme Court sustained an ordinance establishing a beach setback line for structures in a coastal area subject to extreme flooding. Conceding that no buildings could be constructed on some lots, the court noted that since the burden of demonstrating undue restriction on beneficial use was upon the plaintiffs, an essential element of any plaintiff's case was the existence of "some present or potential beneficial use of which he has been deprived."[147] The court observed:[148]

> Plaintiffs failed to adduce proof of any economic use to which the property could be put. The borough, on the other hand, adduced unrebutted proof that it would be unsafe to construct houses oceanward of the building line (apparently the only use to which lands similarly located in defendant municipality have been put), because of the possibility that they would be destroyed during a severe storm--a result which occurred during the storm of March 1962. Additionally, defendant submitted proof that there was great peril to life and health arising through the likely destruction of streets, sewer, water and gas mains, and electric power lines in the proscribed area in an ordinary storm. The gist of this testimony was that such regulation prescribed only such conduct as good husbandry would dictate that plaintiffs should themselves impose on the use of their own lands. Consequently, we find that plaintiffs did not sustain the burden of proving that the ordinance resulted in a taking of any beneficial economic use of their lands.

A similar result has been reached in cases where all practical uses are nuisance-like. In **Consolidated Rock Products Co. v. City of Los Angeles,**[149] the California Supreme Court upheld restrictive regulations that prevented sand and gravel extraction — the only practical use for the land — in a floodplain area because the operations would threaten nearby residential areas. The court found no taking of property and observed:[150]

> The primary purpose of comprehensive zoning is to protect others, and the general public, from uses of property which will, if permitted, prove injurious to them.

Cases upholding regulations that protect the public from threats to safety or nuisances reason that landowners do not have a right to activities causing such problems, even though no practical use remains for the land. This reasoning was applied by the U.S. Supreme Court in **Mugler v. Kansas**[151] in upholding a statute that prohibited the manufacture of alcoholic beverages (then considered a nuisance). While not a wetland case, the language of the Court is applicable:[152]

> The exercise of the police power by the destruction of property which is itself a public nuisance, or the prohibition of its use in a particular way, whereby its value becomes

PLOWING AROUND BUT NOT IN WETLAND. Photo source: Virginia Carter.

depreciated, is very different from taking property for public use, or from depriving a person of his property without due process of law. In the one case, a nuisance only is abated; in the other, unoffending property is taken away from an innocent owner.

Application of a similar approach to wetlands will be discussed shortly.

Exception Two: Where a landowner fails to protest a restriction in a timely manner. Courts in several cases have upheld tight restrictions which prevented all practical use of lands where landowners failed to contest restrictions in a timely manner and less stringent restrictions would have harmed adjacent landowners. In **Hodge v. Luckett,**[153] a Kentucky court upheld residential zoning restrictions for an area 50 to 80 percent low and marshy, noting that the time for an owner to protest restrictions is when a zoning ordinance is first adopted and not after others, in reliance on the restriction, have invested in neighboring property. The court stated:[154]

True, his property ought not to be forever consigned to oblivion, but if he has remained silent when he should have spoken, it is no injustice to impose the condition that in order to justify a reclassification he show by clear and convincing proof that there will be no substantial resulting detriment to others.

This rationale was strongly endorsed by the Minnesota Supreme Court in **Filister v. City of Minneapolis,**[155] which upheld a low density residential zoning classification for 8.43 acres, most of which was a marshland, despite claims by a purchaser that the restrictions prevented all practical uses. The court held that proposed apartment uses were inconsistent with surrounding residential uses and that the landowner had failed to meet the double burden of proof required to prove the regulations invalid. To establish invalidity the landowner would need to have shown that the regulations were both confiscatory and "that the relief...sought would not result in any substantial detriment to the neighboring property improved in reliance on the validity of the ordinance."[156]

Exception Three: Where special permits are available. Regulations are rarely held to be a taking where special permits are available for structures, fills or other practical uses. In this way regulations do not, on their face, deny all practical uses. For example, the Connecticut Supreme Court in **Vartelas v. Water Resources Commission**[157] upheld the denial of a permit under a State floodway protection law. The court observed that the denial of a permit for one proposed use was not equivalent to denial of all possible uses. The applicant could submit another application. Similarly, the Wisconsin court in **Just v. Marinette County**[158] upheld tight wetland regulations against a claim of taking, noting that special excep-

93

tions were authorized by the ordinance. The potential for special permits was also considered significant by the Massachusetts Supreme Court in upholding flood-plain regulations in **Turnpike Realty Co. v. Town of Dedham.**[159]

Despite these holdings, the New Jersey court in an early case, **Morris County Land Improvement Co. v. Parsippany-Troy Hills Township,**[160] held that very restrictive wetland "conservancy" regulations were invalid as a taking despite the inclusion of special exception procedures. The court concluded that the standards for the special exceptions were so restrictive that no practical use was possible under the special exception procedure.

Exception Four: Where regulations affect a portion of a property. In more traditional land use control contexts, courts have often sustained highly restrictive regulations for only part of a property—such as building setback lines[161] and official mapping of roads—where practical uses may be made of other portions.[162] This approach to the taking issue was endorsed by the U.S. Supreme Court in the important 1978 decision of **Penn Central Transportation Co. v. New York City**[163] and has been widely followed in wetland cases since then. The Court stated:[164]

"Taking" jurisprudence does not divide a single parcel into discrete segments and attempt to determine whether rights in a particular segment have been entirely abrogated. In deciding whether a particular government action has effected a taking, this Court focuses rather both on the character of the action and on the nature and extent of the interference with rights in the parcel as a whole...

Citing **Penn Central,** the U.S. Court of Claims held that denials of 404 permits by the Corps of Engineers for mangrove wetlands were not a taking in several recent cases.[165]

At the State level, a New Jersey court in **American Dredging Co. v. N.J. Department of Environmental Protection,**[166] upheld a restriction against the filling of 80 acres out of 2,500 acres owned by the plaintiff, noting that the impact of the regulations upon the entire parcel not simply the wetland should be considered:[167]

In the determination that the prohibition of deposit of dredge spoils on the 80-acre tract is not a "taking" we are not limited to a consideration of the 80 acre tract per se; consideration may be given of the entirety of the 2,500 acres. Each segment is not to be viewed microscopically; rather, the vision must encompass the whole.

Lot size becomes significant in determining whether regulations prevent all practical use of the entire properties. Courts have sustained large lot sizes of two[168] and five[169] acres for lands with flooding or wetland problems. A New York court in **Gignoux v. Kings Point,**[170] noted that the "best possible use...(of a marshy area) would be in connection with its absorption into plots of larger dimensions."

Exception Five: Where the landowner purchases land with knowledge of restrictions. In recent years

courts have often held that when a landowner purchases land with knowledge of restrictions he is in a weakened position to claim a taking. For example, in **Chokecherry Hills Estates, Inc. v. Devel County,**[171] the South Dakota Supreme Court upheld a highly restrictive "natural resource district" as applied to a 13 acre parcel along a small, muddy lake. The Natural Resource District allowed for the following:[172]

A. Permitted Uses
1. Wildlife production areas;
2. Game refuges;
3. Historic sites and/or monuments;
4. Designated natural prairies;
5. Public hunting and fishing access areas.

B. Uses Permitted by Special Permit if Deemed Not Detrimental to District
1. Transportation and utility easements and rights of way;
2. Utility substations;
3. Public parks and/or playgrounds;
4. Horticulture uses and livestock grazing.

Chokecherry Estates had purchased the land "knowing that the land was zoned a Natural Resource District...."[173] The court held that the town's refusal to rezone for single family dwellings was justified and that there was no taking. The court noted that the purchase price reflected farmland value and stated he had been using the land for agricultural purposes at the time of this lawsuit. The court concluded that, "On the whole, the evidence paints a picture of Mr. Kalhoff taking a gamble that he could succeed in changing the existing zoning law so that he could realize a higher profit."[174]

It further observed:

In **Just v. Marinette County,** the Supreme Court of Wisconsin stated that the police power was properly exercised in preventing a public harm by protecting the natural environment of shorelands. No taking was found and no compensation given in **Just,** despite the fact that the landowners had purchased the land before it was restrictively zoned for natural uses. Appellant in the instant case is in a weaker position than the landowner in **Just,** due to the lack of evidence to counter the reasons set forth by the commission and the fact that he purchased the land with full knowledge of the zoning restrictions.[175]

Similarly, in **Graham v. Estuary Properties,**[176] the Florida Supreme Court in upholding the denial of a permit to dredge mangroves, that "Estuary purchased the property in question from a private property owner with full knowledge that part of it was totally unsuitable for development."[177]

Exception Six: Where wetland protection is needed to meet the open space, recreation or other needs of a subdivision. Courts have consistently upheld subdivision regulations requiring that sub-dividers provide open space and recreation areas to meet the needs of subdivision residents. Several courts have specifically upheld wetland protection requirements to meet open space needs. In **Patende v. Town of Meredith,**[178] the New Hampshire Supreme Court held that the Meredith, New Hampshire Planning Board acted within its authority in denying a sub-

FENCING TO PROTECT STREAM AND WETLANDS. Fencing protects wildlife and water quality. Photo source: U.S. Soil Conservation Service.

HOUSE ELEVATED ON PILINGS. Elevation on pilings interferes less with vegetation and water flows than fill. Photo source: Federal Emergency Management Agency.

REVEGETATION OF STREAM BANKS. Revegetation reduces the impacts of channelization. Photo source: U.S. Soil Conservation Service.

REVEGETATION OF DREDGE SPOIL. Where wetland destruction is unavoidable, revegetation of exposed areas and creation of new wetlands may be required. Photo source: Dave Davis.

division plan for a 20 acre wetland area and a shore parcel along Lake Winnipesaukee. There was evidence that the soil type in the area was "unsuitable for development," the area was "wildlife habitat," and that the parcel's development would have been inconsistent with the town's comprehensive plan "which called for preservation of natural features and maintenance of wildlife areas."[179] The court concluded that there was no taking of property in part because the area was needed by the subdivision residents as a recreation area and "the limitation in use is necessitated by the subdivision itself...."[180]

Similarly in **Manor Development Corp. v. Conservation Commission of Town of Simsbury**,[181] the Connecticut Supreme Court held that town denial of a permit to fill and develop seven lots in a wetland area was proper. Denial had been based on several factors including potential health problems, destruction of natural habitat and because the area "may also serve as a significant aquifer recharge area and a means of sustaining stream flow."[182] The court noted that the town had approved permission for development of other lots in the subdivision and concluded that there was no taking of property although the total value of the property had been reduced somewhat.

Exception Seven: Where public rights in navigable waters are affected. A number of recent cases have sustained tight wetland regulations based upon the theory that public interests in navigable waters are paramount to the right of private land-owners to carry out activities resulting in wetland destruction. Therefore, regulations that prevent such activities do not take property.

Several theories have been used in holding that landowners have no constitutional right to destroy or damage wetlands. The New Hampshire Supreme Court in **Sibson v. State** noted that:

> (R)ights of littoral landowners on public waters are always subject to the paramount right of the State to control them reason-ably in the interests of navigation, fishing, and other public purposes.[183]

Similarly, the Michigan Court of Appeals in **Township of Grosse Isle v. Dunbar & Sullivan Dredging County**,[184] enjoined dike and fill operations in the Detroit River on the theory that the operations impaired the public trust in navigable waters and public rights of navigation, fishing, duck hunting, and so forth. A New York court in **People, Town of Smithtown v. Poveromo**[185] strongly endorsed the trust concept and the superiority of public rights in trust lands, although the court invalidated the local ordinance in question for different reasons.

With somewhat similar reasoning, a U.S. Court of Appeals in **Zabel v. Tabb**[186] sustained a denial of a U.S. Army Corps of Engineers permit to fill 11 acres of tide land in Boca Ciega Bay in Florida against claims of taking. This decision was based, in part, upon a holding that "waters and underlying land are subject to the paramount servitude of the Federal government..."[187]

While the State public trust concept and the Federal doctrine of a navigable servitude are not wholly equivalent, both doctrines recognize public interests in navigable waters and the superiority of public interests to private rights. Traditionally, trust and navigable servitude concepts were applied only to waters and lands within the high water mark of public waters.[188] However, the public trust doctrine has been applied more broadly in recent years.[189]

Exception Eight: Where the essential "natural character" of land is destroyed with harm to public rights. Several significant cases have held that landowners have no inherent right to destroy wetlands and, therefore, regulations that prevent destructive activities do not take property. These cases are conceptually similar to the public trust and navigable servitude cases, but take the reasoning of these cases a step further. In the best known case, **Just v. Marinette County**,[190] the Wisconsin Supreme Court strongly endorsed tight wetland regulations adopted by a county pursuant to a state-supervised shoreland zoning program. The court faced the key issue in most wetland taking cases—that regulations severely restrict potential development value -- and rejected the landowner's claim that potential development was a right:[191]

> The Justs argue their property has been severely depreciated in value. But this depreciation of value is not based on the use of the land in its natural state but on what the land would be worth if it could be filled and used for the location of a dwelling. While loss of value is to be considered in determining whether a restriction is a constructive taking, value based upon changing the character of the land at the expense of harm to public rights is not an essential factor or controlling.

The court observed:[192]

> This case causes us to re-examine the concepts of public benefit in contrast to public harm and the scope of an owner's right to use of his property....What makes this case different from most condemnation or police power zoning cases is the inter-relationship of the wetlands, the swamps and the natural environment of shorelands to the purity of the water and to such natural resources as navigation, fishing, and scenic beauty.

Continuing, the court held:[193]

> Is the ownership of a parcel of land so absolute that man can change its nature to suit any of his purposes? The great forests of our State were stripped on the theory man's ownership was unlimited. But in forestry, the land at least was used naturally, only the natural fruit of the land (the trees) were taken. The despoilage was in the failure to look to the future and provide for the reforestation of the land. An owner of land has no absolute and unlimited right to change the essential natural character of his land so as to use it for a purpose for which it was unsuited in its natural state and which injures the rights of others. The exercise of the police power in zoning must be reasonable and we think it is not an unreasonable exercise of that power to prevent harm to public rights

by limiting the use of private property to its natural uses.

The court considered contrary wetland cases and flatly disagreed with them. Restating Chief Justice Holmes' warning in **Pennsylvania Coal** that "We are in danger of forgetting that a strong desire to improve the public condition is not enough to warrant achieving the desire by a shorter cut than the constitutional way of paying for the change...",[194] the court responded:

> This observation refers to the improvement of the public condition, the securing of a benefit not presently enjoyed and to which the public is not entitled. The shoreland zoning ordinance preserves nature, the environment, and natural resources as they were created and to which the people have a present right. The ordinance does not create or improve the public condition but only preserves nature from the despoilage and harm resulting from the unrestricted activities of humans.

The rationale and the language of the Wisconsin court was partially endorsed in a New Hampshire decision, **Sibson v. State**,[195] upholding coastal wetland regulations.

The application of the **Just** rationale in future decisions remains to be seen. Yet, the case is a landmark step in recognizing public as well as private interests in the nation's natural resources including its wetlands. Public interests in private resource lands have been recognized in cases sustaining the regulation of forestry operations[196] and oil and gas extraction,[197] but never with such scope.

Avoiding Legal Problems

Courts will, no doubt, be called upon many additional times to determine whether wetland regulations are legally sound as applied to specific properties. Favorable decisions in the 1980's reduce the threat of successful legal challenges. How can a community avoid problems?

Some suggestions include the following.
--Regulations should be applied fairly with some consideration of landowners' as well as wetland needs.
--The hazards which may result from wetland destruction such as increased flood flows should be documented since courts are particularly willing to support regulations preventing threats to safety or nuisances.
--Real estate tax policies and regulations should be coordinated to reduce the financial burden of regulations on private landowners.
--Wetlands should be mapped with reasonable accuracy to provide a sound factual basis for regulation. Procedures should be available to resolve boundary disputes during administration of a program.
--Similarly situated landowners should be regulated to the same standard to avoid claims of discrimination.
--Where appropriate, innovative regulations should be adopted such as cluster subdivision regulations and transfer of development rights ordinances to reduce the burden on landowners while achieving wetland protection goals.
--Conditions should be attached to permits to reduce development impact on wetlands where denial of a permit is undesirable.
--Acquisition and regulatory efforts should be coordinated and used to complement one another. Zoning should not be used solely to reduce future acquisition costs. Acquisition should be applied where positive public uses such as public access are needed.

In summary, communities can now regulate wetlands with considerable confidence in light of the many favorable decisions. But the regulations should be drawn carefully and administered fairly.

CHAPTER 10: TAXATION AND ACQUISITION

10.1 Introduction

Regulations are the backbone of most local wetland protection programs and, therefore, have been the principal topic of this report. However, regulations are subject to political, legal, and administrative drawbacks. For example, local zoning controls generally do not apply to agricultural, governmental, or existing uses that damage wetland areas. Because of their negative approach to land uses (they tell landowners what they cannot do but not what they should do), regulations are less popular than management techniques that offer incentives or rewards for preserving wetlands. Regulations are also inappropriate for achievement of public access to private wetland areas. Further, since regulations can be altered at the whim of the local legislative body, sound wetland regulations may offer only temporary protection and lull conservationists into a false sense of security. In addition, where development pressures are intense and wetlands most need protection, strong interest groups often obstruct wetland regulatory efforts.

For these reasons, regulations can often best be supplemented by nonregulatory techniques to increase their effectiveness and to achieve wetland objectives unobtainable through regulations. Two of the most useful nonregulatory wetland protection techniques are tax incentives and acquisition programs. These techniques, reviewed below, can be used independently or as complementary elements to regulatory programs.

10.2 Tax Incentives for Wetland Protection

Four types of Federal, State, and local taxes affect the use of wetlands: real property tax, estate tax, gift tax, and income tax. Real property taxes are typically imposed by local general purpose and special purpose units of government. Income, gift, and estate taxes are imposed by the Federal government and by many States. A small number of local governments impose income taxes.

Real property taxes, the largest source of revenue for local governments, are based on the "assessed" values of lands and structures, as determined by local assessors in accordance with State-established guidelines. Some States tax the full market value. Land value usually includes potential development value, a factor that encourages development of wetlands.

Federal and State estate taxes must be paid upon an individual's death. These are based on the value of land and assets owned by the deceased. If land is subject to development restrictions that lower its value, estate taxes are correspondingly reduced. On the other hand, beneficiaries may have to subdivide or sell land assessed at its full market value after the owner's death in order to meet stiff estate taxes.

Federal and State gift taxes apply when property is transferred without compensation. Certain tax-free gifts are allowed, but their amount is limited. However, donors can avoid gift taxes by making gifts to government bodies and to qualifying charitable organizations.

Income taxes are by far the most burdensome for most individuals. Income taxes are annually charged against income and are the major source of revenue for the Federal government and most State governments. They do not in themselves necessarily encourage land development. Indeed, certain income tax provisions, such as deductions for charitable donations of wetlands to conservation organizations or governmental agencies, encourage wetland protection.

The following discussion highlights tax techniques or approaches that may either encourage wetland preservation or offset negative tax implications of wetland regulatory statutes. Because the tax laws are complicated and have different impacts on individuals, a tax expert or lawyer should be consulted by anyone contemplating use of the various tax provisions.

Preferential Real Estate Taxes

Preferential real estate tax assessment policies are available in many States for open space agricultural, forestry and in some instances, other conservation lands. These may take the form of either special real estate tax incentive laws or regulatory statutes with tax incentive provisions.[1] Forty-four States have special statutes that offer some form of preferential tax treatment for land in agricultural, open space, forest, or recreational uses. Many of these statutes may be applied to wetland areas such as forested wetlands, although wetland protection is not an express statutory objective.

Statutes affording preferential tax treatment for undeveloped lands are designed to offset development pressures and the increases in market value attributable to those pressures. Preferential assessment is premised on the theory that there are individuals who may want to preserve their land in an undisturbed state but who are forced, through rising property taxes, to sell their land for development. Rising property taxes are often due to two factors. First, development pressures spark an increase in market value and hence assessed value of the land; second, increases in the population of an area result in an increased need for expensive services, such as schools, roads, and police, which must be supported by higher property taxes. Preferential tax laws that reflect use value, rather than the market or development value, of land are designed to assist landowners in resisting encroaching urbanization.

Three approaches are applied in State differential tax assessment programs. The first is pure preferential assessment where eligible land is assessed at present use value, not at its highest and best use or market value. Preferential assessment is available to all qualified landowners. They suffer no penalties if they later decide to withdraw from the program and develop their land.

With the second approach—a deferred taxation system—land is taxed at its use value (open space, forest, agricultural, recreational use), but owners of eligible land who convert their land to noneligible uses must pay some or all of the taxes that would have accrued (absent the tax abatement) during the years of preferential assessment.

The third system, involving restrictive agreements, also assesses land according to its present use and requires payment of deferred taxes for conversion to noneligible uses. Its distinguishing characteristic is the additional requirement that qualifying owners sign contracts restricting the development for a term of years.[2]

The key to wetland protection through preferential assessment is providing landowner incentives for maintaining lands in an undeveloped state while, at the same time, preventing the use of the preferential treatment as a tax dodge. Otherwise, landowners avail themselves of reduced taxes until development pressures and market values increase sufficiently to warrant subdivision. For this reason, deferred taxation and restrictive agreement approaches are desirable, particularly the latter.

Despite advantages, experience to date indicates that deferred taxation and restrictive agreements are often insufficient in themselves to prevent conversion of agricultural and open space lands in urbanizing areas. In addition, landowners are often unwilling to agree to permanent restrictions in areas of intense development because they do not want to forego future profit options.[3] Consequently, experts on preferential taxing schemes advocate that use value assessment schemes supplement, but not replace, regulatory programs to protect open spaces and ecologically critical areas. One study contends that preferential assessment will be beneficial primarily in semi-rural areas where it can help "buy time" prior to adoption of regulatory programs.[4]

In addition to these special real estate tax incentive laws, several States, such as New York and Massachusetts, provide for preferential assessment of wetlands through wetland regulation and other environmental statutes.[5] These statutes also offer the possibility of Federal and State income, gift, and estate tax advantages, which are discussed in later sections of this chapter.

The New York statute governing freshwater wetlands provides that when development is restricted by conservation restriction (a government-imposed regulation) or as the result of a voluntary protection agreement between a landowner and the State Commissioner of Environmental Conservation, the wetland must be assessed for the duration of the agreement according to the use value of the land.[6] The act is, however, quite new, and no landowners have thus far entered into cooperative restriction agreements. Nevertheless, the State agency in charge of implementing the new act has made preliminary contacts with the State Board of Equalization of Assessment to alert it to the future changes that will have to be made in assessment practices.

Massachusetts has more fully implemented a tax incentive scheme for wetland protection. Two regulatory statutes and one nonregulatory statute contain express wetland protection provisions. These statutes work in combination to provide more complete wetland protection than differential assessment statutes in other States. For this reason, the three statutes are examined below in some depth.

The two regulatory acts—the Massachusetts Inland Wetlands Restriction Act[7] and the Coastal Wetlands Restriction Act[8]—provide for government imposition of development restriction orders by the Commissioner of Natural Resources on the use of inland and coastal wetlands. The Coastal and Inland Wetlands Acts provide that once land has been restricted pursuant to these statutes, the land qualifies for reduced property tax assessment.[9] A landowner affected by an order may petition the Superior Court to determine whether the order so restricts the use of the property as to constitute a taking without compensation. If a taking is found, the Department of Natural Resources may condemn the land or an interest in the land in the name of the Commonwealth. This helps avoid "taking" arguments.

A third Massachusetts statute authorizes property tax reductions for wetlands protected through conservation restrictions or agreements to restrict wetland uses.[10] This act, the Massachusetts Conservation Restriction Act of 1969,[11] permits landowners to enter into agreements with government bodies or charitable organizations to restrict development on land or water areas maintained predominately in their natural, scenic, or open condition or in agricultural, farming, or forest use. Conservation restrictions must usually be approved by the selectmen or city council and by the Massachusetts Secretary of Environmental Affairs. Restrictions are binding on subsequent owners of the land.

Massachusetts law provides that real estate that has been permanently restricted under a voluntary conservation restriction agreement must be assessed for real property tax purposes as a separate parcel of land.[12] By removing certain potential uses of land, conservation restrictions reduce the fair market value, thereby resulting in reduced property taxes.

Even land temporarily subject to voluntary conservation restrictions might qualify for reduced property assessment. Under Massachusetts case law, property assessments must reflect the change in fair market value of land subject to a covenant or restrictions limiting its use.[13] Hence, if temporary restrictions reduce fair market value, the taxes should be correspondingly reduced. However, the chances are greater that property values will decrease with more permanent restrictions. Because another Massachusetts case requires that all land be assessed at 100 percent of fair market value, many localities view conservation restriction agreements as one technique for avoiding uncontrolled development.

Massachusetts communities such as Barnstable, Concord, and Dennis have adopted tax assessment guidelines for their assessors that establish lowered tax rates for property subject to conservation restrictions. Other towns have also adopted informal tax reduction policies. Such explicit guidance has proven desirable since assessors often oppose reduced assessments even where authorized by statute.

Income Tax

Income tax advantages are also available to individuals who donate full title of wetlands or conservation restrictions and easements to governmental bodies, publicly supported charities, or a private charitable foundation. Upon making such donations, landowners may take charitable deductions for the value of the gift from their Federal income tax and, in many States, from their State income taxes.

COASTAL WETLANDS, SUFFOLK COUNTY, NEW YORK. New York provides real estate tax incentives for regulated coastal wetlands. Photo source: Jon Kusler.

Where land or an interest in land has appreciated greatly in value since original acquisition, the tax savings may be substantial. As will be discussed in the next chapter, these tax provisions are being widely used by private organizations to encourage private donation of wetland areas.

Section 170(b) of the Internal Revenue Code allows landowners to deduct the full value of the capital gain on property donated to a government or qualifying charitable organization, provided that the total amount of the contribution does not exceed 30 percent of the landowner's adjusted gross income in the year of the donation.[14] If the amount exceeds 30 percent of the taxpayer's adjusted gross income, he can carry over the excess during five succeeding tax years.[15] Or a taxpayer can deduct up to 50 percent of his adjusted gross income if he pays the entire capital gains tax.[16]

There are some restrictions on the use of the charitable deduction for gifts of partial interests in property.[17] The deduction is limited to those donations which are "exclusively for conservation purposes" and granted in perpetuity.[18]

To qualify as an exclusive conservation purpose, the donation must serve one of four objectives:

1) Preserves land areas for outdoor recreation or education of the general public;

2) Protects a relatively natural habitat of fish, wildlife, or plants, or similar ecosystem;

3) Preserves open space for scenic enjoyment of the public or for some governmental conservation policy; or

4) Preserves an historically important land area or structure.[19]

State and Federal Estate Taxes

Upon an individual's death, estate taxes become payable to the Federal and State governments. These are calculated on a progressive scale in direct proportion to the value of assets in the decedent's estate. The greater the value of the estate, the higher the taxes.

Estate taxes have a particularly harsh impact when the decedent's estate is composed largely of land. Unless cash can be obtained from other assets, the property may have to be sold to pay estate taxes. Thus, wetlands and open spaces that the decedent and his heirs had hoped to protect may become the victims of development.

There are several ways to reduce estate taxes while simultaneously protecting wetland areas. Section 2055(a) of the Internal Revenue Code permits deduction from the gross estate of the value of all bequests of property to qualified charitable organizations or government bodies.[20] The Tax Reform Act of 1976 extended this provision to permit deduction of bequests of leases, options to purchase, and easements.[21] The effect of this provision is that

101

the value of the donated land or interest will be neither included in the assets of the estate, nor applied against the estate and gift tax credit allowed to all individuals.

Gift Taxes

Gift taxes resemble estate taxes in that they are progressive and imposed upon the transfer of an interest in property. Unlike estate taxes, however, gift taxes are imposed during the life of the donor, not at his death.

For a number of years the Internal Revenue Code has provided that gifts to governmental units and to qualifying charitable organizations were not subject to gift taxes.[22] As with the charitable deduction for income tax purposes, gifts of conservation easements, restrictions, and remainder interests must qualify as a gift exclusively for conservation purposes.[23]

Examples of How Tax Incentives Work

Several examples will help explain how the various tax incentives work in practice. Mr. Smith owns 100 acres of land containing 20 acres of wetlands that lie in the path of development from a growing urban area. The 80 non-wetland acres are used for farming. Until recently, Mr. Smith paid $1,500 per year in property taxes. Because of development pressures, the land has been reassessed and Mr. Smith now owes $5,000 per year in taxes. Even the wetlands are highly valued because of their prime location. Because of the increase in taxes, Mr. Smith ordinarily might be forced to sell his lands. Assume, however, that the State has adopted a statute that values prime agricultural lands and wetlands under a preferential taxation scheme which assesses such land at use value rather than its fair market value. As long as Mr. Smith does not convert his land to ineligible uses, he will be able to enjoy his wetlands while paying only $300 per year in assessments.

Although Mr. Smith now has the benefit of reduced property tax assessments, he realizes that the differential taxation statute will do nothing to protect his estate after his death. Assume that Mr. Smith's farm, including the wetlands, would be valued at $350,000 by the IRS even though he originally paid only $50,000 for the land. This would result in a large estate tax that his children would have to pay the Federal government. Because Mr. Smith's family is "land poor," his children would have to sell a portion of the land in order to pay the estate taxes. To avoid such a consequence, Mr. Smith enters into a permanent conservation restriction with the local government. That restriction prohibits the development of Mr. Smith's land by Mr. Smith or by any future owner of the land, but it permits Mr. Smith and his heirs to continue living on and using the land. The public has no right of access. The big difference, however, is that the IRS recognizes as a donation the difference between the unrestricted value of the land and its value subject to the development restrictions. In the case of the Smith farm and wetlands, the restrictions reduce the value of the land by $200,000, leaving a value of $150,000; hence, the amount subject to estate taxes is considerably reduced. In addition, Mr. Smith is able to deduct the entire value of his gift of the conservation restriction on his gift tax return because

the gift of the restriction went to the local government. Thus no gift tax is payable upon conveyance of the restriction.

One other important benefit to Mr. Smith should be noted. Since the conservation restriction that he donated to the local government is worth $200,000, Mr. Smith is now entitled to a charitable deduction of that amount from his income tax. Since Mr. Smith's annual adjusted income is not large enough to permit deduction of the full value of the restriction in one year, that deduction may be spread out over a period of six years.

10.3 Acquisition of Wetlands

Introduction

Land acquisition has been used by many communities to protect wetlands. Wetlands may be acquired through gifts from private individuals or organizations, devises, or purchase of a fee or lesser interest. In deciding whether they should acquire wetlands, an agency or community must first weigh the pros and cons of acquisition. It must then decide: (1) what wetlands should be acquired; (2) whether it wants to acquire full title to the wetlands, or only a partial interest; and (3) how the acquisition funds can be obtained. The following discussion examines some of these issues and outlines a general procedure for purchasing wetlands.

Pros and Cons of Acquiring Wetlands

Acquisition of a fee or easement interest is a straightforward but costly method for protecting wetlands. Acquisition of a fee interest ensures public access and 100 percent public control over land. Depending on its terms, an easement may also permit public access. Because acquisition of either full or partial interests avoids the taking issue, it may be a politically attractive alternative to regulation. Under certain circumstances acquisition may ensure permanent protection of the wetland, whereas regulations are much more susceptible to changing political climates.

Despite advantages, public purchase of wetlands is expensive. For example, coastal wetlands in some areas may cost from $10,000 to $80,000 per acre; inland wetlands are usually less costly, except in urban areas. Public purchase will also remove land from the tax rolls, resulting in loss of property tax revenues. Although reduction in taxes may be minimal for remote rural wetlands not subject to development pressures, loss of revenues may be considerable for wetlands in developed areas where the tax reflects market values stemming from development pressures. Even if the acquisition is by gift, the community must often provide management and protection services. In addition, acquisition can be time-consuming and politically unpopular if done on a large scale or by condemnation.

Acquisition of full title has been highly regarded as a protection technique since it provides complete public control over the land. Yet even full control does not guarantee absolute protection. If, for example, only a portion of a wetland is purchased, development on the remainder may destroy the ecological balance in the "protected" area. This has

CONSERVATION EASEMENT, BLACKHEARTH CREEK, WISCONSIN. Wisconsin has acquired conservation easements to protect wetlands. Photo source: Jon Kusler.

happened to Cherokee Marsh in Madison, Wisconsin where the locality bought only 1,000 acres of a 4,000 acre marsh.

Another danger is that a community will later wish to convert the wetland to an incompatible use. Even where the acquiring agency is dedicated to maintenance of wetlands in a natural state, it may be powerless to prevent destruction of the lands by another agency with superior powers. For example, a utility company may construct a power line through locally owned wetlands, or a dam may be built by the State or a Federal agency.[24]

Which Wetlands Should be Acquired?

Ideally, wetland acquisition should be based on careful wetland inventories that identify areas meriting priority attention. In general, they are: (1) wetlands where all private actions must be prohibited because of the unique features of the land, such as habitat for rare and endangered species; (2) wetlands performing important natural functions that are subject to development threats; and (3) wetlands needed for active public use (e.g., recreation or scientific study).

In reality, local acquisition programs have not been systematic. Communities have often acquired wetlands through donation. Here the preferences of the donor, not the community, prevail. Outright purchase has been relatively rare, primarily because of the expense. State and Federal acquisition is more

common, particularly for relatively low-cost rural wetlands with waterfowl or fisheries potential.

Some communities have elected to buy only a partial interest in land rather than a full fee in order to reduce costs. Acquisition of easements or development rights offers many of the protective advantages of acquiring the full title but at lower cost. Moreover, because the original owner retains title to the property, local governments can continue to collect property taxes (although the assessment must be reduced to reflect the decreased value of the land resulting from the sale of development rights). Federal and State tax incentives discussed above are also available to individuals who donate less than total interest in their property to the government or private conservation organizations.

Easements do have limitations. Easements are often unsatisfactory when intensive public use of land is required (e.g., hiking, picnicking). When easements are temporary, as some are, the protection ends upon termination of the easement. In addition, easements are difficult to enforce. Some landowners clear or otherwise alter the lands ostensibly protected by the easements. Finally, easements sometimes cost as much as 70 percent of the fee. When these drawbacks are considered, full fee acquisition is often preferable.

Sources of Funds

Funds for wetland acquisition may come from several sources. Private sources include donated funds from individuals or corporations. These may be used for general acquisition of specific properties. Individuals may also donate properties and leave an endowment for management and protection of the lands. Donations may be made as gifts during life or devises upon death.

General revenues from property taxes or revenues generated by specially enacted sales taxes also may be used. Authority to adopt sales taxes varies from State to State.

Matching Federal grants for State and local acquisition are also important. Although money allocated to States and communities by the Land and Water Conservation Fund (now zero budgeted) for acquisition of open space lands is not directly earmarked for wetlands acquisition, wetlands may be included in the land actually purchased. Another source of Federal funds for local governments is revenue sharing. The U.S. Fish and Wildlife Service provides grants under the Pittman-Robertson Act[25] for State acquisition of wildlife areas. Similarly, it allocates money to States under the Dingell-Johnson Act[26] to cover 75 percent of the cost of fish restoration and management projects. The Coastal Zone Management Act[27] also funds acquisition of estuarine sanctuaries.

Steps in Purchasing Wetlands

Statutes often establish explicit procedures for condemnation of lands by local units of government, State agencies, or Federal agencies. Fewer specific procedures are provided for acquisition through donation or negotiated fee.

Of course, steps in land acquisition vary according to statutes under which land is acquired. Steps also differ from State to State. Nevertheless, several major steps can be identified in land acquisition. These include the following.

1. <u>Mapping and evaluation of wetlands</u>. Conceptually, the first step in acquisition of wetlands is to identify the wetlands in a community or region and determine their relative importance for acquisition in terms of goals such as recreation, education, waterfowl production, flood storage, and so forth. If undertaken, an inventory should indicate the relative importance of the wetlands and the degree to which the threat of development exists.

2. <u>Identification of wetlands - related legislation</u>. Simultaneous with the inventory, the agency interested in acquisition should identify all legislation and implementing regulations affecting the use of wetlands including regulatory statutes pertaining to use of public lands. Statutes and regulations can be checked against the inventoried wetlands to determine which wetlands are already protected by regulation, which wetlands may be protected by regulation, and which ones should be protected by acquisition.

3. <u>Establishing priorities</u>. Because of economic constraints, local governments can best first acquire lands that are threatened by development. Land values are often high in such circumstances, but funds are rarely available for broader acquisition. Other approaches for determining acquisition strategies have been discussed above. The timing and criteria for acquisition will depend on the amount of money available for acquisition.

4. <u>Preliminary negotiations and approvals</u>.

After specific wetlands have been selected for acquisition, the agency contemplating acquisition often begins discussion with landowners, the local legislative body, private organizations (such as The Nature Conservancy) that may assist in the acquisition effort, and Federal and State agencies that may help fund such acquisition. Priorities are often modified in this negotiation process.

5. <u>Appraising the land</u>. Land appraisal is the next step. If localities rely on Federal funding, they must comply with the requirements of the Uniform Relocation Assistance and Real Property Acquisition Policies Program.[28] This law requires that real property must be appraised before the initiation of negotiation and that the owner or his representative must be given an opportunity to accompany the appraiser during his inspection of the property. The owner may not be offered less than the value set by the appraiser.[29] Several factors influence the appraised value of the land. The soil structure, the productivity of the land, the amount of water on the land, the potential for development, and the value of similar land in the neighborhood are all considered.

6. <u>Preparation of impact statements</u>. In States with environmental impact requirements for land acquisition and where Federal funds are used for land acquisition, a determination must be made on whether an environmental impact statement is required. If one is necessary, it must be prepared before the acquisition occurs.

7. <u>Final negotiations with the landowner</u>. If all has gone smoothly up to this point, the agency can then begin final negotiations with the landowner. The U.S. Fish and Wildlife Service, Realty Division, reports that, in general, about 85 percent of the land purchased by the Federal government is acquired through negotiated agreements. In 15 percent of the cases, land must be condemned either because the title of land is unclear and, therefore, the land cannot be acquired through negotiations, or because the owner refuses to sell. While hard figures are not available, negotiated purchase is also the most common approach at the local level.

8. <u>Closing</u>. Assuming that an agreement for purchase of the land is reached, the following general steps may be followed. These usually require legal assistance.

A. All terms and conditions of the sales contract must be developed and fulfilled.

B. The deed must be drawn and executed.

C. The mortgage deed and note, if any, must be drawn and executed.

D. Any exceptions listed on the title policy must meet with the approval of the acquiring agency.

E. The survey must be certified, and the description in the deed must conform with the survey.

F. Real property taxes must be prorated to the date of closing.

9. <u>Eminent domain</u>. A community may, if negotiation is not successful, take the land by eminent domain. Statutory procedures must be carefully followed. Usually a declaration of taking is filed, and the value of the land is determined as of the date of the declaration. When no agreement can be reached with a landowner, a trial to determine the land value may be necessary. Payment is made to the landowner on the basis of the value determined through the judicial proceedings.

CHAPTER 11: WETLAND PROTECTION BY THE PRIVATE SECTOR

11.1 Importance of Citizen Support

Governmental wetland protection programs necessarily reflect the imagination, talents, knowledge, and enthusiasm of interested citizens. Citizens create the political climate in which wetland protection measures rise or fall. Without strong citizen support, chances are slim that governments will adopt wetland protection regulations, acquisition efforts or tax incentives; or if adopted, that the programs will be tough enough to withstand attack from development interests. Almost without exception, strong community wetland programs are led by a single dedicated individual or group of individuals.

Once programs are adopted, citizen help is needed to provide information for evaluation of development permits and to monitor wetland development since agencies often do not have the manpower or financial resources to monitor all wetlands. When an agency approves an application for a destructive activity, the decision is often as much the result of citizen apathy as agency policy. Citizen support for wetland protection is needed on a continuing basis to counterbalance development arguments and pressures.

Even where there is no governmental program, citizens can often play important roles in safeguarding wetlands. They can educate themselves and others to the importance of wetlands, the opportunities for using wetlands in non-harmful ways, and activities that should be avoided because they injure or destroy wetlands. They can campaign for protective guidelines and policies concerning use of government-owned wetlands. They can show other private landowners how to protect their wetlands through enlightened land management practices and explain how deed restrictions and other protective techniques can be used to ensure future protection. They can organize themselves into nonprofit organizations or join existing organizations that acquire wetlands and lobby for governmental protection. Finally, in some instances, they can initiate private court suits to protect wetlands.

An enormous array of talent and energy for wetland protection is often available in the private sector if it can be tapped and mobilized. A local advertising agent may be willing to put together an attractive citizen guidebook on wetlands. An art teacher might illustrate the book. A high school science teacher may help landowners identify common plant and animal species found in their wetlands. Local lawyers might track down wetland owners and informally explain to them some of the tax advantages for charitable donation of wetlands to conservation organizations. Although insignificant when viewed separately, these combined talents can be extremely effective.

11.2 Wetland Protection by Citizen Organizations

Conservation groups often play major roles in wetland protection. The activities of several well known national and local organizations are described below to familiarize the reader with protection approaches. This is a selected sample from among many fine organizations.

The Audubon Society

Founded in 1905 to protect plumed birds that were being slaughtered by the millions, the Audubon Society has grown to an organization with a national membership of 370,000 individuals in 394 local chapters. Although most people are aware of the organization's wildlife films, educational programs, and national magazine, many are not aware of the Audubon Society's important land acquisition and wildlife sanctuary management programs.

Approximately 175,270 acres are owned or leased by the Audubon Society or patrolled by Society wardens. Many sanctuaries incorporate a salt or freshwater marsh, swamp or shallow bay. In addition to the sanctuaries operated by the national organization, local Audubon chapters also own and operate many sanctuaries whose acreage is not included in the above figure. Audubon, like most other conservation societies, does not judge the merits of protecting a particular wetland simply on the basis of its size. Audubon wildlife sanctuaries containing wetlands range from the 10-acre Cowpens Key—a low, mangrove island off the Florida coast where roseate spoonbills and great white herons nest—to the 26,800-acre Rainey Wildlife Sanctuary in Louisiana, where bayou and brackish marshlands offer feeding grounds for geese and ducks.

Although most of the land acquired by the Audubon Society has been donated to the Society, some of the land has been purchased either independently or jointly with other conservation groups. For example, the Francis Beidler Forest, a 3,400-acre sanctuary found in the Four Holes Swamp northwest of Charleston, South Carolina, was purchased jointly by the Audubon Society and The Nature Conservancy, another non-profit conservation organization. In some instances the Audubon Society has combined donations and purchases to assemble tracts of wetlands and wildlife sanctuaries that are unparalleled in beauty. The famous Corkscrew Swamp Sanctuary in Collier County, Florida is a prime example. It contains a virgin forest of bald cypress, with some trees over 700 years old. The timber company that originally owned the entire Corkscrew tract donated some of the swamp to the Sanctuary after the Audubon Society had made an initial purchase.

The Audubon Society does not always purchase the full fee (all the rights) in land and may acquire only a partial interest to prevent development. In addition, where full ownership is transferred to the Society, land may be leased to other groups for management and use. This approach is used in Big Pine Key in Florida, which serves as habitat for the endangered Key deer. It was purchased by the Audubon Society and is leased for one dollar a year to the U.S. Fish and Wildlife Service. Similarly, Audubon land along the Platte River Sanctuary in Nebraska is leased to farmers for agricultural activities compatible with the wildlife sanctuary. In some instances, donated land may be reserved by the donor

AUDUBON SANCTUARY, WELLFLEET, MASSACHUSETTS. Bird watching is a major activity here. Photo source: Jon Kusler.

for his lifetime use. In this way a donor may have continued enjoyment of the land while realizing significant tax deductions for the donation.

In addition to protecting donated and purchased lands, the Audubon Society sometimes provides wardens and management for State and locally-owned land where management funds are not otherwise available. This approach is applied in the Alexander Sprunt, Jr. Bird Sanctuary outside Charleston, South Carolina, where the endangered brown pelican nests.

The Audubon Society's ability to own and manage important natural areas, including wetlands, is limited by its financial resources. Consequently, the Society prefers that gifts or bequests of land be accompanied by endowments or other assurances of continuing funds for warden patrol and maintenance activities. The Society also requires as a condition of a gift that the donor allow the Society to convey title or management responsibility for the property to another protection agency if it becomes impractical for the Society to maintain the area. Areas may be transferred to a chapter, affiliate, or other suitable conservation or educational organization or government agency. The Society also reserves the right to dispose of property if events, such as the construction of a highway next to the property, make it unsuitable for further protection. Exceptions to the rule requiring that endowments accompany gifts of land are made when individuals offer to donate outstanding wildlife habitats or sites containing rare or endangered species.

The Nature Conservancy

The Nature Conservancy, headquartered in Arlington, Virginia also plays a major private role in wetland protection. The Nature Conservancy, established in 1951, has as its goal the protection of areas of natural diversity to maintain biotic diversity.

The Nature Conservancy has 35 chapters in 29 states with a membership of 130,000. In all, it has preserved close to 1.8 million acres of land and participated in approximately 3,000 preservation projects.

The Nature Conservancy maintains an emphasis on donations and land acquisition, but also has programs to identify ecologically important natural areas, to educate landowners and to provide technical assistance to Federal, State and local agencies and to other conservation societies.

The organization's success in land acquisition stems from its wealth of tax experience, a large revolving property acquisition fund, a well established line of credit with institutional lenders and an ability to act quickly and flexibly when natural areas are threatened. In 60 percent of its projects, the Conservancy retains ownership of the acquired land. In others, the land is transferred for management to the Federal government, a State, a university or another conservation organization.

Donations have provided over one-half of the preserves protected by The Nature Conservancy. Donations may involve: outright donation, donation with retention of life estate, gift of purchase the land

LANDS OWNED BY THE UPPER CONNECTICUT WATERSHED COUNCIL, a private land trust and conservation organization.
Photo source: Richard Newton.

and subsequently lease it for a specific use. In many cases, the Conservancy engages in a "bargain sale" in which the seller sells the land for less than full market value and takes advantage of a Federal income tax deduction equal to the difference between the full market value and the actual selling price. In this way, the seller also enjoys a reduction in the Federal capital gains tax.

Each of these methods for land acquisition, whether by donation or purchase, has different tax consequences for the landowner. Any donation, gift, or bargain sale has tax implications noted in Chapter 10. The Conservancy counsels landowners on methods whereby land may be donated or sold to The Nature Conservancy in a manner most beneficial to the landowner and the Conservancy. Yet the Conservancy advises landowners to retain their own attorneys to do the sophisticated analysis necessary to determine the tax consequences of donating or selling land to a non-profit charitable organization.

Several examples illustrate varying approaches that the Conservancy has used to preserve natural areas, including wetlands, while accommodating the interests of donors or sellers; (Note, the names of individuals and organizations involved in the donations have been deleted by request of the Conservancy):

o   <u>Donation from a private organization</u>. In one case, a gun club donated 25,000 acres containing important marshes and wetlands on the South Carolina coast to The Nature Conservancy. The gift, valued at $20 million, may be the most valuable donation of land ever made to a private conservation organization in the United States. The Nature Conservancy did not retain ownership of the land, but transferred most of the property to the State of South Carolina for creation of a wildlife management area.

o   <u>Donation from a commercial corporation</u>. A major timber corporation donated 10,000 acres of southern swampland to The Nature Conservancy when the company discovered that the land was not suitable for growing commercial timber. A public environmental campaign to save the swamp, the company's desire for a good public image, and the existence of Federal and State regulations that might have blocked conversion of the swamp into agricultural land, also contributed to the company's decision. Complicated tax issues had to be resolved prior to the donation, since the corporation, unlike a private individual, could use a charitable deduction to offset only five percent of its taxable income in one year. The swamp's estimated value of $10 million exceeded the amount that could be deducted during the year and during the five succeeding years as permitted by Federal law. After studying the problem, The Nature Conservancy suggested that the company split its donation over a three-year period. This permitted tax benefits over eight, instead of five years, so the charitable donation could be fully deducted. At the time of the first donation, the Conservancy leased the remainder of the property from the company for one dollar, thus assuring control over areas not yet owned.

o   Donation by private individuals. Because of exorbitant real estate taxes, the owners of a $3 million South Carolina plantation donated the property to a private organization while retaining the right to occupy the main house and other buildings. The State Supreme Court ruled, however, that property owned by the organization was not exempt from State real property taxes and that $100,000 in back taxes was due. When an attempt was made to donate the land to The Nature Conservancy, the Conservancy could not accept the gift because it had no way of paying the $100,000 in back taxes and because it was also not exempt from South Carolina real property taxes. The family was reluctant to turn over the plantation to the State because it wished to continue living in the buildings. At this point, The Nature Conservancy intervened and developed restrictive language that permitted the property to be managed in a manner acceptable to the family and State. Satisfied with the restrictive language, the family transferred the land, subject to the restrictions, to the State, while retaining the right of occupancy.

o   Bargain sale by a private individual. The Nature Conservancy has repeatedly demonstrated that a little imagination and alot of tax expertise can go a long way. One of its purchases involved the bargain sale of 1,000 acres in southern California. Although the landowner had an annual income of only $10,000, The Nature Conservancy was able to show the landowner how he could benefit from "bargain sale" of the land to the Conservancy for $200,000, or $50,000 less than its fair market value. The landowner had bought the property for only $10,000. If he had sold the land for $250,000 on the open market, the landowner could have expected a net return after taxes of $136,000. This contrasted with a net return after taxes of $160,500 that he obtained pursuant to the bargain sale for $200,000 to The Nature Conservancy.

o   Assembling land with different owners. Perhaps the most celebrated land acquisition of The Nature Conservancy has been the acquisition of thirteen Virginia barrier islands that form a part of a sixty-mile chain of eighteen uninhabited islands with pristine marshes. Most of the islands were acquired through bargain sales, with some landowners retaining use rights for 20 years. In some instances, when sellers did not wish to publicly acknowledge sale of their land to a conservation organization, The Nature Conservancy created a dummy corporation that negotiated with the sellers and then turned over the land to The Nature Conservancy.

Several factors led to the success of this enormous project. First, The Nature Conservancy was able to get financial backing from a foundation. Second, developers realized that the barrier islands lacked fresh water and easy access, making development a risky proposition. Third, the increasing regulation of wetlands by Federal and State laws created an atmosphere conducive to bargaining.

Fourth, a slump in the money market encouraged some speculators to give up hopes of development and salvage of their remaining investment. With the help of alert individuals and through tough legal negotiations, assisted by external factors, The Nature Conservancy was able to protect one of the largest undisturbed salt marsh systems in the United States.

The Sierra Club

The Sierra Club has also shown a strong interest in wetlands protection through lobbying and public education efforts. It has not engaged in large-scale land acquisition programs comparable to those of The Nature Conservancy and the Audubon Society but has assisted those organizations in their wetlands acquisition efforts. For example, by lobbying a New York based development corporation, the Sierra Club was able to assist The Nature Conservancy in the purchase of three Virginia barrier islands from the corporation.

The Sierra Club has determined that large-scale land management is beyond its present capabilities. Land acquired by the Sierra Club is actually owned by the Sierra Club Foundation, a nonprofit charitable organization.

The National Wildlife Federation

The National Wildlife Federation is the largest nonprofit citizen organization in the world, with 3.5 million members in primary and affiliated organizations in all 50 states, Guam, Puerto Rico, and the Virgin Islands. It strongly advocates wetland protection and conducts widespread advertising campaigns to encourage protection at all levels of government.

Unlike The Nature Conservancy and the Audubon Society, the Federation is neither a large-scale landowner nor a manager of lands owned by others. Rather, it uses its Land Heritage Program as a conduit for channeling gifts of land to private and public organizations that maintain property donations in accordance with the wishes of the donor. In this way the Federation acts as a clearinghouse for conservation land transfers.

Where property of limited wildlife or natural resource value is donated, the Federation will sell or lease the land and invest the proceeds in the purchase of land with high wildlife features or use the funds to sponsor other Federation programs. The Federation has raised large sums from private corporations and individual contributors for the purchase of ecologically important land. Because the Federation is a nonprofit charitable corporation, contributions of land or other assets are tax deductible.

Local Citizen Organizations

In addition to national organizations with large-scale programs, thousands of State and local citizen organizations play wetland protection roles. These include conservation commissions in the New England States, duck and wildlife clubs throughout the nation, historic preservation groups, and private foundations established to administer trusts and estates. For example, town conservation commissions with statutory status in Massachusetts exercise both land acquisition and wetland regulatory powers.

SHEPPARD DUNES SANCTUARY, EASTHAMPTON, NEW YORK. The Nature Conservancy has acquired many coastal and inland wetlands like this one in Easthampton. Photo source: Jon Kusler.

Conservation commissions in New Jersey, New York, and Connecticut are protecting wetlands by gathering data, conducting workshops and commenting on proposed development and acquisition activities. Duck clubs in California and other western States are principal actors in acquiring and protecting wetlands. Private foundations such as the Ford Foundation and the Rockefeller Foundation have funded the preparation of wetland protection guidebooks for use by local governmental officials in Connecticut and Massachusetts.

One recent wetland protection success story is that of Sanibel, an island off the southwest coast of Florida. A 12,500-acre crescent filled with beaches, estuaries, mangrove swamps, tidal flats, a freshwater river, and many plant and animal species, Sanibel is the southernmost of the barrier islands in the Charlotte Harbor chain. The island was relatively undeveloped until 1963, when construction of a three-mile causeway connected the island with the mainland. Development skyrocketed in the early 1970's; the value of building permits issued for Sanibel during one week of 1973 exceeded the value of those issued in all of 1972.[1]

In 1973, the Sanibel-Captiva Conservation Foundation, a concerned citizens' organization, mounted a major campaign against the haphazard construction of condominiums that destroyed the mangrove swamps, taxed the freshwater system, and preempted public access to the beaches. Citizens' groups raised a $20,000 warchest, formed a Sanibel Home Rule Study Group, hired a professional planning consultant, and held public meetings to organize support. On November 5, 1974, Sanibel's residents voted to free themselves from the control of the Lee County government and to incorporate the island as the City of Sanibel, with the power to establish a city council and adopt a master plan and zoning ordinances that would preserve the island's fragile environment. Separate incorporation was necessary because the county would not adopt adequate zoning to control the developers.

Much of the job of fund-raising and organization fell upon retired citizens living in Sanibel who had free time, a dedication to the island, and enormous administrative and creative talents from their years of experience as businessmen, lawyers, artists, and scientists.

Sanibel's citizens prepared a comprehensive land use[2] plan with the assistance of the consulting firm of Ian McHarg, John Clark and other staff and consultants from The Conservation Foundation, and Fred Bosselman, a nationally known land use lawyer. Citizen committees carried out much of the data gathering for the effort. The plan, adopted in 1976, establishes low-density zoning for coastal and inland wetland areas and performance standards for development to minimize impacts on natural systems.

ESTUARINE WETLANDS OWNED BY SMITHSONIAN INSTITUTE, EDGEWATER, MARYLAND. Photo source: Jon Kusler.

This plan does not prevent further development of Sanibel, but it does limit total population and reduce the impact of development in the fragile wetland areas. The Sanibel-Captiva Conservation Foundation and concerned citizens play a central role in implementation of the plan and protection of wetland areas by overseeing building permit applications, studying environmental problems, conducting public education efforts, and generally serving as watchdogs. The Foundation has also acquired wetlands on the island and now manages approximately 500 acres.

11.3 Wetland Protection Through Deed Restrictions, Covenants, and Easements

Through deed restrictions, covenants, and easements, private landowners may protect wetlands on their own lands even after their death or sale of the land. As noted earlier, the Federal and State governments offer tax advantages to encourage the use of these devices. In addition, groups like The Nature Conservancy help by providing model language for conservation agreements, by becoming a party to perservation agreements, and by acting as a recipient of easements.

The materials that follow describe deed restrictions, covenants, and easements, and examine their potential for protecting wetlands. Appendix D contains examples of these devices.

Deed Restrictions

As the name implies, "deed restrictions" are clauses placed in deeds restricting the future use of land. When property containing wetlands is sold, donated, or willed, deed restrictions can prohibit uses or activities by the new owners that would destroy, damage, or modify wetlands.

When land is donated or devised to a government agency or charitable organization, the donor may include a reverter clause that provides that if the land is not managed and used as specified in the deed, the property must be returned to the original owner or his heirs. Alternately, the reverter clause may require that the land revert to a third party such as The Nature Conservancy, the Audubon Society, or any other conservation group capable of maintaining the land according to the terms of the restrictions.

Although deed restrictions, including reverter clauses, have potential for wetland protection, they are unenforceable in some circumstances.

Covenants

Covenants can be used in some situations where deed restrictions, including reverter clauses, are not legally enforceable. A covenant is a contract between a landowner and another party stating that the landowner will use or refrain from using his land in an agreed-upon manner. Covenants, like deed restrictions, can require, for example, that landowners refrain from activities that will damage wetlands. The

110

documents containing the covenants can give the individuals acquiring the covenant, their heirs, or any third party the right to enforce the covenants. However, covenants, like deed restrictions, are not enforceable in all States, particularly against subsequent purchasers without notice of the covenants.

In lieu of purchasing lands and attaching restrictive covenants to deeds, citizen groups may pay wetland owners to attach covenants to their deeds. The covenants can bind the present owners and all future owners to maintain the wetlands in their natural state with the citizen group holding rights of enforcement. Once placed in deeds, covenants become deed restrictions.

Conservation Easements

Conservation easements can be used to transfer certain rights and privileges concerning the use of land to specified individuals or bodies without transferring the title to the land. Easements are known as "affirmative easements" if they allow the party acquiring the easement to perform affirmative acts on a property (e.g., gain access to wetlands) and "negative easements" if they require that landowners refrain from certain activities. In addition, easements are distinguished according to whether or not they benefit an adjoining piece of land and are therefore "appurtenant" or exist merely as an agreement between landowners and are "in gross." For example, an easement by which a landowner agrees not to conduct agricultural activities on a slope adjacent to his neighbor's wetland would be a negative "appurtenant" easement. Such an agreement not involving adjacent land would be "in gross."

In some States, easements in gross cannot be enforced against anyone other than the original parties to the easement agreement. Because of the uncertainty in many States regarding enforcement of easements, Massachusetts, New Hampshire, Maryland, Connecticut, and California have passed legislation that explicitly recognizes the legality of "conservation" easements and binds all subsequent owners of the property to the terms of the easements for their duration. Of course, if an easement is granted only for a term of years, owners of the property subsequent to expiration of the easement would not be subject to its terms.

A party to a conservation easement has the right to seek enforcement of the agreement. Whether or not others have a right of enforcement depends on State law. In Massachusetts, for example, where conservation easements (known as conservation restrictions) must, in many instances, be approved by a government body, the State attorney general and municipalities can sue to enforce a conservation easement. Massachusetts also has a "Citizen Right of Action Law"[3] whereby any 10 persons domiciled in the Commonwealth can sue to enforce conservation restrictions.

Note, there is very little uniformity among the States regarding requirements, validity, enforceability, and tax implications of deed restrictions, covenants, and conservation easements. Consequently, anyone contemplating the use of one of these techniques should consult a lawyer concerning the law of the jurisdiction.

11.4 Citizen Participation in Wetland Regulatory Programs

Well informed citizen groups can contribute to successful public wetland programs by organizing support for wetland protection, suggesting provisions for wetland legislation, closely supervising agency actions, and keeping a sharp lookout for violations and potential public and private threats to wetlands. The following materials summarize several additional avenues for citizen involvement in public programs affecting wetlands.[4]

NEPA

One avenue for citizen action is the National Environmental Policy Act (NEPA).[5] NEPA requires preparation and review of an environmental impact statement before any major Federal action is undertaken that will significantly affect the quality of the human environment. Major Federal actions include those undertaken directly by Federal agencies and those funded, licensed, or approved by Federal agencies. If, for example, the Federal Highway Administration funds extension of a State highway through a wetland, that action may be deemed a major Federal action and requires an environmental impact statement prior to construction of the highway. It is at this juncture that citizens can influence the decision-making process.

Under NEPA, citizens must be given an opportunity to comment on draft environmental impact statements and their comments must be seriously considered by the Federal agency in the preparation of the final environmental impact statement. Although NEPA does not require that activities with adverse environmental impacts be abandoned, the importance of citizen involvement in highlighting the detrimental side effects of a proposed activity cannot be underestimated. Even if a project is not halted as a result of a negative review, it may be significantly modified to alleviate the potential harm. For example, an agency may substitute a bridge on pilings that allows the free flow of water in wetlands for a proposed solid fill structure.

If citizens believe that an environmental impact statement fails to include necessary information, or that statutory requirements for preparing the EIS were not followed, they may be able to bring suit challenging the adequacy of the statement. This tactic is discussed later in the context of citizen suits.

Although NEPA is a Federal statute, 25 States and the Commonwealth of Puerto Rico have adopted State environmental policy acts or regulations patterned after NEPA.[6] Thus, State actions may also be subject to environmental impact statement requirements, including the opportunity for citizen participation and the possibility of citizen suits if requirements of the State act are not met.

Federal Water Pollution Control Act Amendments of 1972

As discussed in Chapter 6, the Federal statute with most direct impact on wetland protection is the Federal Water Pollution Control Act Amendments of 1972.[7] Section 404[8] of that amended Act requires the U.S. Army Corps of Engineers to evaluate permit applications for the discharge of dredged or fill material into waters of the United States including adjacent wetlands.[9] Under the Clean Water Act of 1977, EPA may approve State 404 programs for a portion of the waters affected by Section 404.

A public hearing or a public meeting where citizens are given an opportunity to comment is required for most Federal and State Section 404 permit applications. Citizens who are directly affected by issuance of permits can request public hearings. One way for citizens to stay apprised of permit applications is to write to the Corps' District Engineer, the Environmental Protection Agency or the State wetland protection agency and request that their names be placed on a mailing list for notification of proposed permits affecting wetlands. At public hearings or meetings, citizens should be prepared to present facts that demonstrate the adverse impacts of proposed activities on wetlands. If Federal projects are involved they might also argue that environmental impact statements are necessary prior to issuance of permits.

Individual permits are not required for some dredge or fill activities, either because it is presumed that the impact on the environment would be minimal or because a general permit for all such activities has already been issued. Even in these situations, however, citizen groups should notify the Corps of Engineers or the appropriate State agency of dredge and fill activities that may require special attention. Citizens can also act as watchdogs for the government agencies by reporting activities undertaken without a proper permit or violations of permit conditions.

Coastal Zone Management Act

A third important Federal statute providing citizen input to wetland use is the Coastal Zone Management Act of 1972[10] which makes Federal funds available to the States for comprehensive coastal land and water management plans.

The coastal zone is defined by the act to include salt marshes, wetlands, beaches and transitional, and intertidal areas. In addition, administrative regulations adopted pursuant to the act list coastal wetlands as areas of "particular" concern. All of the states eligible for funding under the Coastal Zone Mangement Act have applied for program development grants. The act requires that citizens play a large role in both the development and implementation of State coastal zone management plans. Because the grant of Federal money under the Coastal Zone Management Act is a major Federal action, an environmental impact statement must be prepared for each State management program that is submitted for Federal approval. This provides another access point for citizen comment and recommendation.

State Wetland and Critical Area Statutes

At the State level, many statutes directly or indirectly affect the use of wetlands. Citizens should familiarize themselves with the provisons of the statutes in their States and ensure that their requirements are met both by individuals subject to the regulations and agencies responsible for carrying them out. For example, where a statute requires a public hearing on a prepared plan or permit application, citizens may attend such hearings and state their positions. Citizens can also comment on environmental impact statements prepared in connection with the issuance of permits.

Early citizen inputs in planning and application processes are most effective in influencing agency decisions.

If a State has not adopted a wetland statute, citizens can, of course, lobby for legislation. Similarly, citizens may push for local adoption of wetland protection ordinances, whether or not a statewide wetland protection statute is adopted.

11.5 Citizen Law Suits

Citizens can have a major impact on wetland decisions with a minor expenditure of resources by assembling information, getting it to the right officials, and maintaining a watchful eye over

Some States authorize citizen suits to protect activities that affect wetlands. Nevertheless, there are times when the initiation of a private citizen suit is necessary to prevent the destruction of wetlands by a Federal, State, or local agency, or another private individual. However, citizen lawsuits are expensive and, for that reason, should be used as a measure of last resort.

In addition to expense, citizens face legal obstacles to private lawsuits. First, citizens must be able to show that a legally protected right is or may be involved. Second, they must demonstrate that they have sufficient stake in the matter to qualify to bring the lawsuit. These concepts are known as "justiciability" and "standing to sue."[11]

Beyond this, to make a lawsuit worthwhile, the citizens must be able to obtain a satisfactory remedy from the court if they win their suit. In some instances, the available relief may be inadequate to achieve wetland protection even though the citizens win their case.

Getting Into Court

There are several ways for a citizen or citizen group to show that an activity that threatens a wetland violates a legally protected right and that the citizen or the group has standing to protect the right. The legally protected right may derive from a Federal or a State statute or local ordinance, from commonly accepted rights that accompany ownership of a portion of the wetland or adjacent lands, from the notion of a public trust interest in navigable waters, or from some other basis. Assuming that a legally protected interest in the wetlands is or will be violated, standing to sue may also be derived from a statute or ordinance, from ownership of a portion of the wetlands or adjacent lands, from a financial interest that is affected by the wetland activity or from public rights to enjoy navigable waters and land subject to the public trust concept. On the other hand, a generalized interest in protecting wetlands with nothing else to support that interest may be insufficient in some States, depending on the challenged activity. Fortunately, several statutes clearly create rights and standing for citizens hoping to challenge wetland activities.

1. Suits under statutes expressly authorizing

citizen suits. In some instances, a statute creates a right (e.g., to enjoy pollution-free waters) and specifically authorizes private suits to enforce that right. For example, the Federal Water Pollution Control Amendments (as further amended by the Clean Water Act of 1977) contain a section authorizing citizen suits against individuals or government agencies that violate water quality standards adopted under the Act including suits against Federal and State permits for the disposal of dredge or fill material into waters of the U.S. and adjacent wetlands.[12] This section gives citizens, with an interest that may be adversely affected, the right to sue both an individual who illegally discharges dredged material on a wetland and the Corps of Engineers, if only the Corps refuses to enforce permit requirements after a violation is found. The statute, however, sets out specific requirements and procedures that must be followed before initiating a lawsuit. Consequently, anyone contemplating a suit should consult a lawyer.

Some States authorize citizen suits to protect the environment. For example, Connecticut, Florida, Indiana, Michigan, Minnesota, Nevada, New Jersey, and South Dakota have adopted State environmental protection acts that contain provisions authorizing and encouraging citizens to bring suits to prevent violations of the acts.[13] In addition, the Washington Shoreline Management Act of 1971[14] and the California Coastal Zone Conservation Act[15] authorize citizen suits to enforce provisions of those acts.

2. Suits under statutes not expressly authorizing citizen suits. Although most statutes do not expressly authorize citizen suits, this omission does not necessarily bar such suits. If the statutes define a legally protected right to protect the environment, and citizens can show that they have sufficient stake in the right and the activity that they wish to challenge—in particular that they are directly and substantially injured by the activity—a lawsuit generally will be allowed. For example, assume that a citizen believes that an environmental impact statement (EIS) required by NEPA prior to Federal funding of a highway through a wetland is inadequate in that it does not consider alternative locations for the highway. Assume also that the citizen owns and has long hunted on part of the wetland where the proposed highway will run. Because the citizen has a financial stake in the site considered for the highway, and because NEPA establishes a clear duty to prepare an adequate environmental impact statement, the citizen would qualify to bring a lawsuit challenging the failure of the environmental impact statement to consider alternative locations. Without NEPA, however, the citizen could not have compelled the preparation of an adequate environmental impact statement, no matter how adversely he or she was affected. That is because at common law a developer or government unit has no duty to prepare an environmental impact statement, and the citizen has no right to demand its preparation.

3. Suits under the "public trust" doctrine. Some interests are commonly recognized as subject to court protection even though there are no explicit statutes defining or safeguarding them. For example, the "public trust doctrine" holds that there are certain public rights in water and related land resources that the government must protect in the public interest and cannot give away, sell, or damage, except under special conditions.[16] The public trust doctrine recognizes public property rights in rivers, lakes, the sea, and the seashore, including navigational, fishing, and recreational interests and has, to some extent, been extended to protection of wetlands. It can be used in some instances as the basis for a citizen lawsuit to restrain governmental or private actions that would damage or destroy wetlands.

Because the concept of the public trust varies from State to State and is often not clearly defined, citizens are on firmer ground when using the trust concept as the basis of a lawsuit if the State has adopted an environmental protection act or other statutes incorporating the notion of the public trust and defining its dimensions. This is true in Michigan, where the State environmental protection act not only allows citizens to sue the government when its actions would destroy or damage natural resources, but also gives citizens the right to challenge private actions performed on private property that can injure public trust land. As noted above, at least eight States have now adopted environmental protection acts similar to the Michigan act. Nevertheless, only three States—Connecticut, Michigan, and South Dakota—explicitly refer to the public trust concept. New Jersey, however, mentions the "interest of the public" in its State environmental protection act.[17]

4. Suits based on common law theories. There are several common law grounds for citizen challenge to potentially destructive wetland activities even though there is no statutory authority protecting their interests. Common law suits are usually available, however, only where activities directly harm a citizen's wetland through water pollution, increased runoff, or flood flows. In these circumstances, the citizen can argue that the activity constitutes a nuisance, results in trespass on his land, or violates his riparian rights. If the individual can show that the activity directly and substantially harms his property, he can obtain, with certain exceptions, relief in court. For example, if someone dumps into a river toxic materials that subsequently wash into a wetland and kill timber, the wetland owner can argue in court that the dumping constitutes an enjoinable nuisance. He can also claim compensation for damages.

One obstacle to suits based on a nuisance theory is that some environmentally harmful activities are public rather than private nuisances. This means that the activity is harmful to the public as a whole but does not specifically affect a private individual. For example, dumping toxic materials that kill all the fish in a river would probably be a public nuisance. Unfortunately, in some States a lawsuit to stop a public nuisance can be brought only by a public official, not a private citizen. Also, if the activity meets statutory standards it may not be deemed a public nuisance, even though injury results. In addition, courts often refuse to restrain nuisances before they occur. This sometimes means that a citizen can only respond to damage, not prevent it.

Finally, as discussed later, even if a private nuisance action is brought, the remedy may be unsatisfactory. In many States, private individuals are awarded only damages, not an injunction to halt the nuisance, if the community as a whole benefits more than it is harmed by the nuisance. Thus, if a local industry dumps polluting materials into a river, the employment value of that industry may outweigh the harm alleged by the individual to his land. Therefore, the remedy may be damages, and the pollution will be allowed to continue.[18]

The common law varies from jurisdiction to jurisdiction so that it is difficult to generalize regarding the nature of a private nuisance, trespass, or violation of a riparian right. Depending on the jurisdiction, a landowner may or may not have an obligation to avoid acts that will affect adjacent wetlands. Thus grading, filling, construction of levees or otherwise altering the quantity or patterns of surface or groundwater may be subject to governmental review. Similarly, jurisdictions differ regarding landowner duties concerning the obstruction of flood flows that may damage adjacent lands.

5. Suits to enforce deed restrictions, covenants or easements. Another basis for a citizen suit designed to protect wetlands is an action for violation of a contract. A citizen can charge violation of the terms of a conservation restriction, easement, or covenant to which the citizen is a party or has a direct interest. Unlike nuisance, trespass, public trust actions, or suits pursuant to a statutory right, this kind of lawsuit does not depend on a publicly created regulation or publicly recognized right. Rather, it stems solely from an agreement between private parties to undertake or refrain from certain activities. Courts will entertain lawsuits to enforce such agreements, although, as noted elsewhere, State laws differ on the validity and enforceability of deed restrictions, covenants, and easements, particularly where innocent purchasers are involved.

6. Intervention. One final approach for citizen action is through "intervention" in legal proceedings that have been initiated by public bodies or other citizens to protect wetlands. Intervention involves the filing of a brief or joinder in the suit as an interested party. Intervention provides an avenue for citizen inputs concerning factual matters, law, and public policy. For instance, four citizen groups—the Environmental Defense Fund, the National Audubon Society, the Florida Audubon Society, and the Collier County Conservancy—were allowed to intervene in review of the Corps of Engineers' denial of a permit to the Deltona Corporation to develop a residential housing complex on the wetlands of Marco Island, Florida.

Legal Remedies

Even if a citizen is able to initiate a successful lawsuit, court remedies may be only partially effective. In some instances, the lawsuit will not result in substantive relief. Instead, courts may only require that offending parties abide by procedures outlined in the statutes such as preparation of environmental impact statements. Where suits are based on statutes expressly authorizing suits, the permissible remedy is usually defined by the statute. If no statute is involved, the legal issue in dispute (e.g., a broken covenant) and the overall circumstances will determine available remedies. Remedies commonly include money damages where the citizen

can show actual damage. The court may also enjoin the offending activity and order that the land be restored to its original condition. Where a law has been violated, the court may impose a fine on the offending party and, in some instances, share the fine with the private litigant who brought the suit. Remedies are discussed individually below.

o   Procedural relief. Under NEPA and many State environmental policy acts, the statute merely prescribes procedures that must be followed before a governmental body can approve or undertake an action that has a significant impact on the environment. Consequently, if the agency is sued for not complying with the statutory requirements, the relief is not to halt an activity or even require modifications, but merely to require preparation of an adequate environmental impact statement before the activity is approved or undertaken. For example, the court may order that the offending party present alternatives to the proposed project, if alternatives were not explored in the original environmental impact statement. Or the court may order a new hearing on the draft environmental impact statement if citizens were not given an opportunity to participate in the previous hearing. Courts typically order a temporary halt to activities until procedures are met. When an adequate EIS is prepared, the agency may decide that the adverse impacts of the proposed project are so severe or that public opposition is so great that the project should not be approved. But that decision is left to the discretion of the agency; it cannot be ordered by the court unless an abuse of discretion is found.

o   Stopping or modifying the activity. The environmental policy acts of several States offer more than procedural relief. In Michigan, for example, once a citizen has shown that the activity harms or is likely to harm the environment, the burden shifts to the defendant to justify the activity by showing that there will be no significant environmental impact or that no feasible and prudent alternatives exist and that the activity is in the public interest. If the defendant cannot meet this test, substantive rather than procedural relief is granted and the project may be halted unless modified. The most common form of relief in environmental cases—alteration of a project to reduce its adverse impacts—is a standard remedy.

o   Money damages. Some statutes, such as the Washington Shoreline Management Act,[19] authorize citizens to seek only money damages for violation of the statute. The Washington statute provides that a citizen may also bring actions for damages on behalf of all persons similarly situated, but that they may not sue to restrain an activity. Only the attorney general or the attorney for the local government can seek such relief. In contrast, California's Coastal Zone Conservation Act[20] authorizes private citizens to sue to stop violations of the Act and to recover civil penalties for violations. That State is in the minority, for most statutes affecting wetlands, like Washington's, authorize only the attorney general or the attorney for the local government to bring actions to halt violations.

As noted earlier, private citizens may seek damages in suits brought on the theories of trespass and nuisance and in some cases may also obtain an injunction against the offending action. Usually, damages alone are not the preferred remedy because the damages are calculated according to the injury suffered to date by the complaining party. Damages payable to one person or even a small group of people may not be sufficiently onerous to make the defendant stop engaging in the offending activity. On the other hand, payment of damages, unlike an injunction, penalizes defendants for past practices that are destructive of wetlands.

o   Requiring public officials to enforce a statute or regulation. Private citizens generally do not have authority to sue to compel governmental agencies to initiate lawsuits protecting the environment. Some exceptions exist, notably in Florida, where private citizens are encouraged to bring such actions.[21] Nevertheless, as long as the statute does not require that government attorneys prosecute all violators, the matter is left to the prosecutor's discretion.

o   Imposing fines. Some wetland statutes impose a civil or criminal penalty on individuals who violate the statute. Rhode Island offers an interesting approach in that its wetland statute permits private citizens reporting violations of the statute to receive one half of the $500 fine that is assessed against the violator for each violation The rest of the money goes to the State.[22]

o   Obtaining remedies outlined in conservation deed restrictions, covenants, and easements. Often a deed restriction, covenant, or easement will specify the remedies available when conditions for use of property are breached. For example, the property may revert to a third party, the offensive action may be enjoined, or the violator may have to restore the property to its original condition, or pay reasonable damages that are specified in advance in the agreement. If no remedies are outlined in the deed restriction, covenant, or easement, the court will be required to fashion the remedy, which could range from monetary damages to requiring the violator to adhere to the terms of the restrictions.

11.6 Summary

This concludes our review of approaches which may be used by communities, private organizations, and landowners to protect our valuable but threatened national wetland heritage and the precious waters which they convey from the mountains to the sea. Creative partnerships and innovative combinations of techniques are needed.

FOOTNOTES

CHAPTER 1

1. S. P. Shaw and C. G. Fredine, Wetlands of the United States, U.S. Department of the Interior, Fish and Wildlife Service, Circular 39 (1956).
2. J. and M. Teal, Life and Death of a Salt Marsh, Ballantine, New York (1969).
3. W. A. Niering, "Wetlands and the Cities," Massachusetts Audubon (1968).
4. Dewey and Klopper, Report of Effect of Loss of Valley Storage Due to Encroachment—Connecticut River, Connecticut Water Resource Commission, Hartford, Connecticut (1964).
5. Massachusetts Water Resources Commission, Neponset River Basin and Wetland Encroachment Study, Massachusetts Water Resources Comm., Boston, Massachusetts (1971).
6. U.S. Army Corps of Engineers, Natural Valley Storage: A Partnership with Nature, Corps of Engineers, Waltham, Massachusetts (1975).
7. R.R. Grant and R. Patrick, "Tinicum Marsh as a Water Purifier," in Two Studies of Tinicum Marsh, The Conservation Foundation, Washington, D.C. (1970).
8. I. Jonata and O. L. Loucks, An Analysis of the Value of Wetlands for Holding Inorganic Phosphorous, University of Wisconsin, Center of Biotic Systems, Mimeographed report (1975).
9. D. L. Tilton, R. H. Kadlee and C. J. Richardson (eds.) National Symposium, Freshwater Wetlands and Sewage Effluent Disposal, University of Michigan Wetlands Ecosystem Group, Ann Arbor, Michigan (1976).
10. J. and M. Teal, Life and Death of a Salt Marsh, Ballantine, New York (1969).
11. Id.
12. R. M. Darnell, et al., Impacts of Construction Activities in Wetlands of the United States, U.S. Environmental Protection Agency, Corvallis Environmental Research Laboratory, Corvallis, Oregon (1976).
13. F. C. Golet, Classification and Evaluation of Freshwater Wetlands as Wildlife Habitats in the Glaciated Northeast. Ph.D. Dissertation, University of Massachusetts, Amherst (1972).
14. Id.
15. Bureau of Sport Fisheries and Wildlife, Rare and Endangered Fish and Wildlife of the United States, U.S. Department of Interior, Resource Publication 34, Washington, D.C. (1966).
16. W. S. Motts and R. W. Haley, "Wetlands and Ground Water," A Guide to Important Characteristics and Values of Freshwater Wetlands in the Northeast, J. Larson, ed., University of Massachusetts Water Resources Center, Publication No. 31 (1973).
17. R. R. Grant and R. Patrick, "Tinicum Marsh as a Water Purifier," in Two Studies of Tinicum Marsh, The Conservation Foundation, Washington, D.C. (1970).
18. J. and M. Teal, Life and Death of a Salt Marsh, Ballantine, New York (1969).
19. J. Clark, "Food Production in the Nation's Coastal Zone," Institute of Ecology Working Paper (1974).

20. J. and M. Teal, Life and Death of a Salt Marsh, Ballantine, New York (1969).
21. Reported in Peter L. Johnson, Wetlands Preservation, Open Space Institute, New York (1969).
22. G. H. Wharton, The Southern River Swamp--A Multiple Use Environment, Bureau of Business and Economic Research, Georgia State University (1970).
23. R. C. Smardon, Assessing Visual-cultural Values of Inland Wetlands in Massachusetts, MLA Thesis, University of Massachusetts, Amherst (1972).
24. Id.
25. H.R.B.-Singer, Inc., The Nature and Distribution of Subsidence Problems Affecting H.U.D. and Urban Areas. Prepared for the Office of Policy Development and Research, Department of Housing and Urban Development, Contract No. H-2385, Washington, D.C. (April, 1977).
26. Id. This report estimated a total damage and extra construction cost of $57,656,900 annually (in 1977 dollars) for construction on organic wetlands.
27. J. Kusler, Regulations for Disposal of Rural Domestic Wastes in Wisconsin, p. 17. Published by the Upper Great Lakes Regional Commission (1971).
28. S. P. Shaw and C. G. Fredine, Wetlands of the United States, U.S. Department of the Interior, Fish and Wildlife Service Circular 39 (1956).
29. Id. The States are: Arkansas, California, Florida, Illinois, Indiana, Iowa, and Missouri.
30. J. and M. Teal, Life and Death of the Salt Marsh, Ballantine, New York (1969).
31. R. M. Darnell, et al., Impacts of Construction Activities in Wetlands of the United States, U.S. Environmental Protection Agency, Corvallis Environmental Research Laboratory, Corvallis, Oregon (1976).

CHAPTER 2

1. L.M. Cowardin, V. Carter, F.C. Golet, and E.T. LaRoe. Classification of Wetlands and Deep-Water Habitats of the United States, USDI Fish and Wildlife Service Publication FWS/OBS-79/31, Washington, D.C. (1979).
2. S. P. Shaw and C. G. Fredine, Wetlands of the United States, U.S. Department of the Interior, Fish and Wildlife Service, Circular 39 (1956).
3. L.M. Cowardin, V. Carter, F.C. Golet, and E.T. LaRoe. Classification of Wetlands and Deepwater Habitats of the United States, USDI Fish and Wildlife Service Publication FWS/OBS-79/31, Washington, D.C. (1979).

CHAPTER 3

1. See J. Kusler, Strengthening State Wetland Regulations, U.S. Department of the Interior, Fish and Wildlife Service (1978), pp. 14-16 and Appendix C.
2. Va. Code, Section 62.1-13.2(f) (1973 and Supp. 1981).

3. See Strengthening State Wetland Regulations, supra, note 1, pp. 16-18 and Appendix C.

4. See Martel Laboratories, Existing State and Local Wetlands Surveys, Vols. I and II, U.S. Department of the Interior, U.S. Fish and Wildlife Service, Washington, D.C. (1976).

5. 56 Wis. 2d 7, 201 N.W.2d 761, 3 ELR 20167 (1972).

6. G. M. Silberhorn, G. M. Dawes, and T. A. Bernard, Jr., Coastal Wetlands of Virginia, Guidelines for Activities Affecting Virginia Wetlands, Interim Report No. 3, Virginia Institute of Marine Science, Glouster Point, Virginia (1974).

7. B. Bedford, E. Zimmerman, and J. Zimmerman, Wetlands of Dane County, Wisconsin, Dane County Regional Planning Commission, Madison, Wisconsin (1974).

8. Id.

9. J. Larson, "Evaluation Models for Public Management of Freshwater Wetlands," paper presented at the 40th North American Wildlife and Natural Resources Conference, Pittsburgh, Pennsylvania (Mar. 16-19, 1975).

10. Id. This study suggested that wetlands with any one of the following attributes should be preserved:

1. Rare, restricted, endemic or relict flora or fauna;
2. Flora of usually high visual quality and infrequent occurrence;
3. Flora or fauna at, or very near, the limits of their range;
4. Juxtaposition, in sequence, of several seral stages of dydracch succession;
5. High production of native water, marsh, or shore bird species;
6. Use by great numbers of migratory water, marsh, or shore birds;
7. Outstanding or uncommon geomorphological features;
8. An established record of scientific research on the site;
9. Known presence of archaeological evidence;
10. Wetlands that are integral links in a system of waterways or whose size dominates a regional watershed.

11. See, for example, W. Tans, "Priority Ranking of Biotic Natural Areas," 13 Mich. Bot. 31 (1974), which describes the rating system used in the Wisconsin scientific area program. Threat is one of several factors considered. The article observes:

Degree of threat is, unfortunately, a very important consideration in evaluating natural area priorities. Were there sufficient funds available to protect all of the choice natural areas, and better understanding of the need, threat would be of little consequence in a priority rating. Because only limited funds are at hand, those areas that are threatened must be acted upon first in a crisis-by-crisis approach.

Threat may be defined as a rating of an area's security in respect to the maintenance of the structure and integrity of its plant communities and other natural features. In this evaluation, threat for the foreseeable future is considered. Points to consider are:

1. Region of the State, land use patterns in the vicinity, local and State zoning or their lack.

2. Potential of the tract for development, construction, drainage or impoundment, grazing, lumbering, windbreak planting, reforestation, plant introduction, etc.

3. Vulnerability to such projects as sewer, highway, pipeline, mining or other noncompatible use.

4. Owner attitude toward preservation.

5. Possibility of increasing taxes, especially on lakeshore property.

CHAPTER 4

1. The New York Inland Wetland Law states that an "applicant shall have the burden of demonstrating that the proposed activity will be in accord with the policies and provisions of this article." N.Y. Environmental Conservation Law, Section 25-0402 C. McKinney (Supp. 1980). North Carolina provides that the "burden of proof at any hearing shall be upon the person or agency, as the case may be, at whose insistance the hearing is being held." N.C. Codes, Section 113-229 (g)(5) (1978).

2. These principles are compiled from goals and standards contained in state and local wetland protection statutes, administrative regulations and ordinances.

3. See Appendix E in J. Kusler, Strengthening State Wetland Regulations, Office of Biological Services, U.S. Fish and Wildlife Service, U.S. Department of Interior, Washington, D.C. (1978), for a listing of these statutes.

CHAPTER 5

1. For other reports describing permitting procedures, see Department of the Army, Office of the Chief of Engineers, U.S. Army Corps of Engineers Permit Program, A Guide for Applicants, U.S. Army Corps of Engineers, EP 1145-2-1, Washington, D.C. (1977); U.S. Army Corps of Engineers, Florida Department of Environmental Regulation, Florida Department of Natural Resources, State of Florida, Joint Permit Application for Dredge, Fill, Structures, U.S. Army Corps of Engineers, Jacksonville District, Jacksonville (1977); J. C. Coleman and E. Kline, A Guide to Understanding and Administering The Massachusetts Wetlands Protection Act, Massachusetts Audubon Society, Lincoln, Mass. (1977). See also infra, note 4.

2. R. Darnell, Impacts of Construction Activities in Wetlands of the United States, Office of Research and Development, U.S. Environmental Protection Agency, Corvallis, Oregon (1976).

3. North Carolina Department of Natural and Economic Resources, Applying for Permit to Alter Marshland, Estuarine Waters, Tidelands and State-Owned Lands, North Carolina Department of Natural and Economic Resources, Division of Marine Fisheries, Raleigh, N.C. (1975).

4. For example, the Georgia Coastal Wetland Protection Act (Ga. Code Ann., Section 43-2401 et seq. (1978)) provides that the regulatory agency will issue a permit to a permit applicant if it finds that the application "is not contrary to the public interest." The Rhode Island Inland Protection Act (R.I. Gen.

Laws, Section 2-1-21(a) (1976)) provides that a permit will be denied if "in the opinion of the director granting of such approval would not be in the best public interest."

A determination of the public interest is carried out by the Corps of Engineers in evaluating permits for the discharge of dredged or fill materials into waters and wetlands pursuant to Section 404 of the Water Pollution Control Amendments of 1977. Regulations issued by the Corps provide

(a)   Public interest review.   (1) The decision whether to issue a permit will be based on an evaluation of the probable impact of the proposed activity and its intended use on the public interest. Evaluation of the probable impact which the proposed activity may have on the public interest requires a careful weighing of all those factors which become relevant in each particular case.   The benefit which reasonably may be expected to accrue from the proposal must be balanced against its reasonably foreseeable detriments. The decision whether to authorize a proposal, and if so, the conditions under which it will be allowed to occur, are therefore determined by the outcome of the general balancing process (e.g., see 33 CFR 209.400, Guidelines for Assessment of Economic, Social and Environmental Effects of Civil Works Projects). That decision should reflect the national concern for both protection and utilization of important resources. All factors which may be relevant to the proposal must be considered, among those are conservation, economics, aesthetics, general environmental concerns, historic values, fish and wildlife values, flood damage prevention, land use, navigation, recreation, water supply, water quality, energy needs, safety, food production, in general, the needs and welfare of the people. No permit will be granted unless its issuance is found to be in the public interest. 42 Fed. Reg. 37136.

See Section 6.4 of Chapter 6 for a listing of criteria applied by the Corps.

CHAPTER 6

1.   Pub. L. No. 95-217, 91 Stat. 1566 et seq., 33 U.S.C.A. Section 1251 et seq.
2.   33 U.S.C.A. Section 1288(b)(4)(B) (1978).
3.   33 U.S.C.A. Section 1288(i)(2) (1978).
4.   33 U.S.C.A. Section 1285(g) (As Amended, 1981).
5.   33 U.S.C.A. Section 1344(t) (1978).
6.   33 U.S.C.A. Section 1344(r) (1978).
7.   See generally 43 U.S.C.A. Section 981 et seq. (1964).
8.   38 Fed. Reg. 10834-35 (March 20, 1973).
9.   Soil Conservation Service Planning Memorandum 15 (1975).
10.   S.P. Shaw, and C. G. Fredine, Wetlands of the United States, U.S. Department of the Interior, Fish and Wildlife Service Circular 39 (2nd ed., 1971).
11.   16 U.S.C.A. Section 669 (1974 and Supp. 1980).
12.   16 U.S.C.A. Section 4601-4 et seq. (1974).
13.   16 U.S.C.A. Section 1451 et seq. (1974 and Supp. 1980).
14.   16 U.S.C.A. Section 777 (1974 and Supp. 1980).
15.   16 U.S.C.A. Section 1531 et seq. (1974 and Supp. 1980).
16.   Housing and Community Development Act of 1954, Section 701; 40 U.S.C.A. Section 461 et seq. (1977).
17.   42 U.S.C.A. Section 1962 et seq. (1981).
18.   33 U.S.C.A. Section 1288(f).
19.   Id.
20.   33 U.S.C.A. Section 1285(g) (Supp. 1980 and as Amended in Pub. L. No. 97-117, 95 Stat. 1623 (1981)).
21.   16 U.S.C.A. Section 1454 (1974 and Supp. 1980).
22.   42 U.S.C.A. Section 4001 et seq. (1977).
23.   44 C.F.R. Part 60 (1980).
24.   Flood Disaster Protection Act of 1973, Pub. L. No. 93-234.
25.   Pub. L. No. 95-128, Title VII, Section 703(a); 91 Stat. 1144 (1977).
26.   33 U.S.C.A. Section 1288(i)(1) (1978).
27.   43 U.S.C.A. Section 1711 (Supp. 1980).
28.   16 U.S.C.A. Section 661 et seq. (1974 and Supp. 1980).
29.   16 U.S.C.A. Section 1536 (Supp. 1980).
30.   33 U.S.C.A. Section 1344(r) (1978).
31.   42 U.S.C.A. Section 4321 et seq. (1977).
32.   33 U.S.C.A. Section 1344(t) (1978).
33.   16 U.S.C.A. Section 1456(c) (1974 and Supp. 1980).
34.   33 U.S.C.A. Section 407 (1978); 33 C.F.R. 323 (1981).
35.   33 C.F.R. 209.120 (1968).
36.   430 F.2d 199 (5th Cir. 1970), cert den. 401 U.S. 910 (1972).
37.   33 U.S.C.A. 1251 et seq. (1978).
38.   33 U.S.C.A. 1344 (1978).
39.   392 F. Supp. 685 (D.D.C. 1975).
40.   42 Fed. Reg. 37136 (July 19, 1977).
41.   Id., p. 37136.
42.   Id., p. 37137.
43.   Id., p. 37137.
44.   Id., pp. 37136-7.

CHAPTER 7

1.   J. Kusler, Strengthening State Wetland Regulations, FWS/OBS-78/98, U.S. Fish and Wildlife Service, U.S. Department of the Interior, Washington, D.C. (1978).
2.   See discussion of these elements in greater depth in Chapters 1 and 2 of Strengthening State Wetland Regulations, supra, note 1.
3.   See Appendix C of Strengthening State Wetland Regulations, supra, note 1, which reproduces State statutory definitions.
4.   Conn. Gen. Stat. Ann., Section 22a-36 et seq. (1975).
5.   See Martel Laboratories, Inc., Existing State and Local Wetlands Surveys, Vols. I and II, U.S. Department of the Interior, Fish and Wildlife Service, Washington, D.C. (1976).
6.   These are: Massachusetts, Rhode Island, Maine, New Jersey, North Carolina, Maryland, New York, and Delaware.

CHAPTER 8

1.   Zoning Ordinance, Lexington, Mass. (1976).

2. Municipal Ordinance Relating to Marshes, Wetlands, and Lands Abutting Meandered Lakes and Watercourses (1970).

3. Zoning Ordinance, Lincoln, Mass. (1973).

4. Inland Wetland and Water Course Regulations, Glastonbury, Conn. (1974).

5. Zoning Ordinance, Woburn, Mass. (1973).

6. Wisconsin Model Shoreland Protection Ordinance, Wisconsin Department of Natural Resources, Madison, Wisc. (1976).

7. Zoning Ordinance, Brockton, Mass. (1975).

8. Zoning Ordinance, Lexington, Mass. (1976).

9. Watershed Protection District Regulations, Waybud, Mass. (1967).

10. Zoning Ordinance, Lincoln, Mass. (1973).

11. Watershed Protection District Regulations, Wayland, Mass. (1967).

12. Zoning Ordinance, Lexington, Mass. (1976).

13. Zoning Ordinance, Clearwater, Fla. (1973, 1975).

14. Inland Wetlands and Watercourses Regulations, Ledyard, Conn. (1974).

15. Zoning Ordinance, Brockton, Mass. (1975).

16. New York State Department of Environmental Conservation, Model Local Law/Ordinance for the Protection of Freshwater Wetlands, State Department of Environmental Conservation, Albany, N.Y. (1976).

17. Inland Wetlands and Water Courses Regulations, Easton, Conn. (1973).

18. Inland Wetlands and Watercourses Regulations, Ledyard, Conn. (1974).

CHAPTER 9

1. E.g., Spiegle v. Borough of Beach Haven, 46 N.J. 479, 218 A.2d 129 (1966), cert. denied, 385 U.S. 831 (1966).

2. 272 U.S. 365 (1926).

3. 277 U.S. 183 (1928).

4. 56 Wis. 2d 7, 201 N.W.2d 761 (1972).

5. E.g., J.M. Mills, Inc. v. Murphy, 352 A.2d 661 (R.I. 1976).

6. E.g., Spears v. Beale, 422 N.Y.S.2d 636, 48 N.Y.2d 254, 397 N.E.2d 1304 (1979); Monroe v. Carey, 96 Misc. 2d 238, 412 N.Y.S.2d 939 (1977).

7. E.g., East Haven Economic Development Commission v. Department of Environmental Protection, 36 Conn. Supp. 1, 409 A.2d 158 (1979).

8. Moskow v. Commissioner of Department of Environmental Management, 427 N.E.2d 750, (Mass. 1981).

9. 427 N.E.2d 750 (Mass. 1981).

10. Id. 427 N.E.2d at 753.

11. 430 F.2d 199 (1970).

12. E.g. P.F.Z. Properties, Inc. v. Train, 393 F. Supp. 1370 (D.D.C. 1975); United States v. Joseph Mavetti, Inc., 331 F. Supp. 151 (S.D. Fla.), as modified, 478 F.2d 418 (5th Cir. 1973).

13. E.g., Conservation Council of North Carolina v. Costanzo, 398 F. Supp. 653 (E.D.N.C. 1975), aff'd, 528 F.2d 250 (4th Cir. 1975).

14. 399 So.2d 1374 (1981).

15. Just v. Marinette Co., 56 Wis. 2d at 17, 201 N.W. 2d at 768 (1972), cited at 399 So.2d 1382.

16. American Dredging Co. v. State Department of Environmental Protection et al, 169 N.J. Super. 18, 404 A.2d 42 (1979).

17. Sibson v. State of New Hampshire, 336 A.2d 239 (1975); Town of Hampton v. Special Board of New Hampshire, 116 N.H. 644, 365 A.2d 741 (1976).

18. Potomac Savel & Gravel Co. v. Governor of Maryland et. al., 266 Md. 358, 293 A.2d 241 (Md. Ct. App. 1972), cert. denied, 409 U.S. 1040 (1972).

19. Thompson v. Water Resources Commission, 159 Conn. 82, 267 A.2d 434 (1970).

20. Candelstick Properties, Inc. v. San Francisco Bay Conservation and Development Commission, 11 Cal. App. 3d 557, 89 Cal. Rptr. 897 (1970).

21. Bernhard v. Caso, 19 N.Y.2d 192, 225 N.E.2d 521 (1967).

22. In Re Board and Gales Creek Community Association, 300 N.C. 267, 266 S.E.2d 645 (N.C. 1980).

23. Most states have adopted the model language from the Department of Commerce, Standard State Zoning Enabling Act (1926).

24. Id.

25. E.g., Calif. Gov't Code, Section 65502 (West 1966); S.D. Compiled Laws Ann., Section 11-1-13 (1967). See also E. Strauss and J. Kusler, Statutory Land Use Control Enabling Authority in the Fifty States, U.S. Department of Housing and Urban Development, Federal Insurance Administration (1975), pp. 65-73, for a listing of State statutes authorizing local floodplain regulations.

26. 362 Mass. 221, 284 N.E.2d 891 (1972) cert. denied, 409 U.S. 1108 (1973).

27. Id. 284 N.E.2d at 896.

28. Statutory Land Use Control Enabling Authority in the Fifty States, supra, note 25.

29. 356 Mass. 635, 255 N.E.2d 347 (1970).

30. Id. 255 N.E.2d at 349.

31. See a listing of home rule statutes and constitutional provisions in table 4, p. 19, Statutory Land Use Control Enabling Authority in the Fifty States, supra note 25.

32. 379 Mass. 7, 393 N.E.2d 858 (1979).

33. Id., Statutory Land Use Control Enabling Authority in Fifty States, supra, note 25, table 5 at p. 28 and discussion at p. 29.

34. Id., table 5 p. 28 and discussion at p. 26.

35. Lauricella v. Planning and Zoning Bd. of Appeals, 32 Conn. Supp. 104, 342 A.2d 374 (1974).

36. People of Smithtown v. Poveromo, 71 Misc. 2d 524, 336 N.Y.S.2d 764 (1972), rev'd on other grounds, 79 Misc. 2d 42, 359 N.Y.S.2d 848 Dist. Ct. (Sup. Ct. 1973).

37. E.g., Del. Code, Title 7, Section 6604 (1974).

38. Golden v. Board of Selectmen, 358 Mass. 519, 265 N.E.2d 573 (1970).

39. Gordon v. Reid, 43 Misc. 2d 175, 250 N.Y.S.2d 603 (Sup. Ct. 1964).

40. J.M. Mills, Inc. v. Murphy, 352 A.2d 661 (R.I. 1976).

41. 283 N.W.2d 918 (Minn. 1979).

42. See e.g., Walker v. Board of County Commissioners, 208 Md. 72, 116 A.2d 393 (1955), cert. denied, 350 U.S. 902 (1955).

43. E.g., Kozesnik v. Montgomery Township, 24 N.J. 154, 131 A.2d 1 (1957); De Meo v. Zoning Commission, 148 Conn. 68, 167 A.2d 454 (1961); Cleaver v. Board of Adjustment, 414 Pa. 367, 200 A.2d 408 (1964).

44. See generally cases cited in Annot., 58 A.L.R. 2d 1083 (1958).

45. See cases cited in D. Mandelker, "Delegation of Power and Function in Zoning," 1963 Wash. U.L.Q. 60. Mandelker comments at p. 74: "Judicial approval of nuisance standards has been overwhelming, and in many instances the fact that a noxious use is being regulated has encouraged the court to uphold the delegation."

46. 352 A.2d 661 (R.I. 1976).

47. 356 Mass. 635, 255 N.E.2d 347 (1970).

48. 362 Mass. 221, 284 N.E.2d 891 (1972) cert. denied, 409 U.S. 1108 (1973). Special exceptions were to be granted only where land was not subject to flooding or was unsuitable because of drainage conditions and the proposed use would not interfere with the general purposes of the floodplain district, or be detrimental to the public health, safety or welfare.

49. E.g., Berman v. Parker, 348 U.S. 26 (1954).

50. See, e.g., Barney & Carey Co. v. Town of Milton, 324 Mass. 440, 86 N.E.2d 9 (1949); Cooper Lumber Co. v. Dammers, 2 N.J. Misc. 289, 125 A. 325 (1924).

51. E.g., Jordan v. Village of Menomonee Falls, 28 Wis.2d 608, 137 N.W.2d 442 (1965), appeal dismissed, 385 U.S. 4 (1966).

52. See, for example, Bismark v. Village of Bayville, 49 Misc. 2d 604, 267 N.Y.S.2d 1002 (Sup. Ct. 1966) in which the court generally endorsed the adoption of regulations to protect aesthetic values but held that regulations that reduced property values by 58 percent to serve aesthetic objectives were unreasonable.

53. E.g., Long v. City of Highland Park, 329 Mich. 146, 45 N.W.2d 10 (1950); City of Miami v. Romer, 73 So. 2d 285 (Fla. 1954); Galt v. Cook County, 405 Ill. 396, 91 N.E.2d 395 (1950).

54. E.g., Headley v. City of Rochester, 272 N.Y. 197, 5 N.E.2d 198 (1936); State ex rel. Miller v. Manders, 2 Wis. 2d 365, 86 N.W.2d 469 (1957).

55. 24 Cal. App. 3d 311, 101 Cal. Rptr. 93 (1972).

56. 328 U.S. 80, 83 (1946).

57. See, e.g., Cleaners Guild v. City of Chicago, 312 Ill. App. 102, 37 N.E.2d 857 (1941); Denver & Rio Grande R.R. Co. v. City and County of Denver, 250 U.S. 241 (1919).

58. E.g., Hadacheck v. City of Los Angeles, 239 U.S. 394 (1915); Reinman v. City of Little Rock, 237 U.S. 171 (1915); Pierce Oil Corp. v. City of Hope, 248 U.S. 498 (1919).

59. 57 Cal. 2d 515, 370 P.2d 342, 20 Cal. Rptr. 638 (1962), appeal dismissed, 371 U.S. 36 (1962).

60. 270 Minn. 53, 133 N.W. 2d 500 (1964), cert. denied, 382 U.S. 14 (1965).

61. For cases generally supporting the regulation of land to protect purchasers, see Coffman v. James, 177 So.2d 25 (Fla. Dist. Ct. App. 1965); In re Sidebottom, 12 Cal. 2d 434, 85 P.2d 453 (1938), cert. denied, 307 U.S. 634 (1939). For cases upholding subdivision regulations for flood areas, see Brown v. City of Joliet, 108 Ill. App. 2d 230, 247 N.E.2d 47 (1969); and Ardolino v. Board of Adjustment of Borough of Florham Park, 24 N.J. 94, 130 A.2d 847 (1957).

62. 41 F.2d 484 (1st Cir. 1930).

63. Id., at 490.

64. 430 F.2d 199 (5th Cir. 1970), cert. denied, 401 U.S. 910 (1971). See also; P.F.Z. Properties, Inc. v. Train, 393 F. Supp. 1370 (D.D.C. 1975); Conservation Council of North Carolina v. Costanzo, 398 F. Supp. 653 (E.D.N.C. 1975), aff'd, 528 F.2d 250 (4th Cir.

1975); United States v. Joseph G. Moretti, Inc., 331 F. Supp. 151 (S.D. Fla. 1971), modified, 478 F.2d 418 (5th Cir. 1973).

65. Id. 430 F. 2d at 203-204.

66. 266 Md. 358, 293 A.2d 241 (Md. Ct. App. 1972), cert. denied, 409 U.S. 1040 (1972).

67. Id. 293 A.2d at 249.

68. Id. at 251.

69. Commissioner of Natural Resources v. S. Volpe & Co., Inc., 349 Mass. 104, 206 N.E.2d 666 (1965).

70. Sioson v. State, 111 N.H. 305, 282 A.2d 664 (1971).

71. Just v. Marinette County, 56 Wis.2d 7, 201 N.W. 2d 761 (1972).

72. 24 Cal. App. 3d 311, 101 Cal. Rptr. 93 (1972).

73. 362 Mass. 221, 284 N.E.2d 891 (1972), cert. denied, 409 U.S. 1108 (1973).

74. Id. 284 N.E.2d at 899.

75. 395 N.E.2d 880 (Mass. 1979).

76. 43 Wis. 2d 272, 168 N.W.2d 860 (1969).

77. 56 Wis. 2d 7, 201 N.W.2d at 768.

78. Id. 201 N.W.2d at 768.

79. Gordon v. Reid, 43 Misc. 2d 175, 250 N.Y.S.2d 603 (Sup. Ct. 1964); Harbor Farms, Inc. v. Nassau County Planning Commission, 334 N.Y.S.2d 412, 40 A.D.2d 517 (1972).

80. 265 A.2d 711 (Me. 1970).

81. Id. at 717.

82. See cases cited in notes 183-187 infra.

83. 56 Wis. 2d 7, 201 N.W.2d 761 (1972).

84. 336 A.2d 239 (N.H. 1975).

85. Graham v. Estuary Properties, Inc., 399 So. 2d 1374 (Fla. 1981).

86. See, e.g., State v. Heller, 123 Conn. 492, 196 A. 337 (1937) where the Court sustained a Connecticut statute prohibiting anyone from bathing in any stream or tributary to a city water reservoir.

87. 249 U.S. 510 (1919).

88. 393 N.E.2d 858 (Mass. 1979).

89. Id. 393 N.E.2d at 865.

90. See, e.g., Kozesnik v. Montgomery Township, 24 N.J. 154, 131 A.2d 1 (1957).

91. E.g., Zahn v. Board of Public Works, 195 Cal. 497, 234 P. 388 (1925), aff'd, 274 U.S. 325 (1927).

92. E.g., Scarborough v. Mayor & Council, 303 A.2d 701 (Del. Ch. 1973); Ann Arundel County v. Ward, 186 Md. 330, 46 A.2d 684 (1946); Town of Marblehead v. Rosenthal, 316 Mass. 124, 55 N.E.2d 13 (1944).

93. In Re Sports Complex in Hackensack Meadowland, 62 N.J. 248, 300 A.2d 337 (1973), cert. denied, 414 U.S. 989 (1973).

94. 136 N.J. Super. 436, 346 A.2d 612 (Super. Ct. App. Div. 1975).

95. Id. 346 A.2d at 614.

96. 266 Md. 358, 293 A.2d 241 (Md. Ct. App. 1972), cert. denied, 409 U.S. 1040 (1972).

97. 352 A.2d 661 (R.I. 1976).

98. 95 W. Va. 377, 121 S.E. 165 (1924).

99. 40 N.J. 539, 193 A.2d 232 (1963).

100. E.g., Nectow v. City of Cambridge, 277 U.S. 183 (1928).

101. Sturdy Homes, Inc. v. Town of Redford, 30 Mich. App. 53, 186 N.W.2d 43 (1971).

102. Kesselring v. Wakefield Realty Co., Inc., 306 Ky. 725, 209 S.W.2d 63 (1948).

103. E.g., North Suburban Sanitary Sewer Dist. v.

Water Pollution Control Commission, 281 Minn. 524, 162 N.W.2d 249 (1968); Zoning Bd. of Adjustment v. Dragon Run Terrance, Inc., 222 A.2d 315 (Del. 1966).

104.   123 Conn. 275, 193 A. 754, 759 (1937).

105.   Just v. Marinette County, 56 Wis. 2d 7, 201 N.W.2d 761 (1972).

106.   Id. 201 N.W.2d at 766. The court at this point quotes section 2.29 of the county ordinance.

107.   137 N.J. Super. 179, 348 A.2d 540 (Super. Ct. App. Div. 1975).

108.   384 A.2d 610 (R.I. 1978).

109.   261 Iowa 1287, 158 N.W.2d 111 (1968).

110.   30 Mich. App. 53, 186 N.W.2d 43 (1971).

111.   361 Mass. 221, 284 N.E.2d 891 (1972), cert. denied, 409 U.S. 1108 (1973).

112.   270 Md. 652, 313 A.2d 820 (1974).

113.   Morris County Land Improvement Co. v. Parsippany-Troy Hills Township, 40 N.J. 539, 193 A.2d 232 (1963).

114.   Dooley v. Town Plan and Zoning Commission, 151 Conn. 304, 197 A.2d 770 (1964).

115.   32 Wis. 2d 608, 146 N.W.2d 577 (1966).

116.   Id. 146 N.W.2d at 589.

117.   Candlestick Properties, Inc. v. San Francisco Bay Conservation and Development Commission, 11 Cal. App. 3d 557, 89 Cal. Rptr. 897 (1970).

118.   149 F. Supp. 771 (D. Md. 1957), aff'd., 355 U.S. 37 (1957).

119.   Id. at 774.

120.   See, e.g., National Land & Investment Co. v. Kohn, 419 Pa. 504, 215 A.2d 597 (1965) in which the court held invalid four acre minimum lot size zoning for a county, despite arguments by the county that the cumulative effects of higher density development would, over a period of years, cause water pollution. The court was dissatisfied with the evidence of potential pollution in the case and the hypothesis that the entire township would be developed. Similarly, a Michigan court in Christine Bldg. Co. v. City of Troy, 367 Mich. 508, 116 N.W.2d 816 (1962) disagreed with arguments of long term anticipated development to justify present restrictions.

121.   657 F.2d 1184 (1981).

122.   Id. at 1194.

123.   372 N.Y.S.2d 146 (1975).

124.   119 N.Y.S. Super. 572, 293 A.2d 192 (1972).

125.   See J. Kusler, "Open Space Zoning: Valid Regulation or Invalid Taking", 57 Minn. L. Rev. 1 (1972). J. Sax, "Takings and the Police Power," 74 Yale L. J. 36 (1964).

126.   136 N.J. Super. 436, 346 A.2d 612 (Super. Ct. App. Div. 1975).

127.   266 Md. 358, 293 A.2d 241 (Md. Ct. App. 1972), cert. denied, 409 U.S. 1040 (1972).

128.   80 U.S. 166 (1871).

129.   Lorio v. Sea Isle City, 88 N.J. Super. 506, 212 A.2d 802 (1965).

130.   260 U.S. 393 (1922).

131.   Id. at 413.

132.   Goldblatt v. Town of Hempstead, 369 U.S. 590 (1962).

133.   See, e.g., Commissioner of Natural Resources v. S. Volpe & Co., Inc., 349 Mass. 104, 206 N.E.2d 666 (1965); Morris County Land Improvement Co. v. Parsippany-Troy Hills Township, 40 N.J. 539, 193 A.2d 232 (1963).

134.   336 A.2d 239 (N.H. 1975).

135.   Id. at 241.

136.   349 Mass. 104, 206 N.E.2d 666 (1965).

137.   Id. 206 N.E.2d at 669.

138.   208 Md. 72, 116 A.2d 393 (1955), cert. denied, 350 U.S. 902 (1955).

139.   Id. 166 A.2d at 405.

140.   349 Mass. 104, 206 N.E.2d 666 (1965).

141.   Id. 206 N.E.2d at 671-672.

142.   See generally, Cleaners Guild v. City of Chicago, 312 Ill. App. 102, 37 N.E.2d 857 (1941).

143.   369 U.S. 590 (1962).

144.   41 Cal. 2d 879, 264 P.2d 932 (1953), cert. denied, 348 U.S. 817 (1954).

145.   Id. 264 P.2d at 937.

146.   46 N.J. 479, 218 A.2d 129 (1966), cert. denied, 385 U.S. 831 (1966).

147.   Id. 218 A.2d at 137.

148.   Id.

149.   57 Cal. 2d 515, 370 P.2d 342, 20 Cal. Rptr. 638 (1962), appeal dismissed, 371 U.S. 36 (1962).

150.   Id. 370 P.2d at 348.

151.   123 U.S. 623 (1887).

152.   Id. at 669.

153.   357 S.W.2d 303 (1962).

154.   Id. at 305.

155.   270 Minn. 53, 133 N.W.2d 500 (1964), cert. denied, 382 U.S. 14 (1965).

156.   Id. 133 N.W.2d at 505.

157.   146 Conn. 650, 153 A.2d 822 (1959).

158.   56 Wis. 2d 7, 201 N.W.2d 761 (1972).

159.   362 Mass. 221, 284 N.E.2d 891 (1972), cert. denied, 409 U.S. 1108 (1973).

160.   40 N.J. 539, 193 A.2d 232 (1963).

161.   E.g., Gorieb v. Fox, 274 U.S. 603 (1927); State ex rel. McKusick v. Houghton, 171 Minn. 231, 213 N.W.2d 907 (1927); Sierra Construction Co. v. Board of Appeals, 12 N.Y.2d 79, 187 N.E.2d 123, 236 N.Y.S.2d 53 (1962).

162.   E.g., Headley v. Rochester, 272 N.Y. 197, 5 N.E.2d 198 (1936); State ex rel. Miller v. Manders, 2 Wis. 2d 365, 86 N.W.2d 469 (1957).

163.   438 U.S. 104 (1978).

164.   Id. at 130-131.

165.   Deltona Corporation v. United States, 657 F.2d 1184 (1981); Jentgen v. United States, 657 F.2d 1210 (1981).

166.   161 N.J. Super. 504, 391 A.2d 1265 (1978).

167.   Id. 391 A.2d at 1270.

168.   E.g., State ex rel. Grant v. Kiefaber, 114 Ohio App. 279, 181 N.E.2d 905 (1960), aff'd., 171 Ohio St. 326, 170 N.E.2d 848 (1960).

169.   E.g., County Commissioners v. Miles, 246 Md. 355, 228 A.2d 450 (1967) (Coastal area).

170.   199 Misc. 485, 99 N.Y.S.2d 280, 285 (Sup. Ct. 1950).

171.   294 N.W.2d 654 (S.D. 1980).

172.   Id. 294 N.W.2d at 656.

173.   Id.

174.   Id.

175.   Id. 294 N.W.2d at 657.

176.   399 So.2d 1374 (Fla. 1981).

177.   Id., 399 So.2d at 1381, 1382.

178.   392 A.2d 582 (N.H. 1978).

179.   Id. 393 A.2d at 584, 585.

180.   Id. 392 A.2d at 586.

181. 180 Conn. 692, 433 A.2d 999 (1980).
182. Id. 433 A.2d at 1001.
183. 336 A.2d 239 (N.H. 1975).
184. 15 Mich. App. 556, 167 N.W.2d 311 (1969).
185. 71 Misc. 2d 524, 336 N.Y.S.2d 764 (Dist. Ct. 1972), rev'd on other grounds, 79 Misc. 42, 359 N.Y.S.2d 848 (Sup. Ct. 1973).
186. 430 F.2d 199 (5th Cir. 1970), cert. denied, 401 U.S. 910 (1971).
187. Id. at 215.
188. See generally, J. Sax, "The Public Trust Doctrine in Natural Resource Law: Effective Judicial Intervention," 68 Mich. L. Rev. 471 (1970); "The Public Trust in Tidal Areas: A Sometimes Submerged Traditional Doctrine," 79 Yale L.J. 762 (1970); "The State Navigation Servitude," 4 Land and Water L. Rev. 521 (1969).
189. Id. See, e.g., Just v. Marinette County, 56 Wis.2d 7, 201 N.W.2d 761 (1972).
190. 56 Wis. 2d 7, 201 N.W.2d 781 (1972).
191. Id. 201 N.W.2d at 771.
192. Id. at 767 and 768.
193. Id. at 768.
194. Id. at 771.
195. 336 A.2d 239 (N.H. 1975).
196. E.g., State v. Dexter, 32 Wash. 2d 551, 202 P.2d 906, aff'd. per curiam, 338 U.S. 863 (1949).
197. E.g., Lindsley v. Natural Carbonic Gas Co., 220 U.S. 61 (1911); Ohio Oil Co. v. Indiana, 177 U.S. 190 (1900).

CHAPTER 10

1. Several excellent studies explore State differential assessment programs in greater detail. See J. C. Keene, et al., Untaxing Open Space/An Evaluation of the Effectiveness of Differential Assessment of Farms and Open Space, prepared for the U.S. Council on Environmental Quality (Washington, D.C.: U.S. Government Printing Office, April 1976); T. F. Hardy and A. G. Sibold, "State Programs for the Differential Assessment of Farm and Open Space Land," Agricultural Economic Report No. 256 (Washington, D.C.: Economic Research Service, U.S. Department of Agriculture, April 1974); and R. Barlowe and T. R. Alter, "Use-Value Assessment of Farm and Open Space Lands," Michigan State University Agricultural Experiment Station Research Report 308 (East Lansing, Michigan: September 1976).
2. There are additional distinctions among the three kinds of differential assessment laws. For example, States differ in their definition of eligible agricultural land or open space. In some States, the local land use planning or zoning ordinances must designate the land for the eligible uses. Penalty provisions for conversion of land to noneligible uses also vary from State to State. Tax rollback provisions recoup deferred taxes for periods ranging from two to 15 years prior to the conversion, and some States charge interest on the deferred taxes. In several States, landowners must apply for preferential taxation; but in most States with pure preferential assessment schemes, the preferential assessment is automatically applied to eligible lands.
3. See Hardy, supra note 1, at 11.
4. See Barlowe, supra note 1, at 33.
5. Mississippi and Connecticut also have adopted preferential tax provisions that specifically apply to wetlands, but these provisions do not serve as a true tax incentive since they come into operation not at the option of the landowner but only where regulations are exercised by the State.

The preferential assessment provision in the Connecticut wetlands statute states that any wetland owner, who is denied a permit to modify or develop the wetland, can apply to the local assessor for a revaluation of the property to reflect its fair market value in light of the use restrictions (Conn. Gen. Stat., Section 22a-36, et seq. (1975)). In actuality, one expert estimates that 95 to 97 percent of all permits for development in wetland areas in Connecticut have been accepted. In the small number of instances in which permits have been denied, there has been no follow-up to determine whether the provisions for tax relief have been used. Since an individual cannot apply for a permit to modify the wetland without coming in with fully developed plans, maps, and charts, it seems clear that anyone applying for a development permit has made a commitment to development and will not view the tax provision as a true incentive but only as a technique for relieving a burden imposed by the regulation. Consequently, Connecticut's general differential assessment statute, not its wetland statute, offers a far greater incentive for wetland protection. Indeed, when wetland development has been prevented because of government-imposed regulations, a developer may best donate the land to a charitable organization or governmental body, thereby qualifying for a charitable donation, rather than hold property with reduced property taxes. Tax advantages stemming from charitable donations are discussed elsewhere in the text.

Another example of a special wetland tax provision is found in the Mississippi Coastal Wetland Protection Act, which excludes coastal wetlands from assessment for ad valorem, or property taxes (Miss. Code Ann. Section 49-27-67) (Supp. 1980)). However, other sections of the statute may make this provision unnecessary. These sections establish that certain coastal wetlands are public trust lands and, therefore, neither owned by private individuals nor subject to property taxes.
6. N. Y. Envir. Conserv. Law Section 24-0905 (McKinney Supp. 1980). The New York Tidal Wetlands Act also contains a provision for use valuation of tidal wetlands the use of which has been restricted because of a development permit denial (N. Y. Envir. Conserv. Law Section 25-0302-2 (McKinney Supp. 1980)). Like the Connecticut provision, however, this language helps relieve the burden on landowners rather than offer a true incentive.
7. Mass. Gen. Laws Ch. 131, Section 40A.
8. Mass. Gen. Laws Ch. 130, Section 105.
9. Mass. Gen. Laws Ch. 59, Section 11.
10. Examples of conservation restrictions are set forth in Appendix D.
11. Mass. Gen. Laws Ch. 184, Sections 23-33.
12. Mass Gen. Laws Ch. 59, Section 11.
13. Lodge v. Swampscott, 216 Mass. 260, 103 N.E. 635 (1913).
14. I.R.C. Section 170(b)(1)(C)(i).
15. I.R.C. Section 170(b)(1)(C)(ii).
16. I.R.C. Section 170(b)(1)(C)(iii).

17. I.R.C. Section 170(f)(3)(B).
18. The valuation of remainder interests in real property for contributions made after July 31, 1969, are set out in the tables in Income Tax Regulations 1.170 A-12. Standards for valuing easements in gross (easements that give a personal interest in or right to use land) in perpetuity are illustrated in several revenue rulings.
19. 94 Stat. 3207.
20. I.R.C. Section 2055(a).
21. I.R.C. Section 2055(e)(2).
22. I.R.C. Section 2522(a)(2).
23. I.R.C. Section 2522(c)(2), which refers to Section 170f(B)(3).
24. See The Nature Conservancy, "Tools for the Protection of Natural Diversity," draft, pp. 1-13. Language to help mitigate this problem is included in a land acquisition statute adopted by Ohio. In order to protect a certain State-controlled natural area from improper use by agencies that have no stake in their protection, the Ohio statute prohibits the land from being "taken for any other use except another public use after a finding . . . of the existence of an imperative and unavoidable public necessity for such other public use, and with the approval of the governor" (emphasis added). Ohio Rev. Code Ann. Section 1517.06 (Page). See The Nature Conservancy, supra, pp. 15-16.
25. 50 Stat. 917 (1937).
26. 64 Stat. 430 (1950).
27. 16 U.S.C. Section 1455a(b) (Supp. 1980).
28. 42 U.S.C. Section 4601 et seq. (1977).
29. 42 U.S.C. Section 4651 (1977).

CHAPTER 11

1. R. Kennedy, "Eden Fights Back," Sports Illustrated, February 3, 1975, p. 29.
2. For a review of the Sanibel comprehensive plan, see J. Clark, The Sanibel Report: Formulation of a Comprehensive Plan Based on Natural Resources (Washington, D.C.: The Conservation Foundation, 1977).
3. Mass. Gen. Laws, Ch. 214, Section 7A.
4. See Natural Resources Defense Council, Land Use Controls in the United States/A Handbook on the Legal Rights of Citizens (New York: The Dial Press, 1977) for a discussion of a citizen action in enforcing regulations that control land use. This section draws heavily from that book.

5. 42 U.S.C.A. Section 4321 et seq. (1977); and ELR Stats. & Regs. 41009 et seq.
6. N. C. Yost, "State Legislation Patterned on NEPA—Overview", The Environmental Impact Statement Process Under NEPA, a conference co-sponsored by the Center for Administrative Justice of the American Bar Association and the Environmental Law Institute (Washington, D.C.: June 3-5, 1976).
7. 33 U.S.C. Section 1251 et seq. (1978); and ELR Stats. & Regs. 42101 et seq.
8. 33 U.S.C. Section 407; and ELR Stats. & Regs. 41141.
9. See Natural Resources Defense Council v. Callaway, 392 F. Supp. 685, 5 ELR 20285 (D.D.C. 1975); Report on Application for Department of the Army Permits to Dredge and Fill at Marco Island, Florida, 6 ELR 30020 (Chief of Engineers, Dept. of the Army, Apr. 15, 1976).
10. 16 U.S.C. Section 1451 et seq. (1974 & Supp. 1980); and ELR Stats. & Regs. 41701 et seq.
11. Other legal issues, such as the jurisdiction of the court to hear the lawsuit, also exist, but they are best explained in the specific context of a proposed lawsuit, not through generalizations.
12. 33 U.S.C. Section 1365 (1978); and ELR Stats. and Regs. 42147.
13. See J. F. DiMento, "Citizen Environmental Legislation In the States: An Overview," 53 Journal of Urban Law, 413, 460 (February, 1976).
14. Wash. Rev. Code, Section 90.58 et seq. (Supp. 1980).
15. Cal. Pub. Res. Code, Section 30000 et seq. (1977 and Supp. 1980).
16. See J. Sax, "The Public Trust Doctrine in Natural Resource Law: Effective Judicial Intervention," 68 Mich. L. Rev. 471 (1970), for a discussion of the origin of the public trust doctrine.
17. DiMento, supra note 13.
18. See, for example, Boomer v. Atlantic Cement Co., 26 N.Y.2d 219, 309 N.Y.S.2d 312, 257 N.E.2d 870 (1970) which denied injunctive relief to a private plaintiff when the injury to the defendant caused by the injunction would be unduly harsh in comparison with the injuries suffered by the plaintiff.
19. Wash. Rev. Code, Section 90.58.230 (Supp. 1980).
20. Cal. Pub. Res. Code, Section 30805 (1977 and Supp. 1980).
21. Fla. Stat. Ann., Section 403.412(2) (1973).
22. R. I. Gen Laws, Section 11-46.1-1 (1981).

APPENDIX A
GUIDE TO FEDERAL WETLANDS-RELATED PROGRAMS
DEPARTMENT OF AGRICULTURE

Soil Conservation Service

Rural Clean Water Program

Secretary authorized to enter into contracts lasting 5-10 years with rural landowners or operators, to share costs of implementing Best Management Practices under an approved §208 plan.

- o   Authority: 33 U.S.C. §1288, as amended.
- o   Contact: Soil Conservation Service, USDA, Washington, D.C. 20205; (202) 447-2470.

Small Watershed Management

Technical and cost sharing assistance provided to States and localities for agricultural water management projects, which may affect wetlands.
- o   Authority: Small Watershed Project Act (Watershed Protection and Flood Prevention Act), 43 U.S.C. §422a-422h.
- o   Contact: Deputy Administrator's Office, Natural Resource's Project, SCS, P.O. Box 2890, Washington, D.C. 20013; (202) 447-4527

Rural Development Act

SCS authorized to inventory, monitor, and classify wetlands. Various inventories have been conducted.
- o   Authority: 7 U.S.C. §1010a.
- o   Contact: Soil Conservation Service, Rural Development Staff, P.O. Box 2890, Washington, D.C. 20013; (202) 382-1861.

Agriculture Stabilization and Conservation Service

Water Bank Act of 1970

Secretary authorized to enter into 10-year contracts with landowners for preservation of wetlands determined to be important for the nesting and breeding of migratory waterfowl.
Annual fee paid to landowners.
- o   Authority: 16 U.S.C. §§1301-1311.
- o   Contact: Conservation & Environmental Protection Division, USDA-ASCS (Agriculture Stabilization Conservation Service), P.O. Box 2415, Washington, D.C. 20013; (202) 447-6221.

Agriculture and Conservation Program

Designed, in part, to preserve habitat of migratory waterfowl and other wildlife, increase fish and wildlife and recreation resources, promote management and planning, and improve game habitat, through contracts and easements with landowners.
- o   Authority: Agriculture and Consumer Protection Act, 16 U.S.C. §§1501-1510.
- o   Contact: Conservation & Environmental Protection Division, USDA-ASCS, P.O. Box 2415, Washington, D.C.; (202) 447-7333.

Forest Service

Renewable Resources Planning Act

Requires assessment of all renewable resources on all U.S. forest and range lands, including wetlands.
- o   Authority: 16 U.S.C. §§1600-1614.
- o   Contact: Forest Service, USDA, P.O. 2417, Washington, D.C. 20012; (202) 447-6663.

Land and Water Conservation Fund Act

The fund provides for the purchase of outdoor recreation areas. At least 40% of the fund must be used for Federal purposes; the rest goes to the States as matching grants. The Federal portion of this fund is allocated directly to BLM, the Fish & Wildlife Service, the Forest Service and the National Park Service.

- o Authority: 16 U.S.C. §§4601-4 to 4601-11.
- o Contact: Land Staff, U.S. Forest Service, P.O. Box 2417, Room 1010 (RP-E), Washington, D.C. 20013; (202) 235-8212.

DEPARTMENT OF COMMERCE

Office of Coastal Zone Management

Coastal Zone Management Act

Provides Federal grants for development of coastal management and preservation programs, including the planning for the impact of offshore energy development on coastal States (Coastal Energy Impact Program).
- o Authority: 16 U.S.C. §§1454-1456a.
- o Contact: OCZM, 3300 Whitehaven St., N.W., Washington, D.C. 20235; (202) 634-4235.

Estuarine Sanctuary Program

Provides matching grants to States for acquisition of acreas to be maintained and operated as estuarine sanctuaries.
- o Authority: 16 U.S.C. §1461.
- o Contact: Estuarine Sanctuary Program, 2001 Wisconsin Ave., N.W., Washington, D.C. 20235; (202) 634-4236.

Marine Sanctuary Program

Authorizes designation of marine areas as sanctuaries in order to preserve, restore, or enhance conservation, recreation, ecological or aesthetic values of these water resources.
- o Authority: 16 U.S.C. §§1431-1434.
- o Contact: (See above contact).

National Marine Fisheries Service

Fish and Wildlife Coordination Act

Review of activities, by the Federal government or requiring Federal permits, in wetlands, with respect to impacts on fish resources.
- o Authority: 16 U.S.C. §§661-661c.
- o Contact: Environmental Assessment Division (F-53), NMFS, 3300 Whitehaven St., N.W., Washington, D.C. 20235; (202) 634-7490.

COUNCIL ON ENVIRONMENTAL QUALITY

National Environmental Policy

Responsible for receiving and reviewing Environmental Impact Statements; sponsors research and advise the President.
- o Authority: NEPA, 42 U.S.C. §§4321 et seq.; Environmental Quality Improvement Act, 42 U.S.C. §§4371 et seq.
- o Contact: Council on Environmental Quality, General Counsel's Office, 722 Jackson Place, N.W., Washington, D.C. 20006; (202) 395-5754.

DEPARTMENT OF DEFENSE

Army Corps of Engineers

Clean Water Act §404

Provides jurisdiction over discharges of dredged and fill material into the waters of the United States, which includes wetlands contiguous or adjacent to navigable waters and their tributaries. If States adopt an EPA-approved program, Corps jurisdiction restricted to navigable waters and adjacent wetlands. Coordination with EPA required (see below).
- o Authority: 33 U.S.C. §1344.
- o Contact: U.S. Army Corps of Engineers, Construction Operations Division, Regulations Branch, Office of Chief Engineer, 20 Massachusetts Ave., N.W., Washington, D.C. 20314; (202) 272-0200.

Rivers and Harbors Act of 1899

    Authorizes permits for structures and discharges in navigable waters, considering navigation, flood control, fish and wildlife management, and environmental impacts.
- o   Authority: 33 U.S.C. §§401, 403, 404, 406, 407.
- o   Contact: (See above contact).

Dredged Material Research Program

    Conducts research on the disposal and reuse of dredged material in order to minimize adverse impacts on wetlands.
- o   Authority: 33 U.S.C. §1165a.
- o   Contact: (See above contact).

ENVIRONMENTAL PROTECTION AGENCY

Clean Water Act §404

    EPA and Corps must set §404(b)(1) guidelines regulating the discharge of dredged and fill material in sensitive areas. EPA also reviews Federal projects claimed to be exempt under §404(r). Under §404(c), EPA may prohibit use of a specific site for the disposal of dredged material on the basis of environmental impacts. EPA is also responsible for overseeing the transition of authority to States which develop §404 permit programs that meet EPA's regulatory requirements.
- o   Authority: 33 U.S.C. §1344.
- o   Contact: EPA, Aquatic Protection Branch (A-104), 401 M Street, S.W., Washington, D.C. 20460; (202) 472-2798.

Clean Water Act §208

    Plans may now regulate certain discharges of dredged and fill material, where State has an approved §404 program, in accordance with Best Management Practices. Also governs water quality of areas under areawide waste treatment plans. Grants available, §§205, 208.
- o   Authority: 33 U.S.C. §§1285,1288.
- o   Contact: EPA, Office of Federal Activities (A-104), 401 M Street, S.W., Washington, D.C. 20460; (202) 755-0770.

Safe Drinking Water Act

    EPA may designate an aquifer as a principal water supply source, requiring review of any project affecting the aquifer; no Federal assistance to project if it would contaminate the water source.
- o   Authority: Safe Drinking Water Act §144c.
- o   Contact: EPA, State Programs Division (WH-550), 401 M Street, S.W., Washington, D.C. 20460; (202) 426-8290.

Research and Development

    Conducts research on various aspects of wetlands pollution, etc.
- o   Contact: EPA, Wetlands Research Coordinator, Environmental Research Lab, 200 S.W. 35th St., Corvallis, OR 97330; (503) 757-4764.

FEDERAL EMERGENCY MANAGEMENT AGENCY

National Flood Insurance Program

    Provision for a flood insurance program to provide Federally-subsidized insurance against loss of real or personal property due to floods or the results of floods. To qualify for insurance, communities must adopt land use regulations which meet Federal standards.
- o   Authority: 42 U.S.C. §§4001-4128; Housing and Community Development Act.
- o   Contact: Federal Insurance Administration, Federal Emergency Management Agency, 500 C Street, S.W., Washington, D.C. 20472; (202) 287-0750.

DEPARTMENT OF HOUSING AND URBAN DEVELOPMENT

Interstate Land Sales Full Disclosure Act of 1973

Interstate Land Sales Office requires distribution to purchasers of subdivision lots of a report stating, among other things, whether or not dredge and fill permits needed.

- o   Authority: 15 U.S.C. §§1701-1720.
- o   Contact: Office of Interstate Land Sale Office, HUD Building, 451 7th Street, S.W., Washington, D.C. 20410; (202) 755-5860.

DEPARTMENT OF THE INTERIOR

Bureau of Land Management

Public Lands

Requires protection, maintenance, and enhancement of wildlife habitats on the public lands; BLM must prepare Habitat Management Plans.

- o   Authority: Federal Land Policy and Management Act, 43 U.S.C. §§1701 et seq.
- o   Contact: Division of Wildlife, BLM, Dept. of the Interior, 18 & C Streets, N.W., Washington, D.C. 20240; (202) 653-9202.

Land and Water Conservation Fund Act
The fund provides for the purchase of outdoor recreation areas. At least 40% of the fund must be used for Federal purposes; the rest goes to the States as matching grants. The Federal portion of the fund is allocated directly by Congress to BLM, the Fish & Wildlife Service, the Forest Service and the National Park Service.

- o   Authority: 16 U.S.C. §§4601-4 to 4601-11.
- o   Contact: Office of the Asst. Director of Land Resources, BLM (310), Dept. of the Interior, Washington, D.C. 20240; (202) 343-6757.

Bureau of Reclamation

Reclamation Act

Constructs and operates irrigation, flood control, and power projects in 17 western States; operates fish and wildlife sanctuaries on reclamation land.

- o   Authority: Reclamation Act, 43 U.S.C. §§411 et seq.
- o   Contact: Office of Environmental Affairs, Bureau of Reclamation Dept. of the Interior, Washington, D.C. 20240; (202) 343-4991; or the Operation & Maintenance Staff, Land Resources Management Branch, Bureau of Reclamation, Dept. of the Interior, Washington, D.C. 20240; (202) 343-5204.

Fish and Wildlife Service

Land and Water Resource Development Planning Program

Consultation required on impacts on fish and wildlife of any Federal agency action which will modify waters of the U.S.

- o   Authority: Fish and Wildlife Coordination Act, 16 U.S.C. §§661-666C.
- o   Contact: Branch of Permits and Licenses, Fish and Wildlife Services (E.S.), Dept. of the Interior, Washington, D.C. 20240; (202) 343-8814.

National Wetlands Inventory Project

Classifying, identifying, and mapping wetlands, in order to create a data base to aid management, particularly by the States.

- o   Authority: Fish and Wildlife Act, 16, U.S.C. §§742a et seq.; Fish and Wildlife Coordination Act, 16 U.S.C. §§661-666c.
- o   Contact: Office of Biological Services, Fish and Wildlife Services, Dept. of the Interior, Washington, D.C. 20240; (202) 343-4767.

Coastal Ecosystem Project

Studying special problems associated with coastal areas.

- o   Contact: Office of Biological Services, (see above contact).

Clean Water Act §§208, 404

Required to assist States in developing dredge and fill programs under §208; must review State 404 programs prior to EPA approval.
- o   Authority: 33 U.S.C. §§1288, 1344.
- o   Contact: Division of Ecological Services, Fish and Wildlife Services, Dept. of the Interior, Washington, D.C. 20240; (202) 343-4767.

Migratory Bird Program

Authorizes inventory of significant waterfowl habitats and purchase in fee or easement of land necessary for refuges. Waterfowl Production Areas purchased.
- o   Authority: Migratory Bird Conservation Act, Wetland Acquisition Act, 16 U.S.C. §§715a-715s; Migratory Bird Hunting Stamp Act, 16 U.S.C. §718.
- o   Contact: Office of Migratory Bird Management, Fish and Wildlife Services, Dept. of the Interior, Washington, D.C. 20240; (202) 254-3207.

Endangered Species Act

Protects and restores threatened and endangered species and their critical habitats; provides for permit program for import/export of certain animals. Federal actions must avoid harm to species and their habitats; if differences between Office and project sponsor irreconcilable, Endangered Species Committee rules on whether or not project should be exempt from Act.
- o   Authority: 16 U.S.C. §§1531 et seq. as amended.
- o   Contact: Office of Endangered Species, U.S. Fish and Wildlife Services, 1000 North Glebe Road, Arlington, VA 22207; (703) 235-2771.

Water Resources Analysis Project

Studies the effect of instream flow on fish species; produces River Reach Files and maps which evaluate the nation's streams as fish habitats.
- o   Contact: Office of Biological Services, (see above contact).

Land and Water Conservation Fund Act

The fund provides for the purchase of land primarily for the protection of fish and wildlife and endangered or threatened species but also for outdoor recreation. Allows purchase of fee and easement interests in land for the protection of fish and wildlife and endangered and threatened species. Administered by Heritage Conservation and Recreation Service (see below). At least 40% of the fund must be used for Federal purposes; the rest goes to the States as matching grants. The Federal portion of the fund is allocated by Congress directly to BLM, the Fish & Wildlife Service, Forest Service, & the National Park Service.
- o   Authority: 16 U.S.C. §§4601-4 to 4601-11.
- o   Contact: Division of Realty, Fish and Wildlife Services, Dept. of the Interior, Washington, D.C. 20240; (202) 272-3365.

Pittman-Robinson and Dingell-Johnson Acts.

Grants-in-aid all available to the States for habitat and species restoration.
- o   Authority: Federal Aid to Wildlife Restoration Act, 16 U.S.C. §§669-669i; Federal Aid to Fish Restoration Act, 16 U.S.C. §§669-669i; Federal Aid to Fish Restoration Act, 16 U.S.C. §§777-777k.
- o   Contact: Associate Director Federal Assistance, Fish and Wildlife Services (AFA), Dept. of the Interior, Washington, D.C. 20240; (202) 343-4646.

Geological Survey

Surveys

Has collected and analyzed land use data, and has mapped and classified wetlands.
- o   Authority: Varied.
- o   Contact: Geological Research, USGS, Mail Stop 521, Reston, VA 22092; (703) 860-6341, or, Water Resources Division, Branch of Surface Water, Wetlands Research, (703) 860-6892.

National Park Service

National Park System

     The Service maintains the Park System, and studies areas for nationally significant natural areas that may qualify as natural landmarks or parks.
- o   Authority: 16 U.S.C. §§1-3, and 461.
- o   Contact: Natural Landmarks and Theme Studies Unit, National Park Service, Denver Service Center, P.O. Box 25287, Denver, CO 80225; (303) 234-4500.

Land and Water Conservation Fund Act

     The fund provides for the purchase of outdoor recreation areas. At least 40% of the fund must be used for Federal purposes; the rest goes to the States as matching grants. The Federal portion of this fund is allocated directly to BLM, the Fish & Wildlife Services the Forest Service and the National Park Service.
- o   Authority: 16 U.S.C. §§4601-4 to 4601-11.
- o   Contact: Land Resources Division, National Park Service, Dept. of the Interior, Washington, D.C. 20240; (202) 523-5252.
     The National Park Service also administers the State matching grant sections of this Act.
- o   Contact: State and Urban Programs, National Park Service, 440 G Street, N.W., Washington, D.C. 20240.

Office of Water Research and Technology

Water Resources Research Act

     Grants and matching grants assist research on water-related problems of interest to the States and regions.
- o   Authority: 42 U.S.C. §§1961a-1961c.
- o   Contact: Office of Water Research and Technology, Dept. of the Interior, Washington, D.C. 20240; (202) 343-5975.

TENNESSEE VALLEY AUTHORITY

TVA Projects

     Manages reservoir system containing wetlands; involved in fisheries and wildlife management in that context.
- o   Authority: 16 U.S.C. §831.
- o   Contact: Office of Natural Resources, Div. of Water Resources, END Bldg., Muscle Shoal, Alabama 35660; (205) 386-2276.

DEPARTMENT OF TRANSPORTATION

Preservation of the Nation's Wetlands

     Policy to protect wetlands to fullest extent possible during planning, construction, and operation of Federal and Federally-financed projects. May assist in acquisition or mitigation where destruction of wetlands inevitable.
- o   Authority: DOT Order 5660. 1A
- o   Contact: Environmental Division, Office of Economics (P-37), 400 7th Str., S.W. Washington, D.C. 20590; (202) 426-4366; or, Office of Environmental Policy HEV1, Nassif Building, Washington, D.C. 20540; (202) 426-0160.

APPENDIX B

EXAMPLES OF WETLAND PROTECTION ORDINANCES

Several model wetland protection ordinances developed by other studies and several local ordinances actually adopted by communities are included in the following materials to suggest alternative approaches to the draft ordinances contained in Appendix C of the present report. The rationale for inclusion of each is explained below.

1. Wetland Protection Provisions: Model Shoreland Protection Ordinance, Wisconsin Department of Natural Resources, 1967. The wetland protection provisions are contained in a broader shoreland protection ordinance adopted by many of the 72 Wisconsin counties. It is a brief, straightforward ordinance for use with wetland maps based either on USGS topographic maps or soil surveys. Similar wetland zoning provisions were sustained by the Wisconsin court in Just v. Marinette Co., 56 Wis. 2d 7, 201 N.W. 2d 761 (1972).

2. Model Wetland Ordinance contained in the Virginia Coastal Wetland Protection Statute, Va. Code §§62.1-13.1 to 62.1-13.20. This is the only model ordinance contained in an enabling statute. It is a relatively brief but sophisticated ordinance applying to coastal areas and has been adopted by at least 25 local governments.

3. Wetland Protection Provisions, Village of Orono, Minnesota. This is an adopted ordinance applying to inland wetland areas. USGS maps are used for defining wetland areas. Several amendments to the ordinance have not been reproduced here. This ordinance is one of the more extensive local ordinances reviewed in the present report. It has a particularly detailed statement of purposes and standards for uses.

Wetland Protection Provisions Model Shoreland Ordinance Promulgated by the Wisconsin Department of Natural Resources in 1967 and Adopted By Many Counties.

Section 12.0 Conservancy District

12.1 Designation. This district includes all shorelands designated as swamps or marshes on the United States Geological Survey Quadrangle map sheets which have been designated the Shoreland Zoning Map of _____ County, Wisconsin or on the detailed Insert Shoreland Zoning Maps.

Or In the Alternative

This district shall include all lands within the jurisdiction of this ordinance which are designated on map sheets 1 through ___ inclusive of the Soil Survey ___ County, Wisconsin. (USDA SCS Series ___, No. ___) by the following letter symbols:

Map Symbol   Map Unit Name
1.
2.
3.

12.2 Purpose. Wetlands are areas where groundwater is at or near the surface much of the year. Tamarack, sphagnum moss, sedge, cattail, reed and bullrush are typical wetland vegetation types. Wetlands are seldom suitable for building for the following reasons:
(1) Septic tank systems will not function because of high groundwater; (2) Water supplies are often polluted by septic tank wastes that have not been adequately absorbed by the soil; (3) Foundations and roads crack due to poor support capabilities and frost action; (4) Flooding is common in spring and other times of high water. Filling rarely solves all those problems so that the land often cannot be safely improved even at great expense.

Wetlands provide fish spawning grounds and wildlife habitat. The natural plant and animal communities found here provide ecological balance to a watercourse. To maintain safe and healthful conditions, to prevent water pollution, to protect fish spawning grounds and aquatic life, and to preserve shore cover and natural beauty, building development in wetlands should be limited.

12.3 Permitted Uses.
12.31 The harvesting of any wild crop such as marsh hays, ferns, mosses, wild rice, berries, tree fruits and tree seeds,
12.32 Forestry,
12.33 Utilities such as, but not restricted to, telephone, telegraph and power transmission lines,
12.34 Hunting, fishing, preservation of scenic, historic and scientific areas, wildlife preserves,
12.35 Non-residential buildings used solely in conjunction with the raising of waterfowl, minnows, and other similar lowland animals, fowl or fish,
12.36 Hiking trails and bridle paths,
12.37 Accessory uses,

12.38 Public and private parks, picnic areas, golf courses and similar uses,

12.39 Signs, subject to the restrictions of 13.35., and

12.4 Special Exceptions

The following uses upon issuance of a Special Exception Permit as provided in Section 18.4 of this ordinance and issuance of a Division of Resource Development permit, where required by Sections 30.11, 30.12, 30.19, 30.195, and 31.05, Wisconsin Statutes.

12.41 General farming provided farm animals shall be housed at least 100 feet from any non-farm residence. Farm buildings housing animals, barnyards or feedlots shall be at least one hundred (100) feet from any navigable water and shall be so located that manure will not drain into any navigable water.

12.42 Dams, power plants, flowages, ponds.

12.43 Relocation of any watercourse.

12.44 Filling, drainage or dredging of wetlands according to the provisions of Section 9.0 of this ordinance.

12.45 Removal of topsoil or peat.

12.46 Cranberry bogs.

12.47 Piers, docks, boathouses.

12.48 Solid waste disposal (See Section 4.3).

12.5 Tree-cutting Regulations

Tree-cutting regulations as set forth in section 8.0 of this ordinance shall apply.

Model Wetland Ordinance Contained in Virginia Coastal Wetland Protection Statue, (VA. CODE §62.1 - 13.1 to 62.1 - 13.20) and Adopted By At Least 28 Counties.

§ 62.1-13.5. Counties, cities and towns authorized to adopt wetlands zoning ordinance; terms of ordinance. — Any county, city or town may adopt the following ordinance:

Wetlands Zoning Ordinance

§ 1. The governing body of ...., acting pursuant to Chapter 2.1 of Title 62.1 of the Code of Virginia, for purposes of fulfilling the policy standards set forth in such chapter, adopts this ordinance regulating the use and development of wetlands.

§ 2. Definitions. — For the purposes of this ordinance:

(a) "Commission" means the Virginia Marine Resources Commission.

(b) "Commissioner" means the Commissioner of Marine Resources.

(c) "Person" means any corporation, association or partnership, one or more individuals, or any unit of government or agency thereof.

(d) "Governmental services" means any or all of the services provided by this .... to its citizens for the purpose of maintaining this .... and shall include but shall not be limited to such services as constructing, repairing and maintaining roads, sewage facilities, supplying and treating water, street lights and construction of public buildings.

(e) "Wetlands" means all that land lying between and contiguous to mean low water and an elevation above mean low water equal to the factor 1.5 times the mean tide range at the site of the proposed project in this ....; and upon which is growing on the effective date of this act or grown thereon subsequent thereto, any one or more of the following: saltmarsh cordgrass (Spartina alterniflora), saltmeadow hay (Spartina patens), saltgrass (Distichlis spicata), black needlerush (Juncus roemerianus), saltwort (Salicornia spp.), sea lavender (Limonium spp.), marsh elder (Iva frutescens), groundsel bush (Baccharis halimifolia), wax myrtle (Myrica sp.), sea oxeye (Borrichia frutescens), arrow arum (Peltandra virginica), pickerelweed (Pontederia cordata), big cordgrass (Spartina cynosuroides), rice cutgrass (Leersia oryzoides), wildrice (Zizania aquatica), bulrush (Scirpus validus), spikerush (Eleocharis sp.), sea rocket (Cakile ecentula), southern wildrice (Zizaniopsis miliacea), cattails (Typha spp.), three-squares (Scirpus spp.), buttonbush (Cephalanthus occidentalis), bald cypress (Taxodium distichum), black gum (Nyssa sylvatica), tupelo (Nyssa aquatica), dock (Rumex spp.), yellow pond lily (Nuphar spp.), marsh fleabane (Pluchea purpurascens), royal fern (Osmunda regalis), Marsh hibiscus (Hibiscus moscheutos), beggar's ticks (Bidens sp.), smartweeds (Polygonum sp.), arrowhead (Sagittaria spp.), sweet flag (Acorus calamus), water hemp (Amaranthus cannabinus), reed grass (Phragmites communis), and switch grass (Panicum virgatum).

The wetlands of Back Bay and its tributaries and the wetlands of the North Landing river and its tributaries shall mean all marshes subject to regular or occasional flooding by tides, including wind tides, provided this shall not include hurricane or tropical storm tides, and upon which one or more of the following vegetation species are growing or grows thereon subsequent to the passage of this amendment: saltwater [saltmarsh] cordgrass (Spartina alterniflora), saltmeadow hay (Spartina patens), black needlerush (Juncus reomerianus), marsh elder (Iva frutescens), groundsel bush (Baccharis halimifolia), wax myrtle (Myrica sp.), arrow arum (Peltandra virginica), pickerelweed (Pontederia cordata), big cordgrass (Spartina cynosuroides), rice cutgrass (Leersia oryzoides), wildrice (Zizania aquatica), bulrush (Scirpus validus), spikerush (Eleocharis sp.), cattails (Typha spp.), three-squares (Scirpus spp.), dock (Rumex sp.), smartweeds (Polygonum sp.), yellow pond lily (Nuphar spp.), royal fern (Osmunda regalis), marsh hibiscus (Hibiscus moscheutos), beggar's ticks (Bidens sp.), arrowhead (Sagittaria spp.), water hemp (Amaranthus cannabinus), reed grass (Phragmites communis), and switch grass (Panicum virgatum).

(f) "Wetlands board" or "board" means a board created as provided in §62.1-13.6 of the Code of Virginia.

(g) "Back Bay and its tributaries" means the following as shown on the U.S. Geological Survey Quadrangle Sheets for Virginia Beach, North Bay, and Knotts Island: Back Bay north of the Virginia-North Carolina State Line; Capsies creek north of the Virginia-North Carolina State Line; Deal creek; Devil creek; Nawney creek; Redhead Bay, Sand Bay, Snipps Bay, North Bay, and the waters connecting them; Beggars Bridge creek; Muddy creek; Ashville Bridge creek; Hells Point creek; Black Gut; and all coves, ponds and natural waterways adjacent to or connecting with the above-named bodies of water.

(h) "North Landing river and its tributaries" means the following as based on the United States Geological Survey Quadrangle Sheets for Pleasant Ridge, Creeds, and Fentres: the North Landing river from the Virginia-North Carolina Line to Virginia Highway 165 at North Landing Bridge; the Chesapeake and Albemarle canal from Virginia Highway 165 at North Landing Bridge to the locks at Great Bridge; all named and unnamed streams, creeks, and rivers flowing into the North Landing river and the Chesapeake and Albemarle canal except the following: West Neck creek north of Indian River Road; Pocaty river west of Blackwater Road; Blackwater river west of its forks located at a point approximately 6400 feet due west of the point where the Blackwater Road crosses the Blackwater river at the village of Blackwater; Millbank creek west of Blackwater Road.

§ 3. The following uses of and activities on wetlands are permitted if otherwise permitted by law:

(a) The construction and maintenance of noncommercial catwalks, piers, boathouses, boat shelters, fences, duckblinds, wildlife management shelters, footbridges, observation decks and shelters and other similar structures; provided that such structures are so constructed on pilings as to permit the reasonably unobstructed flow of the tide and preserve the natural contour of the marsh;

(b) The cultivation and harvesting of shellfish, and worms for bait;

(c) Noncommercial outdoor recreational activities, including hiking, boating, trapping, hunting, fishing, shellfishing, horseback riding, swimming, skeet and trap shooting, and shooting preserves, provided that no structure shall be constructed except as permitted in subsection (a) of this section;

(d) The cultivation and harvesting of agricultural or horticultural products; grazing and haying;

(e) Conservation, repletion and research activities of the Virginia Marine Resources Commission, the Virginia Institute of Marine Science, Commission of Game and Inland Fisheries and other related conservation agencies;

(f) The construction or maintenance of aids to navigation which are authorized by governmental authority;

(g) Emergency decrees of any duly appointed health officer of a governmental subdivision acting to protect the public health;

(h) The normal maintenance, repair or addition to presently existing roads, highways, railroad beds, or the facilities of any person, firm, corporation, utility, Federal, State, county, city or town abutting on or crossing wetlands, provided that no waterway is altered and no additional wetlands are covered;

(i) Governmental activity on wetlands owned or leased by the Commonwealth of Virginia, or a political subdivision thereof;

(j) The normal maintenance of man-made drainage ditches, provided that no additional wetlands are covered; and provided further, that this paragraph shall not be deemed to authorize construction of any drainage ditch.

§ 4.   (a)   Any person who desires to use or develop any wetland within this .... (county, city or town), other than for those activities specified in § 3 above, shall first file an application for a permit with the wetlands board and shall send copies to the Commission and the Virginia Institute of Marine Science.

(b)   An application shall include the following: the name and address of the applicant; a detailed description of the proposed activity and a map, drawn to an appropriate and uniform scale, showing the area of wetland directly affected, with the location of the proposed work thereon, indicating the area of existing and proposed fill and excavation, especially the location, width, depth and length of any proposed channel and the disposal area, all existing and proposed structures; sewage collection and treatment facilities, utility installations, roadways, and other related appurtenances or facilities, including those on adjacent uplands, and the type of equipment to be used and the means of equipment access to the activity site; the names and addresses of owners of record of adjacent land and known claimants of water rights in or adjacent to the wetland of whom the applicant has notice; and estimate of cost; the primary purpose of the project; any secondary purposes of the project, including further projects; the public benefit to be derived from the proposed project; a complete description of measures to be taken during and after the alteration to reduce detrimental offsite effects; the completion date of the proposed work, project, or structure and such additional materials and documentation as the wetlands board may deem necessary.

(c) A nonrefundable processing fee to cover the cost of processing the application, set by the applicable governing body with due regard for the services to be rendered, including the time, skill, and administrator's expense involved, shall accompany each application.

§ 5. All applications and maps and documents relating thereto shall be open for public inspection at the office of the recording officer of this .... (county, city or town).

§ 6. Not later than sixty days after receipt of such application, the wetlands board shall hold a public hearing on such application. The applicant, the local governing body, the Commissioner, the owner of record of any land adjacent to the wetlands in question, known claimants of water rights in or adjacent to the wetlands in question, the Virginia Institute of Marine Science, the Division of State Planning and Community Affairs, the Department of Game and Inland Fisheries, Water Control Board, the Department of Highways and governmental agencies expressing an interest therein shall be notified of the hearing by mail not less than twenty days prior to the date set for the hearing. The wetlands board shall also cause notice of such hearing to be published at least once a week for two weeks prior to such hearing in the newspaper having a general circulation in this .... (county, city or town). The costs of such publication shall be paid by the applicant.

§ 7. In acting on any application for a permit, the board shall grant the application upon the concurring vote of three members. The chairman of the board, or in his absence the acting chairman, may administer oaths and compel the attendance of witnesses. Any person may appear and be heard at the public hearing. Each witness at the hearing may submit a concise written statement of his testimony. The board shall make a record of the proceeding, which shall include the application, any written statements of witnesses, a summary of statements of all witnesses, the findings and decision of the board, and the rationale for the decision. The board shall make its determination within thiry days from the hearing. If the board fails to act within such time, the application shall be deemed approved. Within forty-eight hours of its determination, the board shall notify the applicant and the Commissioner of such determination and if the board has not made a determination, it shall notify the applicant and the Commission that thirty days has passed and that the application is deemed approved.

The board shall transmit a copy of the permit to the Commissioner. If the application is reviewed or appealed, then the board shall transmit the record of its hearing to the Commissioner. Upon a final determination by the Commission, the record shall be returned to the board. The record shall be open for public inspection at the office of the recording officer of this .... (county, city or town).

§ 8. The board may require a reasonable bond in an amount and with surety and conditions satisfactory to it securing to the Commonwealth compliance with the conditions and limitations set forth in the permit. The board may, after hearing as provided herein, suspend or revoke a permit if the board finds that the applicant has failed to comply with any of the conditions or limitations set forth in the permit or has exceeded the scope of the work as set forth in the application. The board after hearing may suspend a permit if the applicant fails to comply with the terms and conditions set forth in the application.

§ 9. (a) In making its decision whether to grant, to grant in modified form, or to deny an application for a permit the board shall base its decision on these factors:

(1) Such matters raised through the testimony of any person in support of or in rebuttal to the permit application.

(2) Impact of the development on the public health and welfare as expressed by the policy and standards of chapter 2.1 of Title 62.1 of the Code of Virginia and any guidelines which may have been promulgated thereunder by the Commission.

(b) If the board, in applying the standards above, finds that the anticipated public and private benefit of the proposed activity exceeds the anticipated public and private detriment and that the proposed activity would not violate or tend to violate the purposes and intent of Chapter 2.1 of Title 62.1 of the Code of Virginia and of this ordinance, the board shall grant the permit, subject to any reasonable condition or modification designed to minimize the impact of the activity on the ability of this .... (county, city or town), to provide governmental services and on the rights of any other person and to carry out the public policy set forth in Chapter 2.1 of Title 62.1 of the Code of Virginia and in this ordinance. Nothing in this section shall be construed as affecting the right of any person to seek compensation for any injury in fact incurred by him because of the proposed activity. If the board finds that the anticipated public and private benefit from the proposed activity is exceeded by the anticipated public and private detriment or that the proposed activity would violate or tend to violate the purposes and intent of Chapter 2.1 of Title 62.1 of the Code of Virginia and of this ordinance, the board shall deny the permit application with leave to the applicant to resubmit the application in modified form.

§ 10. The permit shall be in writing, signed by the chairman of the board and notarized.

§ 11. No permit shall be granted without an expiration date, and the board, in the exercise of its discretion, shall designate an expiration date for completion of such work specified in the permit from the date the board granted such permit. The board, however, may, upon proper application therefor, grant extensions.

Village Of Orono, Minnesota Ordinance No. 125

AN ORDINANCE RELATING TO MARSHES, WETLANDS AND LANDS ABUTTING MEANDERED LAKES AND WATERCOURSES: PROHIBITING DEVELOPMENT OF THOSE LANDS AND PROVIDING FOR THE ISSUANCE OF PERMITS BY AMENDING CHAPTER 31 OF THE MUNICIPAL CODE OF ORONO BY ADDING SECTIONS THERETO. THE VILLAGE COUNCIL OF THE VILLAGE OF ORONO ORDAINS AS FOLLOWS:

Section 1. Chapter 31 of the Municipal Code of the Village of Orono is amended as follows:

31.800. Statement of Policy. It is in the public interest to protect against uncoordinated and unplanned land development which affect marshes, swamps, wetlands, drainage ways, lakes and watercourses within the Village of Orono, which development, if allowed to continue, will result in loss and damage to public and private improvements through inundation by flood waters and subsequent expensive construction of storm sewers and other public projects, in the permanent destructions of these natural resources, loss of water retention facilities, open space and wildlife habitats, and impairment of public and private water supplies. The objectives of this ordinance are to permit and encourage a coordinated land and water management program and the retention of open land uses which will locate permanent structures and artificial obstructions so as not to obstruct the passage of waters nor destroy the natural public water areas, marshes and wetlands within the Village. The Village Council has in mind its statutory obligation to adopt a flood plain ordinance pursuant to Minnesota Statutes 1969, Chapter 104, the proposed regulations of the Minnetonka Conservation District, the open space policies of the Metropolitan Council and its guidelines encouraging protection of marshes, wetlands and the flood plain area, and the public interest in preventing irreparable destruction of valuable natural resources as expressed by numerous persons and organizations.

In addition to these general purposes, the specific intent of this ordinance is to:

(a) Reduce danger to health by protecting surface and groundwater supplies from the impairment which results from incompatible land uses by providing safe and sanitary drainage.

(b) Reduce the financial burdens imposed both on this community and on communities within the Minnehaha Creek Watershed District and the individuals therein by frequent floods and overflow of water on lands.

(c) Permit and encourage planned development land uses which will not impede the flow of flood water or cause danger to life or property.

(d) Permit and encourage land uses compatible with the preservation of the natural vegetation and marshes which are a principal factor in the maintenance of constant rates of water flow through the year and which sustain many species of wildlife and plant growth.

(e) Avoid fast runoff of surface waters from developed areas to prevent pollutional materials such as animal feces, motor oils, paper, sand, salt and other debris, garbage and foreign materials from being carried directly into the nearest natural stream, lake or other public waters.

(f) Encourage a suitable system of ponding areas to permit the temporary withholding of rapid water runoff which presently contributes to downstream flooding and general water pollution giving preference to areas which contribute to groundwater infiltration and recharge, thereby reducing the need for public projects to contain, store and control such runoff.

(g) Provide sufficient land area to carry abnormal flows of storm water in periods of heavy precipitation, and to prevent needless expenditures of public funds for storm sewers and flood protection devices which proper planning could have avoided.

(h) Prevent the development of structures in areas unfit for human usage by reason of danger from flooding, unsanitary conditions or other hazards.

(i) Prevent the placement of artificial obstructions which restrict the right of public passage and use of the bed, bank and water of any creeks, marshes or watercourses within the Village.

31.810. Definitions. For the purpose of this ordinance, the terms defined in this section shall have the following meanings:

(a) Obstruction means any dam, wall, wharf, embankment, levee, dike, pile, abutment, projection, excavation, bridge, conduit, pole, culvert, building, wire, fence, fill, other structure or matter in, along, across or projecting into the Flood Plain and Wetlands Conservation Area.

(b) Natural obstruction means any rock, tree, gravel or analogous natural matter that is an obstruction and has been located within the flood plain by a nonhuman cause.

(c) Artificial obstruction means any obstruction which is not a natural obstruction.

(d) Flood plain means the land area adjacent to a watercourse, drainage way or creek which has been or may be covered by flood waters.

31.820. Definition and Establishment of Protected Area. The "Flood Plain and Wetlands Conservation Area" within the Village of Orono, hereinafter referred to as the protected area, is defined and established to be the low areas and flood plain adjoining and including any watercourse or drainage way or body or water subject to periodic flooding or overflow; and those areas designated and shown as marsh, wooded marsh, submerged marsh, inundation area, intermittent lake or intermittent streams by the United States Department of the Interior, through the Geological Survey on maps and supporting data designated as Mound Quadrangle, Minnesota, (NW/4 Lake Minnetonka, (1958)) and Excelsior Quandrangle, Minnesota (NW/4 Lake Minnetonka, (1958)). Those maps are hereby made a part of this ordinance and two copies thereof shall remain on file in the office of the Village Administrator for public inspection. For purposes of defining the application of this map to any specific area, the maps, data and other available source material for this survey shall be on file in the office of the Village Administrator and shall be proof of the intended limits of the Flood Plain and Wetlands Conservation Area. Any change in the Flood Plain and Wetlands Conservation Area as may from time to time be determined to be proper shall be reflected on those maps.

31.830. Development Prohibited.
(a) Prohibition. No filling, grading, dredging, excavation or construction shall be allowed within the Flood Plain and Wetlands Conservation Area; nor on lands abutting, adjoining or affecting said area if such activity upon those adjacent areas is incompatible with the policies expressed in this ordinance and the preservation of those wetlands in their natural state; nor shall land within the protected area be used in determining minimum area requirements for building sites except as provided in Section 31.841 herein. To specifically further define the specific boundaries of the Flood Plain and Wetlands Conservation Area as described in the official maps thereof, and to ensure the policies in this ordinance are properly implemented, any persons undertaking improvements to or on any land abutting or adjacent to the protected area shall, prior to commecing the work, obtain a permit therefor from the Village of Orono. Approval may be expressly given in conjunction with other permits applied for, but no approval shall be implied from the grant of such permits nor from the necessity to apply for a permit as described herein.

(b) Variances. In extraordinary cases, variances may be granted upon application therefor, but only when the proposed use is determined to be in the public interest, and no variance shall be granted which the Council determines will or has a tendency to:

(1) Increase the height or duration of flood water in or along the Minnehaha Creek.

(2) Result in the placement of an artificial obstruction which will restrict the passage of flood water in such a manner as to increase the height of flooding, except obstructions approved by the Minnehaha Creek Watershed District in conjunction with sound flood plain management.

(3) Result in incompatible land uses or which would be detrimental to the protection of surface and ground water supplies.

(4) Increase the financial burdens imposed on the community through increasing floods and overflow of water onto land areas within this Village or onto land areas adjacent to Minnehaha Creek.

(5) Be not in keeping with land use plans and planning objectives for the Village of Orono or which will increase or cause danger to life or property.

(6) Be inconsistent with the objectives of encouraging land uses compatible with the preservation of the natural land forms, vegetation and the marshes and wetlands within the Village of Orono.

(7) Includes development of land and water areas essential to continue the temporary withholding of rapid runoff of surface water which presently contributes to downstream flooding or water pollution or for land and water areas which provide groundwater infiltration which diminishes the land area necessary to carry increased flows or storm water following periods of heavy precipitation.

(c) Supporting Data. No permit or variance shall be issued unless the applicant, in support of his application, shall submit engineering data, surveys, site plans and other information as the Village may require in order to determine the effects of such development on the affected land and water areas. The applicant shall submit four copies of the application and the information. One copy shall be sent by the Village to the secretary of the Minnehaha Creek Watershed District. The District shall file its comments and recommendations with the Village within 20 days after receipt of the information, unless additional time is authorized by the Village.

31.840. Land Development and Platting. No part of any lot within the Flood Plain and Wetlands Conservation Area shall be platted for residential occupancy or for other uses which will increase the danger to health, life, property or the public welfare. Whenever a portion of the Flood Plain and Wetlands Conservation Area is located within or adjoins a land area that is being subdivided, the subdividor shall dedicate an adequate easement over the land within the protected area and along each side of such area for the purpose of improving or protecting the area for drainage or other purposes expressed in this ordinance and other recreational uses. Public or private streets, driveways, drainage openings and culverts shall not be constructed unless the design thereof has been approved by the Village, and such structures shall be designed so as not to restrict the flow of water.

31.841. Limited Credit Allowed. When land to be developed is connected to a public sanitary sewer line and includes land within the Flood Plain and Wetlands Conservation Area, the owner or developer thereof will be credited with an amount of his land within the Flood Plain and Wetlands Conservation Area equal to but not exceeding the amount of his adjacent land which otherwise qualifies for development under these ordinances for purposes of complying with the land use density, open space, building unit to land area ratios or other similar requirements of the land development and zoning ordinances of, the Village except for requirements for recreational uses.

31.850. Special Assessments. The land area in the Flood Plain and Wetlands Conservation Area which is not to be developed and which is dedicated as an easement shall not be subject to special assessments to defray the cost of other municipal improvement projects, including but not limited to trunk sanitary sewer and water mains and storm sewer improvements.

31.860. Nuisance. Any filling, alteration, construction or artificial obstruction of the Flood Plain and Wetlands Conservation Area is declared to be and to constitute a public nuisance unless a permit to construct and maintain the obstruction has been obtained in the manner provided herein.

31.861. Removal of Artificial Obstructions. If an artificial obstruction is found after investigation by the Village, an order shall be issued to the owner, following ten days written notice and hearing thereon, for removal within a reasonable time as may be prescribed by the condition and type of artificial obstruction. If the owner shall fail to remove the artificial obstruction or if the owner cannot be found or determined, the Village shall have the power to make or cause such removal to be made, the cost of which shall be borne by the owner or specially assessed against the lands in the same manner as prescribed by law for the levy of special assessments for municipal improvements notwithstanding Section 31.850 herein. The special assessment shall be certified to the county auditor for collection in the same manner as the ad valorem real property of tax of the Village.

31.870. Effect of Permit. The granting of a permit under the provision of this ordinance shall in no way affect the owner's responsibility to obtain the approval required by any other statute, ordinance or regulation of any State agency or subdivision thereof.

31.880. Penalties. Any person who violates the provisions of this ordinance shall be guilty of a misdemenor and may be fined in such amount and be imprisoned for such time as authorized by law. Each day a violation exists shall be deemed a separate and distinct offense. The imposition of a criminal penalty shall not constitute a waiver of the right of the village of others to secure removal of obstructions by injunction or other civil legal remedy.

31.881. Separability. Every section, provision or part of this ordinance is declared separable from every other section, provision or part; and if any section, provision or part thereof shall be held invalid, it shall not affect any other section, provision or part.

Section 2. Sections 31.700, 31.705 and 31.710 of Chapter 31 of the Municipal Code of Orono are hereby amended to read:

31.700. Prohibition. It shall be unlawful for any person, firm or corporation to remove, fill, or use for fill, dredge, store or excavate rock, sand, gravel, dirt or similar material within the limits of the Village of Orono; to fill or reclaim any land by depositing such material or by grading of existing land so as to elevate or alter the existing natural grade; or to build, alter, or repair any seawall, retaining wall, to riprap or to otherwise change the grade or shore of lakeshore property without a conditional use permit issued by the Village Council. Granting of such permits is subject to other regulations and prohibitions of these ordinances, and other applicable statutes or ordinances of other governmental bodies.

31.705. Permit. An application for such permit shall be accompanied by a drawing made by a registered

137

surveyor or other competent person showing the location of the proposed excavation or storage and shall state the amount of material which is to be removed, excavated or stored, filled or graded, and such other information as the Council may require from time to time. Applications shall be filed with the Village Administrator and shall be accompanied by a fee of $10.00 payable to the Village.

31.710. Exception. The requirements of Section 31.700 are not intended to govern the normal and customary grading in the area of an existing or a newly constructed building, or the grading of the driveway serving such building. Such grading and earth moving shall be approved by the Building Inspector at the time of issuance of the Building Permit, providing that a plan showing proper drainage and protection of adjoining property has been submitted. Any unusual earth filling or removal of grading shall be referred by the Building Inspector to the Planning Commission and Village Council for action in accordance with this ordinance.

Section 3. Section 39.150 of Chapter 39 of the Municipal Code of Orono is hereby amended to read:

39.150. Flood Plain Areas and Wetlands. Areas within the Flood Plain and Wetlands Conservation Area will not be considered for subdivision purposes except in accordance with Sections 31.800 through 31.880 of this Code. Easements as required by Section 31.840 shall be granted by the subdivider.

Section 4. Review. This ordinance shall be reviewed two years from its effective date by the Council. At that time the Council shall review any development plans and studies of the Planning Commission and laws and ordinances of other governmental bodies which have reference to the policies and subject matter of this ordinance, and the Council shall consider whether amendments to the provisions of this ordinance can be made consistent with the purposes of this ordinance.

Section 5. Publication. This ordinance shall be published in the Mound-Westonka Minnetonka Sun and shall be effective upon publication.

Adopted by the Village Council of the Village of Orono on the 28th day of December, 1970, by a vote of 4 ayes and 0 nays.

APPENDIX C
DRAFT WETLAND PROTECTION ORDINANCES

INTRODUCTION

Two draft wetland protection ordinances are provided below to aid local governments in their own drafting efforts. The approaches taken in these ordinances are only two of many possible approaches and should be tailored to local needs.

The first of the two ordinances is an interim ordinance intended for the use in a community without detailed wetland maps but with severe development pressures. This ordinance may be adopted pursuant to interim zoning authority, home rule power, or special wetland regulatory authority, available in some States. It is a relatively simple ordinance which provides the following regulatory framework:

(1) Wetland areas are defined or mapped on an interim basis through use of written definition criteria, elevations, distances from streams or lakes, topographic maps, soil maps, or other available data.

(2) Limited open space uses without severe impact upon wetlands are permitted as of right; and other uses are prohibited unless permitted as variances.

(3) The local governing body is authorized to issue variances. However, the applicant must meet a variety of conditions including a showing that no practical use is possible for his entire property without a variance and that the use will have minimal impact upon the wetland.

The ordinance continues in effect for a period of up to three years unless renewed. This will permit more detailed mapping of wetlands and the adoption of a more permanent ordinance.

The second ordinance is intended for more permanent use by a community. This ordinance may be adopted pursuant to zoning enabling authority, special wetland regulatory enabling statutes, or home rule powers. It is intended for use as a free-standing ordinance or as overlay ordinance where comprehensive zoning regulations have been adopted. With the latter approach, the wetland ordinance provisions may be adopted as a separate, integrated amendment. In the alternative, ordinance provisions may be integrated into appropriate sections of a broader community zoning ordinance or floodplain zoning ordinance.

The second ordinance provides the following regulatory framework:

(1) Wetland areas are mapped at relatively large scale. However, the ordinance also provides a procedure for locating zoning boundary lines with more precision in case of boundary disputes.

(2) Limited open space uses without severe impact upon wetlands are permitted as of right; all other uses are permitted only as "special permit" uses.

(3) A special wetland regulatory board or the zoning board of adjustment is delegated power to issue special permits. Detailed criteria and procedures are provided for evaluation of permit applications. A landowner must show compliance with these criteria.

(4) The ordinance contains special provisions pertaining to existing uses, amendments, judicial review, special assessments, and other matters.

Discussion concerning the rationale for inclusion of various ordinance provisions is provided in the commentary that follows each ordinance.

DRAFT 1: EMERGENCY WETLAND PROTECTION ORDINANCE

Section 1: Findings of Fact

The wetlands of (local unit of government) are indispensable but fragile natural resources subject to flood, erosion, soil bearing capacity limitations, and other hazards. In their natural state they serve multiple functions for wildlife, pollution control, storage and passage of flood waters, aquifer recharge, erosion control, education, scientific study, open space, and recreation. Immediate threats are posed to wetland resources due to uncontrolled use of land and waters. Destruction or damage to wetlands threatens public safety and the general welfare.

It is therefore necessary for (local unit of government) to discourage further activities in wetland areas which may be located at upland sites and to insure maximum protection for wetland values.

Section 2: Lands to Which the Ordinance Applies

This ordinance shall apply to all lands within the jurisdiction of (local unit of government):

(OPTIONS: CHOOSE ONE OR MORE OF THE FOLLOWING)
—Within _____ feet horizontal distance of the mean water level of the following bodies of water: (list)

—Within _____ feet, vertical elevation of the mean water level of the following bodies of water: (list)

—Mapped as wetlands on USGS topographic maps (specific series and dates)

—Consisting of soil types designated as poorly drained, very poorly drained, alluvial, and floodplain by the Soil Conservation Service or the United States Department of Agriculture Cooperative Soils Survey on soil maps (describe series, dates)

—Mapped wetlands on _____ (specify wetland maps or other maps with wetland designations).

Section 3: Permitted and Prohibited Activities

The following activities shall be permitted as of right within designated wetland areas to the extent they are not prohibited by any other ordinance, State statute, or Federal statute or regulation and provided they do not require structures, grading, fill, dredging, or draining:

(1) Conservation of soil, water, vegetation, fish, shellfish, and wildlife;

(2) Agricultural uses such as general farming, pasture, wildcrop harvesting, haying;

(3) Outdoor recreational activities including hunting, birdwatching, hiking, boating, trapping, fishing, horseback riding, swimming, skeet and trap shooting, and shooting preserves;

(4) Commercial shellfishing and trapping;

(5) Education and scientific research, nature trails;

(6) Forestry;

(7) Wilderness areas and wildlife preservation and refuges.

In addition, the following structural uses are permitted providing they do not involve grading, fill, dredging, or draining: catwalks, piers, boathouses, boat shelters, fences, duck blinds, wildlife management shelters, footbridges, observation decks and shelters and other similar water-related structures, provided that such structures are constructed on piling so as to permit the unobstructed flow of waters and preserve the natural contour of the wetland.

All other uses and activities involving structures, grading, filling, dredging, vegetation removal, and disturbance of wetland water supply and flora and fauna are prohibited for the effective duration of this ordinance except as they may be permitted as variances.

All uses and activities that were lawful before the passage of this ordinance, but which do not conform with the provisions of the ordinance, may be continued but may not be expanded, changed, enlarged, or altered except as provided in Section 7.

Section 4: Variances

Uses and activities other than those permitted as of right in Section 3 may be authorized in special circumstances through issuance of a variance by the zoning board of adjustment if the applicant can demonstrate all of the following conditions:

(1) No practical use is possible for the entire parcel of land owned by the applicant and alternative locations outside of the wetland are not possible.

(2) The use will not threaten public safety or cause nuisances, increase flooding on other lands, impair public rights to the enjoyment of plant or animal species, or violate pollution control standards or other Federal, State, or local regulations. In addition, the use must be protected against flooding, erosion, and other hazards.

(3) The applicant's circumstances differ from those of wetland landowners as a whole;

(4) The proposed use will not, when viewed by itself and in terms of the cumulative impact of existing and reasonably anticipated future uses of a similar nature, result in: (a) substantial infilling of the wetland or other modification of natural topographic contours; (b) significant disturbance or destruction of natural flora and fauna; (c) significant increases in water turbidity due to influx of sediments or other materials; (d) substantial removal of wetland soils; (e) damaging reduction in wetland water supply; (f) damaging reduction or increases in wetland nutrients; (g) influx of toxic chemicals; and, (h) damaging thermal changes in the wetland.

(5) All other Federal, State, and local permits have been obtained (where this is appropriate).

The (local unit of government) may require data concerning each of these conditions from the applicant. A public hearing shall be held prior to a decision on the application. The (local unit of government) shall attach conditions to the variance to minimize the impact of any proposed activity.

Section 5: Penalties

Any person who commits, takes part in, or assists in any violation of any provision of this ordinance is guilty of a misdemeanor and may be fined not more than _____ dollars for each offense and subject to imprisonment not exceeding _____ months or both. Each violation of this act shall be a separate offense, and , in the case of continuing violation, each day's continuance thereof shall be deemed to be a separate and distinct offense.

The (governing body) shall have jurisdiction to enjoin a violation or threatened violation of this ordinance. All costs, fees, and expenses in connection with such action shall be assessed as damages against the violator.

In the event of a violation, the (governing body) shall have the power to order complete restoration of the wetland area involved by the person or agent responsible for the violation. If such responsible person or agent does not complete such restoration within a reasonable time following the order, the authorized local government shall have the authority to restore the affected wetlands to the prior condition wherever possible and the person or agent responsible for the original violation shall be held liable to the (local unit of government) for the cost of restoration.

Section 6: Effective Date; Duration of Ordinance

This ordinance shall be in force and take effect immediately upon its adoption. It shall continue in effect for a period of 3 years (or other period) from the date of adoption unless renewed by the (local unit of government).

COMMENTARY:
EMERGENCY WETLAND
PROTECTION ORDINANCE

Section 1: Findings of Fact

This section sets forth the justification for adoption of the emergency ordinance. If the ordinance is to apply only to a particular wetland, a community may wish to cite additional specific facts in this section such as severe flood damages or water pollution threats suffered by development in that particular wetland.

Section 2: Lands to Which the Ordinance Applies

The community is given a choice in approaches for defining or mapping wetland areas. The first two approaches--definition in terms of a horizontal distance from specified bodies of water or a vertical elevation from such bodies of water--are, of course, very approximate but may suffice on a temporary basis. Definition in terms of elevation may be satisfactory on even a long-term basis for coastal wetlands. The second two approaches--definition in terms of topographic maps and soil maps—are preferable in most instances but require more data. They have been used by a considerable number of communities for interim and permanent ordinances. The fifth approach—special wetland maps—are also widely used. See discussion of data gathering in Chapter 4.

Section 3: Permitted and Prohibited Uses

The ordinance prohibits all uses that are not permitted as of right or as variances. Permitted uses include open space uses with limited impact upon wetlands. Open space uses are not permitted as of right if they require grading, filling, dredging, or draining.

Section 4: Variances

The ordinance authorizes the zoning board of adjustment to issue variances in special conditions where no practical use is otherwise possible for the land, where the proposed use will not threaten the wetland, and other standards are met. A community might relax the requirement so long as other standards

are met if the applicant can demonstrate that in the absence of a variance, no practical use for his land is available. The ordinance may characterize such uses as "special permits" or "special exemptions", as has been done by the second ordinance, rather than as "variances". However, such an approach is likely to encourage a larger number of permit applications.

The present ordinance is, of course, very restrictive, but it is intended for use for a short period of time. Interim zoning ordinances have been upheld by courts where properly authorized and of limited duration.

The ordinance authorizes the zoning board of adjustment to issue variances because most zoning enabling acts authorize the zoning board of adjustment and no other body to issue variances. However, such a body rarely has expertise in wetland matters. Issuance of permits by a local legislative body, planning commission, conservation commission, or other group may be preferable when such an approach is authorized by statutory or constitutional home rule powers.

Section 5: Penalties

Penalties for violation of wetland ordinances typically include fines and jail sentences. However, additional provisions have been added to require violators to restore the wetland area or to authorize the local unit of government to restore the wetland and charge violators for this restoration.

DRAFT: WETLAND PROTECTION ORDINANCE

Section 1: Findings of Fact and Purpose

1.1 Findings of Fact

The wetlands of (local unit of government) are indispensable but fragile natural resources subject to flood, erosion, soil bearing capacity limitations, and other hazards. In their natural state they serve multiple functions for wildlife, pollution control, storage and passage of flood waters, aquifer recharge, erosion control, education, scientific study, open space, and recreation.

Considerable acreage of these important natural resources has been lost or impaired by draining, dredging, filling, excavating, building, pollution, and other acts inconsistent with the natural uses of such areas. Other wetlands are in jeopardy of being lost, despoiled, or impaired by such acts, contrary to the public safety and welfare.

It is therefore, the policy of (local unit of government) to protect its citizens including generations yet unborn by preventing the despoliation and destruction of wetlands while taking into account varying ecological, economic, development, recreational, and aesthetic values. Activities which may damage wetlands should be located on upland sites.

1.2 Purposes

It is the policy of (local unit of government) that wetland activities conform with all applicable building codes, sediment control regulations, and other regulations and that such activities not threaten public safety or cause nuisances:

(1) By blocking flood flows destroying flood storage areas, or destroying storm barriers, thereby resulting in increased flood heights or velocities on other lands;

(2) By increasing water pollution through location of domestic waste disposal systems in wet soils, unauthorized application of pesticides and algaecides, disposal of solid wastes at inappropriate sites, creation of unstabilized fills, or the destruction of wetland vegetation serving pollution and sediment control functions;

(3) By increasing erosion.

In addition, wetland activities should not destroy natural wetland functions:

(1) By decreasing breeding, nesting, and feeding areas for many forms of waterfowl and shore-birds including rare species;

(2) By interfering with the exchange of nutrients needed by fish and other forms of wildlife;

(3) By decreasing habitat for fish and other forms of wildlife;

(4) By decreasing recharge for groundwater aquifers;

(5) By destroying sites needed for education and scientific research as outdoor biophysical laboratories, living classrooms, and training areas;

(6) By interfering with public rights in navigable waters and the recreation opportunities of wetlands for hunting, fishing, boating, hiking, birdwatching, photography, camping, and other uses; or

(7) By destroying aesthetic and property values.

Section 2: Lands to Which This Ordinance Applies

2.1 Wetland District

This ordinance shall apply to all lands within the jurisdiction of (local unit of government) shown on the Official Zoning Map as being located within the boundaries of the Wetland District. The Official Zoning Map, together with all explanatory matter thereon and attached thereto, is hereby adopted by reference and declared to be a part of this ordinance. The Official Zoning Map shall be on file in the office of the (city clerk, town clerk, etc.)

2.2 Rules for Interpretation of District Boundaries

The boundaries of the Wetland District shall ordinarily be determined by scaling distances on the Official Zoning Map. Where interpretation is needed as to the exact location of the district boundaries due to ambiguity or discrepancy between mapped boundaries and field conditions, the Zoning Administrator shall determine the exact location through field investigation to apply the wetland definition criteria contained in the following section. The Administrator may consult with biologists, hydrologists, soil scientists, or other experts as needed in this determination. The person contesting the location of the district boundary may present his case to the Zoning Board of Adjustment and submit his own technical evidence if dissatisfied with the determination of the Zoning Administrator.

Section 3: Definitions

Words or phrases used in this ordinance shall be interpreted as defined below, and where ambiguity exists, words or phrases shall be interpreted so as to give this ordinance its most reasonable application in carrying out the regulatory goals:

"Filling" means the placing of any soil, sand, gravel, shells, structures, solid waste, or other material which raises, either temporarily or permanently, the elevation of an area.

"Regulated activity" means any dredging, draining, filling, bulkheading, polluting, mining, drilling, or excavating, or engaging in construction of any kind, or in any activity that will kill or materially damage wetland flora or fauna.

"Wetland" (Definition to be provided by the locality.)

Section 4: Permit Requirements, Penalties

4.1 Permit Requirements, Compliance

No regulated activity shall be conducted in a Wetland District without a permit from the Zoning Administrator and full compliance with the terms of this ordinance and other applicable regulations. All activities that are not permitted as of right or as Special Permit uses shall be prohibited.

4.2 Penalties

Any person who commits, takes part in, or assists in any violation of any provision of this ordinance is guilty of a misdemeanor and may be fined not more than _____ dollars for each offense and subject to imprisonment not exceeding _____ months or both. Each violation of this act shall be a separate offense, and, in the case of continuing violation, each day's continuance thereof shall be deemed to be a separate and distinct offense.

The governing body shall have jurisdiction to enjoin a violation or threatened violation of this ordinance. All costs, fees, and expenses in connection with such action shall be assessed as damages against the violator.

In the event of a violation, the shall have the power to order complete restoration of the wetland area involved by the person or agent responsible for the violation. If such responsible person or agent does not complete such restoration within a reasonable time following the order, the authorized local government shall have the authority to restore the affected wetlands to the prior condition wherever possible and the person or agent responsible for the original violation shall be held liable to the (local unit of government) for the cost of restoration.

4.3 Abrogation and Greater Restrictions

It is not intended that this ordinance repeal, abrogate, or impair any existing regulations, easements, convenants, or deed restrictions. However, where this ordinance imposes greater restrictions, the provisions of this ordinance shall prevail.

4.4 Interpretation

The provisions of this ordinance shall be held to be minimum requirements in their interpretation and application and shall be liberally construed to serve the goals of the ordinance.

Section 5: Permitted and Special Permit Uses in the Wetland District

5.1 Permitted Uses

The following uses shall be permitted as of right within the Wetland District to the extent that they are not prohibited by any other ordinance and provided they do not require structures, grading, fill, draining, or dredging except as authorized by Special Permit:

(1) Conservation of soil, water, vegetation, fish, shellfish, and wildlife;

(2) Agricultural uses such as general farming, pasture, wildcrop harvesting, haying;

(3) Outdoor recreational activities including hunting, birdwatching, hiking, boating, trapping, fishing, horseback riding, swimming, skeet and trap shooting, and shooting preserves;

(4) Commercial shellfishing and trapping;

(5) Education and scientific research, nature trails;

(6) Forestry;

(7) Wilderness areas, wildlife preservation and refuges.

In addition, the following structures are permitted providing they do not involve draining, grading, fill, or dredging: catwalks, piers, boathouses, boat shelters, fences, duck blinds, wildlife management shelters, footbridges, observation decks and shelters, and other similar water-related structures. All such structures must be constructed on pilings to permit the unobstructed flow of waters and preserve the natural contour of the wetland except as authorized by Special Permits.

5.2 Special Permit Uses

Regulated activities other than those specified in 5.1 may be permitted upon application to the (conservation commission, board of adjustment, etc.) and issuance of a Special Permit.

Section 6: Standards and Procedures for Special Permit Uses

6.1 Special Permits

No regulated activity shall be conducted without issuance of a permit from the (conservation commission, board of adjustment). Application for a Special Permit shall be made in duplicate to the Zoning Administrator on forms furnished by him. Permits shall ordinarily be valid for a period of three years from the date of issue and shall expire at the end of that time unless a longer time period is specified by the (conservation commission, board of adjustment) upon issuance of the permit. An extension of an original permit may be granted upon written request to the Administrator by the original permit holder or his legal agent at least 90 days prior to the expiration date of the original permit. The (conservation commission, board of adjustment) may require new hearings if, in his judgment, the original intent of the permit is altered or extended by the renewal, or if the applicant has failed to abide by the terms of the original permit in any way. The request for renewal of a permit shall follow the same form and procedure as the original application except that the (conservation commission, board of adjustment) shall have the option of not holding a hearing if the original intent of the permit is not altered or extended in any significant way.

6.2 Permit Applications

Unless the (conservation commission, board of adjustment) waives one or more of the following information requirements, applications for a permit shall include:

(1) A detailed site plan for the proposed activity including a map at a scale of 1 inch equals 50 feet showing the location, width, depth, and length of all existing and proposed structures, roads, sewage treatment, and installation facilities, drainage facilites, utility installations within 200 feet of the mapped wetland;

(2) The exact sites and specifications for all proposed draining, fill, grading, dredging, and vegetation removal including the amount and procedures;

(3) Elevations of the site and adjacent lands within 200 feet of the site at contour intervals of no greater than 5 feet;

(4) A general description of the vegetative

cover of the regulated area including dominant species;

(5) A description of the entire parcel of land owned by the applicant and the location of the wetland on the parcel.

The purposes of the project and an explanation why the proposed activity cannot be located at other sites including an explanation of how the proposed activity is dependent upon wetlands or water-related resources.

The (conservation commission, board of adjustment) may require additional information as needed such as study of flood, erosion, or other hazards at the site and the effect of any protective measures that might be taken to reduce such hazards; and other information deemed necessary to evaluate the proposed use in terms of the goals and standards of this act.

Upon receipt of the completed application, the (conservation commission, board of adjustment) shall notify the individuals and agencies, including federal and state agencies having jurisdiction over or an interest in the subject matter, to provide such individuals and agencies with an opportunity to raise objections.

The (conservation commission, board of adjustment) shall establish a mailing list of all interested persons and agencies who wish to be notified of such applications.

6.3 Public Hearing

No sooner than thirty days and not later than sixty days after receipt of the permit application and after notice of the application has been published by the applicant in one newspaper having general circulation in the area, the (conservation commission, board of adjustment) may hold a public hearing on the application unless the (conservation commission, board of adjustment) finds that the activity is so minor as not to affect the wetland.

All hearings shall be open to the public. A full and complete record of the hearing shall be made.

Any party may present evidence and testimony at the hearing. At the hearing, the applicant shall have the burden of demonstrating that the proposed activity will be in accord with the goals and policies of this ordinance and the standards set forth below.

6.4 Standards for Special Permits

The (conservation commission, board of adjustment) shall deny a permit if the proposed activity may threaten public health and safety, result in fraud, cause nuisances, impair public rights to the enjoyment and use of public waters, threaten a rare or endangered plant or animal species, violate pollution control standards, or violate other Federal, State, or local regulations. In determining the impact of the activity upon public health and safety, rare and endangered species, water quality and additional wetland functions listed in the purposes of this ordinance and below, the (conservation commission, board of adjustment) shall consider existing wetland destruction and the cumulative effect of reasonably anticipated future uses similar to the one proposed.

The (conservation commission, board of adjustment) shall also deny an application if it finds that the detriment to the public measured by the factors listed below that would occur on issuance of the permit outweighs the benefits. The (conservation commission, board of adjustment) shall evaluate wetland functions and the role of the wetland in the hydrologic and ecological system. In this determination it shall consider the following factors:

(1) The goals and purposes of the ordinance;

(2) The impact of the proposed activity and reasonably anticipated similar uses upon flood flows, flood storage, storm barriers, and water quality;

(3) The safety of the proposed activity from flooding, erosion, hurricane winds, soil limitations and other hazards and possible losses to the applicant and subsequent purchasers of the land;

(4) The impact of the use and existing and reasonably anticipated similar uses upon neighboring land uses and wetland functions set forth in the purpose of this ordinance including the impact of the activity upon the: (a) infilling of the wetland or other modification of natural topographic contours; (b) disturbance or destruction of natural flora and fauna; (c) influx of sediments or other materials causing increased water turbidity; (d) removal or disturbance of wetland soils; (e) reductions in wetland water supply; (f) interference with wetland water circulation; (g) damaging reduction or increases in wetland nutrients; (h) influx of toxic chemicals; (i) damaging thermal changes in the wetland water supply; (j) destruction of natural aesthetic values;

(5) The adequacy of water supply and waste disposal for the proposed use;

(6) Consistency with Federal, State, county, and local comprehensive land use plans and regulations; and

(7) Alternatives to the proposed activity and alternative sites for the activity.

Preference will be given to activities that must have a shoreline or wetland location in order to function and that will have as little impact as possible upon the wetland area. In general, permission will not be granted for dredging or ditching solely for the purpose of draining wetlands, lagooning, constructing factories, providing spoil and dump sites, and building roadways that may be located elsewhere. The regulated activity must to the extent feasible, be confined to the portion of a lot outside of a wetland. All reasonable measures must be taken to minimize impact upon the wetland.

In evaluating the proposed activity, the (conservation commission, board of adjustment) may consult with expert persons or agencies.

6.5 Acting on the Application

The (conservation commission, board of adjustment) shall act on the application within (30 days, etc.) of the public hearing, except that where additional information is required by the (conservation commission, board of adjustment) it may extend this period by (15 days, etc.). In acting on the application, the (conservation commission, board of adjustment) shall in writing deny, permit, or conditionally permit the proposed activity.

6.6 Conditions Attached to Special Permits

The (conservation commission, board of adjustment) may attach such conditions to the granting of a Special Use Permit or Variance as it deems necessary to carry out the purposes of the ordinance. Such conditions may include (but shall not be limited to):

(1) Limitations on minimum lot size for any activity;

(2) Limitation on the total portion of any lot or the portion of the wetland on the lot that may be graded, filled, or otherwise modified. This limitation may be linked to an overall protection policy for the particular wetland (e.g., no more than 5% filling for this and all future development);

(3) Requirements that structures be elevated on piles or otherwise protected against natural hazards;

(4) Modification of waste disposal and water supply facilities;

(5) Imposition of operational controls, sureties, and deed restrictions concerning future use and subdivision of lands such as flood warnings, preservation of undeveloped areas in open space use, and limitation of vegetation removal;

(6) Dedication of easements to protect wetlands;

(7) Erosion control measures;

(8) Setbacks for structures, fill, deposit of spoil and other activities from the wetlands;

(9) Modifications in project design to ensure continued water supply to the wetland and circulation of waters; and/or

(10) Replanting of wetland vegetation and construction of new wetland areas to replace damaged or destroyed areas.

The (conservation commission, board of adjustment) may suspend or revoke a permit if it finds that the applicant has not complied with the conditions or limitations set forth in the permit, or has exceeded the scope of the work set forth in the application. The (conservation commission, board of adjustment) shall cause notice of its denial, issuance, conditional issuance, revocation or suspension of a permit to be published in a daily newspaper having a broad circulation in the area wherein the wetland lies.

The (conservation commission, board of adjustment) may require a bond in an amount and with surety and conditions sufficient to secure compliance with the conditions and limitations set forth in the permit. The particular amount and the conditions of the bond shall be consistent with the purposes of this ordinance. In the event of a breach of any condition of any such bond, the (conservation commission, board of adjustment) may institute an action in (Superior Court, etc.) upon such bond and prosecute the same to judgment and execution.

Section 7: Non-conforming Activities

A regulated activity that was lawful before the passage of ordinance but which is not in conformity with the provisions of this ordinance may be continued subject to the following:

7.1 No such activity shall be expanded, changed, enlarged, or altered in a way that increases its non-conformity without a Special Permit.

7.2 No structural alteration or addition to any non-conforming structure over the life of the structure shall exceed 50 percent of its value at the time of its becoming a Non-conforming Activity unless the structure is permanently changed to a Conforming Use.

7.3 If a Non-conforming Activity is discontinued for 12 consecutive months, any resumption of the activity shall conform to this ordinance.

7.4 If any Non-conforming Use or Activity is destroyed by man's activities or an act of God, it shall not be resumed except in conformity with the provisions of this ordinance.

7.5 Activities or adjuncts thereof that are or become nuisances shall not be entitled to continue as Non-conforming Activities.

Section 8: Judicial Review

Any decision of the (conservation commission, board of adjustment) denying, approving, or conditionally approving a Special Permit shall be judicially reviewable in the (Superior Court, etc.). The applicant, his agent, adjacent landowners, any agency and any member of the public may challenge the decision of the (conservation commission, board of adjustment) as being unconstitutional or inconsistent with the goals and standards of this ordinance.

Based upon these proceedings and a decision of the court, the (conservation commission, board of adjustment) may, within the time specified by the court, elect to:

(1) Institute negotiated purchase or condemnation proceedings to acquire an easement or fee interest in applicant's land; or

(2) Approve the permit application with lesser restrictions or conditions.

Section 9: Amendments

These regulations and the official wetland map may from time to time be amended in accordance with procedures and requirements of the general statutes and as new information concerning soils, hydrology, flooding, or botanical species peculiar to wetlands become available.

Any person may submit in writing in a form prescribed by the (conservation commission, board of adjustment) a request for a change in the regulations or the boundaries of a wetland area. The request shall be considered at a public hearing held in accordance with the provisions of the general statutes not less than ninety days after receipt of the written request unless winter conditions prevent investigation of wetland areas. If winter conditions make such investigation impossible, such public hearing shall be held not later than 180 days after receipt of the written application.

Section 10: Assessment Relief

Assessors and boards of assessors shall consider wetland regulations in determining the fair market value of land. Any owner of an undeveloped wetland who has dedicated an easement or entered into a perpetual conservation restriction with (conservation commission, board of adjustment) or a nonprofit organization to permanently control some or all regulated activities in the wetland shall be assessed consistent with those restrictions. Such landowner shall also be exempted from special assessment on the controlled wetland to defray the cost of municipal improvements such as sanitary sewers, storm sewers, and water mains.

COMMENTARY:
DRAFT WETLAND PROTECTION ORDINANCE

Section 1: Statutory Authorization, Findings of Fact and Purpose

The draft ordinance sets forth detailed findings of fact and purposes to explain to the public, landowners, and the courts the rationale for regulating wetland uses. The findings of fact and purposes also aid the local wetland regulatory board in evaluating special permit uses and proposed amendments to the ordinance. It is to be noted that the findings and the purposes emphasize both natural hazards found in wetland areas and the natural values of wetlands.

Section 2: Lands to Which the Ordinance Applies

This section formally incorporates wetland zoning maps. Normally local regulations are adopted only where wetland maps are available. It provides a procedure for locating boundaries in relationship to proposed development and resolving boundary disputes. Written wetland definition criteria are to be applied through field investigations where there are possible inaccuracies in the boundary lines or where uncertainty exists as to their precise location. Some communities have adopted a written definition for wetlands based upon vegetative or other criteria and have not mapped them. This is acceptable in some circumstances (e.g., certain coastal wetlands), but it creates uncertainty as to the application of the ordinance in others.

Section 3: Definitions

Key terms used in the ordinance are defined here. "Regulated activity" is broadly defined to include virtually all activities that may damage wetlands. A community may, however, wish to adopt a more limited definition exempting certain activities. "Wetland" has not been defined in the present ordinance.

Section 4: Permit Requirements, Penalties

This section requires a permit for all regulated activities. Penalties are also provided for violation of the ordinance including fines, jail sentences, injunctions, and orders to restore the wetland. The local unit of government is authorized to restore the wetland in the event a violator fails to do so.

Section 5: Permitted and Special Permit Uses

This section permits as of right (without a permit) uses with limited impact upon wetlands. All other uses are "special permit uses."

Section 6: Standard and Procedures for Special Permit Uses

Relatively detailed criteria and procedures are established for evaluating special permit applications. A special wetland regulatory board or zoning board of adjustment is responsible for issuing special permits. A special wetland regulatory board, such as a local conservation commission, is the preferred approach and is expressly authorized in some States. Such a specialized board has more expertise than a traditional zoning board of adjustment. However, where a community adopts a wetland zoning ordinance pursuant to a traditional zoning enabling act that requires that special exceptions be issued by a zoning board of adjustment, it may be necessary to authorize this board to issue special permits, or the enabling statute may be violated.

The ordinance requires that the applicant for a special permit submit detailed data concerning the design and precise location of the proposed use. This information is essential to evaluate the impact of the use upon the wetland. The ordinance also requires that the applicant supply a portion of the natural resource data required for evaluating the impact of the proposed use. The rest of the data will be gathered by the regulatory board. The regulatory board may require submission of an environmental impact statement or other data. However, this is not required in all instances.

A public hearing must ordinarily be held on the proposed use after notice of the hearing has been published in the local newspaper, unless the local regulatory board finds that the activity is so minor as not to affect the wetland.

If a permit is granted, all reasonable measures must be taken to minimize the impact of the use upon the wetland. Conditions may be attached to a permit. A performance bond may be required to ensure compliance with conditions.

Section 7: Non-conforming Activities

The ordinance imposes minimal restrictions on lawful activities initiated prior to adoption of the ordinance. While limited control over existing uses may, in some instances, effect the ordinance, retroactive regulation often encounters strong political opposition (except for nuisance uses). In addition, control of existing uses is prohibited or restricted by more than one half of the zoning enabling acts. Although the present ordinance does not abate existing uses, it does regulate the enlargement of an existing activity, the major alteration or addition exceeding 50 percent of the value of the use, and the reestablishment of an activity after it has been discontinued or destroyed. These minimal provisions are incorporated in many zoning ordinances.

A community may wish to adopt more stringent regulations for existing uses where regulation of existing uses is authorized by the enabling authority or where nuisance uses are involved. Communities could adopt "amortization" provisions that require a Nonconforming Use to be brought into conformity after a specified period of time (e.g., ten years).

Section 8: Judicial Review

The ordinance provides a special judicial review procedure for the granting or denial of special permits. Often zoning and other land use control enabling acts specify the court to which appeals from regulations adopted under the acts must be taken. This ordinance authorizes the regulatory agency to purchase or condemn an interest in lands, based upon a decision of the court, or approve the permit application with lesser restrictions.

Section 9: Amendements

Amendments to the ordinance may be adopted under specified conditions such as mistake of fact. These standards for amendment supplement those normally contained in zoning enabling acts or other enabling statutes.

Section 10: Assessment Relief

This final section of the ordinance directs tax assessors to consider wetland regulations in determining the fair market value of land.

APPENDIX D

SAMPLE DEED RESTRICTIONS, COVENANTS AND CONSERVATION EASEMENTS

Following are samples of a deed restriction, covenants, and easements designed to protect the natural condition of land by limiting its use. Though none of the documents was specifically drafted for application to wetlands, the provisions are generally transferable. Nevertheless, certain alterations in the conditions may be desirable. For example, the documents should incorporate conditions prohibiting drainage of wetlands and should provide for construction of boardwalks rather than foot trails through marshes. The document might also specify remedies if the conditions are breached. Samples include:

(1) Deed Restriction With Reverter Clause. The first excerpt is a standard reverter clause adopted by the Governing Board of The Nature Conservancy for use when that organization transfers property to other organizations that will use the land for research purposes while protecting it.

(2) Covenants. The second set of excerpts are covenants.

(a) Covenants in Deed Conveying Property. This covenant was included in a deed conveying property from a private individual to The Nature Conservancy.

(b) Covenant Between Private Landowners and The Nature Conservancy To Preserve a River and Adjacent Land. This covenant does not contemplate transfer of property, but rather restricts use of the property by mutual agreement.

(3) Conservation Easements. The final excerpts are easements.

(a) Sample Conservation Easement. This sample easement was drawn up by The Nature Conservancy and reflects the general form that is used when individuals convey an easement to that organization.

(b) Conservation Restriction Over a Whole Parcel. This sample document is provided by a Massachusetts conservation commission to guide individuals who wish to enter into a conservation restriction agreement with a city or town.

EXCERPTS

1. Deed Restriction with Reverter Clause

Standard Reverter Clause adopted by the Governing Board
of The Nature Conservancy

This conveyance is made subject to the express condition and limitation that the premises herein conveyed shall forever be held as a nature preserve, for scientific, educational, and aesthetic purposes, and shall be kept entirely in their natural state, without any disturbance whatever of habitat or plant or animal populations, excepting the undertaking of scientific research and the maintenance of such fences and foot trails as may be appropriate to effectuate the foregoing purposes without impairing the essential natural character of the premises. Should the premises cease to be used solely as provided herein, then the estate hereby granted to the ...., its successors and assigns, shall cease and determine and shall revert to and vest in The Nature Conservancy, its successors and assigns, the said reversion and vesting to be automatic and not requiring any re-entry or other act or deed.

2. Covenants

Covenants included in the Quit-claim deeds conveying Pine Hills

1. Harley H. Hasselman to The Nature Conservancy as Trustee.

"The above described lands shall be and considered as a memorial to the memory of Frank G. Hasselman, and a suitable monument, of a design approved by the Department of Conservation, State of Indiana, shall be erected by The Nature Conservancy on said lands in a location selected by said heirs and approved by said Department;

Subject, however, to the express conditions and limitations that the lands contained in the premises herein conveyed shall be maintained in their natural state, undisturbed by hunting, trapping, organized camping, grazing of domesticated animals, timber-cutting, removal of dead, dying or fallen trees, artificial planting for reforestation or landscaping, or any other activities that might adversely affect the physical habitat or the plant or animal populations of said premises, except that primitive foot trails may be provided and that parking and related facilities for the public may be constructed within fifteen hundred (1500) feet of the existing public road bordering the west side of the premises.

Activities conducted for scientific or education purposes shall be permitted only when in accord with the limitations above set forth, and deemed proper by the Department of Conservation, State of Indiana, and approved in writing by an official of the Division of State Parks, Lands, and Waters, or its successor, of said Department.

In the event that Grantee, The Nature Conservancy, or its successors or assigns, particularly the State of Indiana, should violate any of the foregoing covenants, the right to enforce said covenants or to enjoin the violation of the same shall vest in the Grantors, their heirs, assigns, and successors, and particularly The Nature Conservancy after said tract is conveyed to the State of Indiana, by the remedy of mandatory injunction or by appropriate action at law."

2. The Nature Conservancy as Trustee to the State of Indiana

"The above described lands shall be and considered as a memorial to the memory of Frank G. Hasselman, and his heirs shall have the right to erect a suitable monument, at their expense and of a design approved by the Department of Conservation, State of Indiana, on said lands in a location selected by said heirs and approved by said Department.

This deed is executed to the Grantee by the Grantor as trustee in full satisfaction of trusts created in deeds of..., and this conveyance is made subject to the covenants, restrictions and conditions in said deeds contained."

Restrictive agreement between private land owners and
The Nature Conservancy to provide for the preservation of
the Bantam River in Litchfield, Connecticut

"This Agreement..., by and between (list of owners)..., and The Nature Conservancy,...Witnesseth

Whereas, the parties hereto are owners of land adjacent to and abutting upon the Bantam River in said Town of Litchfield; and

Whereas, the banks of the Bantam River and the land adjacent thereto in the area where the properties of the parties hereto are situated are of rare natural beauty and their terrain, vegetation, and wildlife have not yet been spoiled by the activities of mankind; and

Whereas, the parties hereto are mindful of the dwindling number of regions where nature has been allowed to develop her own plan, uninfluenced and undisturbed by the activities of mankind; and

Whereas, the parties hereto are desirous of conserving this area, as nearly as may be practicable, in its present state in order to preserve its natural beauty for both this and future generations; and

Whereas, other owners of land adjacent to and abutting upon the Bantam River have entered, or it is contemplated that they will enter, into agreement with The Nature Conservancy containing covenants in whole or in part identical with or similar to those contained herein;

Now, Therefore, the parties hereto for and in consideration of the mutual covenants herein set forth, each on behalf of himself, his heirs, executors, administrators, successors, and assigns agree with the others and with their respective heirs, executors, administrators, successors, and assigns that the following shall be covenants running with so much of the land described beneath their respective names in the appendix attached hereto and hereby made a part hereof as lines within two hundred (200) feet of the nearer bank of said Bantam River bounding said property (or if said property is on both sides of said river, then within two hundred (200) feet of each of said banks), and that the same shall be enforceable by the parties hereto and each of them and by their respective heirs, executors, administrators, successors, and assigns, and any of them and by any other owners (and by the successors in title of such owners) of land adjacent to and abutting upon the Bantam River who have heretofore entered or hereafter may enter into covenants in whole or in part identical with or similar to those hereinafter contained.

No sewage, industrial waste, or other objectionable, or offensive material shall be dumped or discharged into said river upon, over, or from such land, insofar as the owner thereof can control the same nor shall said area be used for leaching or for any sewage disposal field;

No billboards or other outdoor advertising signs shall be erected thereon;

No topsoil shall be removed therefrom;

No commercial lumbering operations shall be conducted thereon;

No sand, gravel, or other minerals shall be excavated therefrom;

No pigpens, slaughterhouses, or other structures for the conduct of activities that would be considered a nuisance if conducted in a residential area shall be erected thereon;

No trees shall be cut thereon unless dead, diseased, or decayed or for the better landscaping of the area;

No buildings of any description shall be erected thereon;

There shall be no dumping of refuse, nor burning of refuse thereon;

There shall be no hunting or trapping thereon;

There shall be no stripping of the land in such a way as to promote erosion thereof."

3. Conservation Easements

a. Sample Conservation Easement

THIS INDENTURE, made this _____ day of _____, 198__

WITNESSETH:

WHEREAS, _____ of _____ hereinafter called the Grantor, is the owner in fee simple of certain real property, hereinafter called the "Protected Property," which has aesthetic, scientific, educational and ecological value in its present state as a natural area which has not been subject to development or exploitation, which property is described as follows:

[Legal description of the land]

WHEREAS, [insert name of conservation organization or public body], hereinafter called Grantee, is a [nonprofit corporation incorporated under the laws of _____] or [public body] whose purpose is to [preserve and conserve natural areas for aesthetic, scientific, charitable and educational purposes]; and

WHEREAS, the Grantor and Grantee recognize the natural scenic, aesthetic and special character of the region in which the Protected Property is located, and have the common purpose of conserving the natural values of the Protected Property by the conveyance to the Grantee of a Conservation Easement on, over and across the Protected Property, which shall conserve the natural values of the Protected Property, conserve and protect the animal and plant populations, and prevent the use or development of the property for any purpose or in any manner which would conflict with the maintenance of the Protected Property in its natural, scenic and open condition for both this generation and future generations; and

WHEREAS, "aesthetic, scientific, educational and ecological value," "natural, scenic and open condition" and "natural values" as used herein shall, without limiting the generality of the terms, mean the condition of the Protected Property at the time of this grant, evidenced by reports, photographs, maps and scientific documentation possessed (at present or in the future) by the Grantee which the Grantee shall make available on any reasonable request to the Grantor, his heirs and assigns;

NOW THEREFORE, the Grantor, for and in consideration of the facts above recited and of the mutual covenants, terms, conditions and restrictions herein contained and as an absolute and unconditional gift does hereby give, grant, bargain, sell and convey unto the Grantee, its successors and assigns, forever a Conservation Easement in perpetuity over the Protected Property consisting of the following:

1. The right of view of the Protected Property in its natural, scenic, and open condition;
2. The right of the Grantee, in a reasonable manner and at reasonable times, to enforce by proceedings at law or in equity the covenants hereinafter set forth, including but not limited to, the right to require the restoration of the Protected Property to the condition at the time of this grant. The Grantee, or its successors or assigns, does not waive or forfeit the right to take action as may be necessary to ensure compliance with the covenants and purposes of this grant by any prior failure to act;
3. The right to enter the Protected Property at all reasonable times for the purpose of inspecting the Protected Property to determine if the Grantor, or his heirs or assigns, is complying with the covenants and purposes of this grant; and further to observe and study nature and to make scientific and educational observations and studies in such a manner as will not disturb the quiet enjoyment of the Protected Property by the Grantor, his heirs and assigns.

And in furtherance of the foregoing affirmative rights, the Grantor makes the following covenants, on behalf of himself, his heirs and assigns, which covenants shall run with and bind the Protected Property in perpuity:

Covenants:[*] Without prior express written consent from the Grantee, on the Protected Property:
1. There shall be no construction or placing of buildings, camping accommodations or mobile homes, fences, signs, billboards or other advertising material, or other structures;

---

[*] Note: These clauses may be changed to meet specific variations and situations such as easements over farm lands where continued agricultural use or grazing is permitted; provision may also be made as appropriate for replacing existing buildings, maintaining access, or limited hunting. This sample is of a "Forever Wild" conservation easement.

2. There shall be no filling, excavating, dredging, mining or drilling, removal of topsoil, sand, gravel, rock, minerals or other materials nor any building of roads or change in the topography of the land in any manner excepting the maintenance of foot trails;

3. There shall be no removal, destruction or cutting of trees or plants (except as is necessary to construct and maintain foot trails), planting of trees or plants, spraying with biocides, grazing of domestic animals or disturbance or change in the natural habitat in any manner;

4. There shall be no dumping of ashes, trash, garbage, or other unsightly or offensive material, and no changing of the topography through the placing of soil or other substance or material such as land fill or dredging spoils;

5. There shall be no manipulation or alteration of natural water courses, lake shores, marshes or other water bodies or activities or uses detrimental to water purity;

6. There shall be no operation of snowmobiles, dune-buggies, motorcycles, all-terrain vehicles or any other types of motorized vehicles;

7. There shall be no hunting or trapping except to the extent specifically approved by the Grantee as necessary to keep the animal population within the numbers consistent with the ecological balance of the area.

The Grantor, his heirs and assigns, agree to pay any real estate taxes or assessments levied by competent authorities on the Protected Property and to relieve the Grantee from responsibility for maintaining the Protected Property.

The Grantor agrees that the terms, conditions, restrictions, and purposes of this grant will be inserted by him in any subsequent deed, or other legal instrument, by which the Grantor divests himself of either the fee simple title to or his possessory interest in the Protected Property.

TO HAVE AND TO HOLD the said Conservation Easement unto the said Grantee, its successors and assigns forever.

Except as expressly limited herein, the Grantor reserves for himself, his heirs and assigns, all rights as owner of the Protected Property, including the right to use the property for all purposes not inconsistent with this grant.

The covenants agreed to and the terms, conditions, restrictions, and purposes imposed with this grant shall not only be binding upon the Grantor but also his agents, personal representatives, heirs and assigns, and all other successors to him in interest and shall continue as a servitude running in perpetuity with the Protected Property.

IN WITNESS WHEREOF the Grantor has set his hand the day and year first above written.

_____
(Add acknowledgment form used in
the State where the land is
located.)

b. Conservation Restriction Over a Whole Parcel

We, John Doe and Mary Doe, husband and wife of _____, County of _____, Massachusetts, grant (without covenants - if a gift) (for $_____ consideration paid and with quitclaim covenants - if a purchase) to said town/city, a conservation restriction on a parcel of land located in said town/city, bounded and described as follows:
(description, plan, and title reference, if any)

The terms of the conservation restriction are as follows: that neither we nor our successors or assigns will perform the following acts nor permit others to perform them, hereby granting to the town/city the right to enforce these restrictions against all persons:

1. No building, sign, outdoor advertising display, fence, mobile home, utility pole or other temporary or permanent structure will be constructed, placed or permitted to remain on said parcel. (Optional: except for the following existing structures:..... and except as provided in paragraph five.)

2. No soil, loam, peat, gravel, sand, rock, or other mineral substance, refuse, trash, vehicle bodies or parts, rubbish, debris, junk, waste or unsightly or offensive material will be placed, stored or dumped thereon.

3. No loam, peat, gravel, sand, rock, or other mineral resource or natural deposit shall be excavated or removed from said parcel in such a manner as to affect the surface thereof. (Optional: except as may be provided in paragraph five.)

4. No trees, grasses, or other vegetation shall be cut or otherwise destroyed. (Optional: except as may be provided in paragraph five.)

5. (Optional) notwithstanding anything contained in paragraphs one through four, we reserve to ourselves, our successors and assigns the right to conduct or permit the following activities on said parcel:

a. the cultivation and harvesting of crops, flowers, hay, and shellfish; the planting of trees and shrubs and the mowing of grass; the grazing of livestock; and the construction and maintenance of fences necessary in connection therewith;

b. the cultivation and harvesting of forest products in accordance with recognized forestry conservation practices, including the construction of fire roads, provided that all slash is removed from public view;

c. the construction and maintenance of a small duck blind;

d. the installation of underground utilities;

e. ....

The foregoing restriction is authorized by G. L. Ch. 184, Sec. 31-33, and is intended to retain said parcel predominantly in its natural, scenic and open condition, in agricultural, farming, or forest use (choose appropriate) in order to protect the natural and watershed resources of said town/city. The restriction shall be administered by the conservation commission of said town/city, established under G. L. Ch. 40, Sec. 8C.

The conservation restriction hereby conveyed does not grant either the town/city or the public any right to enter said parcel except as follows:

1. We grant to the town/city a permanent easement of access to enter said parcel, by its conservation commission, for the purpose of inspecting the premises and enforcing the foregoing restrictions and remedying any violation thereof. The right hereby granted shall be in addition to any other remedies available to the town/city for the enforcement of the foregoing restrictions. (Required by G. L. Ch. 184, Sec. 32.)

2. We grant to the town/city a permanent easement to enter said parcel by its conservation commission or its designees to plant or selectively cut or prune trees, brush or other vegetation to improve the scenic view and to implement disease prevention measures. (Optional)

3. We grant to the town/city and its inhabitants an easement to pass and repass upon said parcel on foot for purposes of fishing, hiking, winter sports or nature study, and to permit the town/city through its conservation commission to clear and mark trails for said purposes. (Optional) (No documentary stamps are needed for this instrument, if a gift).

In witness thereof we have hereto set our hands and seals this _____ day of _____, 198___

              John Doe
              Mary Doe

COMMONWEALTH OF MASSACHUSETTS

County of _____ ss

Then personally appeared the above-named John Doe and Mary Doe and acknowledge the foregoing to be their free act and deed, before me.

_____ My commission expires _____

CITY COUNCIL
APPROVAL BY SELECTMEN (if a gift)

We, the undersigned Board of Selectmen (City Council) of the town/city of _____, hereby certify that we approve the receipt of the foregoing deed under G. L. Ch. 40, Sec. 8C as it has been and may be amended as requested by vote of the conservation commission of the town/city of _____ for the protection of the natural and watershed resources of the town/city.

_____
_____
_____

APPROVAL BY THE COMMISSIONER
(required for either purchase or gift)

The Commissioner of the Department of Natural Resources, Commonwealth of Massachusetts, hereby certifies that he approves receipt of the within conservation restriction under G. L. Ch. 184, Sec. 32.

_____
              Commissioner
              Department of Natural Resources

APPENDIX E

ENDANGERED ANIMAL SPECIES DEPENDENT

Note: The following chart lists only representative examples of endangered species dependent on wetlands
in the United States. The chart is not intended as a comprehensive list of endangered species that are
wetlands-dependent; nor does it give the total range of each species listed.

Common Name	Scientific Name	Description	Kind of Wetland On Which Species Is Dependent	Degree of Dependence On Wetlands	Location of Wetlands
MAMMALS					
Salt Marsh Harvest Mouse	Reithrodontomys raviventris	Unusually dark-colored harvest mouse	West coast coastal marshes	Exclusively dependent on wetlands	California
Red Wolf	Canis rufus	Relatively small, dark wolf	Occasionally found in eastern coastal marshes	Not necessarily ever found in wetlands, but present populations sometimes use wetlands for shelter or subsistence	Louisiana, Texas
Florida Panther	Felis concolor coryi	Large, long-tailed cat	Mainly found in inland floodplain wetlands, and sometimes in mangrove swamps and eastern coastal marshes.	Not necessarily ever found in wetlands, but present populations are concentrated there	Florida, possibly other southeastern states
Florida Manatee	Trichechus manatus latirostris	Large aquatic mammal with forelimbs modified as flippers	Often found in mangrove swamps, eastern coastal marshes, and inland floodplains	Dependent on wetlands for subsistence	Florida, Georgia, possibly other coastal states
Columbian White-tailed Deer	Odocoileus virginianus leucurus	Medium-sized deer with small antlers and a long tail	Bottomland forest and meadows	Almost exclusively dependent on wetlands	Washington, Oregon
Key Deer	Odocoileus virginianus clavium	Small deer with small antlers	Sometimes found in mangroves	Sometimes utilizes wetlands	Florida
REPTILES					
American Alligator	Alligator mississippiensis	Huge, roughbacked, lizard-like quadruped	Mangroves, eastern coastal marshes, and inland floodplains	Almost exclusively dependent on wetlands	Texas, Oklahoma, Arkansas, Louisiana, Mississippi, Alabama, Georgia, Florida, South Carolina, North Carolina
American Crocodile	Crocodylus acutus	Huge, roughbacked, lizard-like quadruped	Mangroves and eastern coastal marshes	Largely dependent on wetlands	Florida
San Francisco Garter Snake	Thamnophilis sirtalis tetrataenia	Small snake with yellow, black, and red stripes	West coast coastal marshes	Largely dependent on wetlands	California
AMPHIBIAN					
Santa Cruz Long-toed Salamander	Ambystoma macrodactylum croceum	Long-toed, black and orange salamander	Ponds and nearby lands	Exclusively dependent on wetlands for breeding	California
BIRDS					
Hawaiian Duck	Anas wyvilliana	Small duck, streaked brown and buff	Lagoons, mountain streams, marshes and ponds		Kauai, Hawaii
Laysan Duck	Anas laysanensis	Small, dull brownish duck	Oceanic island with saltwater pond		Laysan Island, Hawaii
Mexican Duck	Anas diazi	Large dabbling duck resembling the black duck, but lighter colored	Inland marshes		Southeastern Arizona, southern New Mexico and central western Texas
Aleutian Canada goose	Branta canadensis leucopareia	Very small goose with dark brown and gray plumage and broad white band at base of neck; pointed bill	Mostly inland California marshes and wetlands		California
Southern bald eagle	Haliaeetus l. leucocephalus	Large, hawk-like bird with dark brown plumage except for pure white tail and head when adult	Inland lakes, reservoirs, large rivers, estuaries	Nesting in estuarine areas	Atlantic and Gulf coasts, from New Jersey to Texas and lower Mississippi Valley southward from eastern Arkansas and western Tennessee and through southern west to California and Baja California
Florida Everglade kite	Rosthrhamus sociabilis plumbeus	Like marsh hawk, adult is predominantly slate grey with black head and wing tip and patches of white on tail; female streaked with dark lines on buffy body and white tail patch	Fresh water shallow marshes	Eats snails found in marshes; nests in marshes	Southern and central Florida
American peregrine falcon	Falco peregrinus anatum	Medium-sized hawk with long, pointed wings and long tail	Estuaries, marshes, oceanic beaches		Western U.S. along Pacific coast, central Arizona to eastern front of Rocky Mountains. (Formerly also in eastern U.S.)

Common Name	Scientific Name	Description	Kind of Wetland On Which Species Is Dependent	Degree of Dependence On Wetlands	Location of Wetlands
Arctic peregrine falcon	Falco peregrinus tundrius	Like American peregrine falcon, but smaller and paler	Estuaries, marshes, oceanic beaches		Migrates in U.S. through eastern and middle North America to Gulf coast of U.S.
Hawaiian coot	Fulica americana alai	Dark slate-grey duck-like bird	Mostly fresh water marshes and ponds		Hawaii
Hawaiian gallinule	Gallinula chloropus sandvicensis	Grayish marsh bird with red-tipped legs and red bill with yellow tip	Mostly fresh water marshes and ponds	Exclusively	Hawaii
California clapper rail	Rallus longirostris obsoletus	Predominantly gray-brown bird with long legs	Brackish marshes		California, especially in San Francisco Bay and Moss Landing and sometimes along coast of central western California at Tomales Bay, Humboldt Bay, Bolings Bay, and Morro Bay
Yuma clapper rail	Rallus longirostris yumanensis	Like small hen, but with long bill and longish legs, short tail	Fresh water marshes	Breeding	Lower Colorado River
Light-footed rail	Rallus longirostris levipes	Similar to California clapper rail, but with smaller legs, feet and bill	Tidal salicernia marshes; formerly all salt marshes from Santa Barbara County, California, to the Mexican border		Santa Barbara County, California, to Mexican border
Mississippi sandhill crane	Grus canadensis pulla	Long legs, neck and bill with dark plumage	Semi-open and wet pine savannah		Jackson County, Mississippi Formerly in Louisiana, Alabama, and more extensively in Mississippi
Whooping Crane	Grus americana	Very large, long-legged, long-necked bird, almost all white with a few black patches	Marshes and estuaries		Texas, Oklahoma, Nebraska, Kansas, North Dakota, South Dakota, Montana
Eskimo curlew	Numenius borealis	Medium-sized brown and black shore bird	Estuaries, tundra		Texas coast
Hawaiian stilt	Himantopus himantopus knudseni	Shore bird with black and white plumage and very long red legs	Estuaries, shallow ponds		Hawaii
California least tern	Sterna albifrons browni	Small white tern with yellow bill	Estuaries		South San Francisco Bay, California to southern Baja, California
Cape Sable sparrow	Ammospiza mirabilis	Dull-colored, olive-gray sparrow	Fresh water and brackish marshes; cordgrass marshes		Southwestern Florida
Dusky seaside sparrow	Ammospiza nigrescens	Dark-colored, sparrow-size bird	Grassy coastal salt marshes		Merritt Island, Florida and on mainland Florida from east side of upper St. Johns River west of Titusville south to Sharpe
Bachman's warbler	Vermivora bachmanii	Very small bird with fine bill and mostly olive green and yellow plumage	Hardwood-cypress swamps		Observed near Lawton, Virginia; Charleston, South Carolina; and in three localities in Alabama. Formerly found in southeastern Missouri, northeastern Arkansas, western Kentucky, central Alabama, and South Carolina
FISHES					
*Threatened, but not on Endangered list				Primary: Fish spawn in shallow areas; young feed on grass in shallows	
				Secondary: Fish feed on invertebrates that in turn feed on detritus produced in wetlands	
Sturgeon, Shortnose	Acipenser brevirostrum	Small, wide-mouthed fish, seldom longer than 3 feet	Found near mouths of rivers in salt and fresh water	Secondary	Florida to Maine
Cisco, Longjaw	Coregonus alpenae	Pale colored, medium-sized fish with relatively short fins		Secondary	Lakes Michigan, Huron &Erie
*Trout, Arizona (Apache)	Salmo apache	Spots on dorsal and anal fins, relatively narrow body and sizeable pectoral, pelvic and dorsal fins	Mountain streams	Probably primary--young may feed in shallows	Arizona
Trout, Gila	Salmo gilae	Fine, profuse spotting on dorsal and anal fins, golden yellow	Mountain streams	Probably primary--young and adult may move into shallows to feed	New Mexico

Common Name	Scientific Name	Description	Kind of Wetland On Which Species Is Dependent	Degree of Dependence On Wetlands	Location of Wetlands
Trout, Greenback cutthroat	Salmo clarki stomias	Small (rarely over one pound) and predominantly green with red throat	Streams and beaver ponds	Primary--feed on insects associated with wetlands grass	Colorado
*Trout, Lahontan cutthroat	Salmo clarki henshawi	Sport fish reaching 12-15 pounds	Mountain streams and lakes	Primary--young feed in shallows	California, Nevada
*Trout, Paiute cutthroat	Salmo clarki seleniris	Highly colored, usually with orange-red dash on dentary, few spots	Mountain streams and lakes	Primary--young feed in shallows	California
Bony tail, Pahranagat	Gila robusta jordani		Desert streams	Secondary	Nevada
Chub, Mohave	Gila mohavensis	Lacustrine-type chub with 18-29 gill rakers	Desert springs and lakes	Primary--wetlands provide food and protection	California
Cui-ui	Chasmistes cujus	Large, heavy-bodied sucker, usually 6 pounds	Pyramid Lake	Primary--obtains food and protection in shallows	Pyramid Lake, Nevada
Dace, Kendall Warm Springs	Rhinichthys osculus thermalis	Two to 3 inches long; males are purple and females green when breeding	Spring marsh area	Primary--obtains food and protection in shallows	Wyoming
Dace, Moapa	Moapa coriacea	Small, deeply embedded scales in leathery-textured skin and a prominent black spot at caudel base	Desert springs and streams	Primary--obtains food and protection in shallows	Nevada
Woundfin	Plagopherus argentissimus	Lacks scales; has flattened head and belly; bright silvery	Desert streams	Secondary at best	Utah
Madtom, Scioto	Noturus trautman	Small catfish	Creek	Secondary at best	Big Darby Creek, Ohio
Gambusia, Big Bend	Gambusia gaigei	Tiny fish with orange and yellow colors	Desert springs, streams or pools	Primary--Use plants in wetlands for protection and feed on insects that feed on wetland vegetation	Big Bend National Park, Texas
Gambusia, Clear Creek	Gambusia leterochis		Texas creek	Primary--Use plants in wetlands for protection and feed on insects that feed on wetland vegetation	Headwaters of Clear Creek in Menard County, Texas
Gambusia, Pecos	Gambusia nobilis		Springs and spring-fed ditches	Primary--Use plants in wetlands for protection and feed on insects that feed on wetlands vegetation	Near Toyahvale and Fort Stockton, Texas
Killifish, Pahrump	Empetrichythys latos		Spring-fed pool	Primary--Use plants in wetlands for protection and feed on insects that feed on wetlands vegetation	Manse Ranch, Pahrump Valley, Nevada
Pupfish, Comanche Springs	Cyprinodon elegans	Slender bodied fish	Irrigation ditches of Phantom Lake Spring	Primary--Use plants in wetlands for protection and feed on insects that feed on wetlands vegetation	Near Toyahvale, Texas
Pupfish, Owens River	Cyprinodon radiosus	Pupfish with dorsal fin far forward, first dorsal ray thickened	Small pond and slough	Primary--Use plants in wetlands for protection and feed on insects that feed on wetlands vegetation	Fish Slough, Owens Valley, California; and small pond north of Big Pine, Owens Valley, California
Pupfish, Tecopa	Cyprinodon nevadensis calidae	Pupfish with large scales	Reservoir and creek	Primary--Use plants in wetlands for protection and feed on insects that feed on wetlands vegetation	South of Shoshone, Inyo County, California
Pupfish, Warm Springs	Cyprinodon nevadensis pectoralis	Pupfish with about 7 pectoral fin rays	Desert springs	Primary--Use plants in wetlands for protection and feed on insects that feed on wetlands vegetation	School Springs and Scruggs Springs in Ash Meadows, Nye County, Nevada
Topminnow, Gila	Poeciliopsis occidentalis		Desert springs	Primary--Use plants in wetlands for protection and feed on insects that feed on wetlands vegetation	Santa Cruz County and San Carlos Indian Reservation, Arizona
Stickelback, unarmored three-spine	Gasterosterus aculeatus williamsoni	Rounded pectoral and caudal fins, weak dorsal spines		Primary--In addition to feeding and seeking protection in wetlands, it builds its nests out of aquatic vegetation	
*Darter, Bayou	Etheostoma Rubrum	Diminutive--maximum length of 46mm; moderately sharp snout and streamlined body; red spots on sides	Streams, shallow gravel shoals	Secondary at best	Mississippi River drainage, Mississippi River and its major tributary, White Oak Creek
Darter, Fountain	Etheostoma fonticola	Small dark darter, usually with only one anal spine	Springs	Primary--derives protection from wetlands and probably feeds on local insects feeding on wetlands vegetation	Comal and San Marcos Springs and their outflows in Hays and Comal Counties, Texas
Darter, Maryland	Etheostoma sellare	One to 2 inches long, reddish-brown with a black spot behind the eye	Springs, shallow shoal area	Secondary at best	Swan Creek near Havre de Grace, Maryland

Common Name	Scientific Name	Description	Kind of Wetland On Which Species Is Dependent	Degree of Dependence On Wetlands	Location of Wetlands
Darter, Okaloosa	Etheostoma okaloosa	Small, medium to dark brown darter lacking breeding tubercles	Several streams	Primary--associated with wetlands vegetation for protection or food	Small streams originating on Elgin Air Force Base and emptying into north-west corner of Chocta-whatchee Bay, Okaloosa County, Florida
Darter, Watercress	Etheostoma nuchale	Small (no more than 2 inches), robust species; breeding males have red-orange and blue fins and red-orange on lower part of body	Springs	Primary--uses watercress for food and protection	Glen Spring at Bessemer, Jefferson County, Alabama
Pike, Blue	Stizostedion vitreum glaucum	Bluish-gray body and whitish-blue pelvic fins	Great Lakes	Secondary at best--sometimes strays into shoals	Lakes Erie and Ontario
Darter, Snail	Percinia tanasi	Bottom dwelling fish 2 to 3 inches long	Big rivers and streams	Secondary at best--reproduces and feeds in shoal areas	Tennessee River system
MUSSELS					
Birdwing pearly mussel	Conradilla caelata			All mussels are dependent on wetlands for nutrients	Powell and Clinch Rivers in Virginia and Tennessee, Duck River in Tennessee
Dromedary pearly mussel	Dromus dromas			Same	Powell and Clinch Rivers in Virginia and Tennessee
Curtis' pearly mussel	Epioblasma (-Dysnomia) florentina curtisi			Same	Black River in Missouri
Yellow-blossom pearly mussel	Epioblasma (-Dysnomia) florentina florentina			Same	Duck River in Tennessee
Sampson's pearly mussel	Epioblasma (-Dysnomia) sampsoni			Same	Wabash River in Indiana and Illinois
White cat's paw pearly mussel	Epioblasma (-Dysnomia) sulcata delicata (including perobliqua)			Same	Detroit River in Michigan and the St. Joseph River in Ohio, Michigan and Indiana
Green-blossom pearly mussel	Epioblasma (-Dysnomia) torulosa gubernaculum			Same	Clinch River in Virginia and Tennessee
Tuberculed-blossom pearly mussel	Epioblasma (-Dysnomia) torulosa torulosa			Same	Lower Ohio River in Kentucky and Illinois, Nolichucky River in Tennessee and Kanawha River in West Virginia
Turgid-blossom pearly mussel	Epioblasma (-Dysnomia) turgidula			Same	Duck River in Tennessee
Fine-rayed pigtoe pearly mussel	Fusconaia cuneolus			Same	Clinch River in Virginia and Tennessee, Powell River in Virginia and Tennessee, and Paint Rock River in northern Alabama
Shiny pigtoe pearly mussel	Fusconaia edgariana			Same	Powell River in Virginia and Tennessee, Clinch River in Virginia and Tennessee, Paint Rock River in Alabama, and Holston River in Virginia
Higgins' eye pearly mussel	Lampsilis higginsi			Same	Mississippi River in Minnesota, Wisconsin and Illinois; Meramec River in Missouri, St. Croix River in Wisconsin and Minnesota
Pink mucket pearly mussel	Lampsilis orbiculata orbiculata			Same	Green River, Kentucky; Kanawha River in West Virginia; Tennessee River (Tenn. and Ala.); Muskingum River, Ohio
Alabama lamp pearly mussel	Lampsilis virescens			Same	Paint Rock River system in Alabama
White warty-back pearly mussel	Plethobasis cicatricosus			Same	Tennessee River, Tennessee and Alabama
Orange-footed pimpleback	Plethobasis cooperianus			Same	Tennessee River, Tennessee and Alabama, Duck River, Tennessee
Rough pigtoe pearly mussel	Pleurobema plenum			Same	Tennessee River, Tennessee; Green River, Kentucky; Clinch River, Virginia and Tennessee
Fat pocketbook pearly mussel	Potamilus (-Proptera) capax			Same	White River, Arkansas, St. Francis River (Ark. and Mo.)

Common Name	Scientific Name	Description	Kind of Wetland On Which Species Is Dependent	Degree of Dependence On Wetlands	Location of Wetlands
Cumberland monkey-face pearly mussel	Quadrula intermedia			Same	Powell and Clinch Rivers (Va. and Tenn.), Duck River, Tennessee
Appalachian monkey-face pearly mussel	Quadrula sparsa			Same	Powell and Clinch Rivers, (Va. and Tenn.)
Pale lilliput pearly mussel	Toxolasma (-Carunculina) cylindrella			Same	Duck River, Tennessee, Paint Rock River, Alabama
Cumberland bean pearly mussel	Villosa (-Micromya) trabilis			Same	Cumberland and Rockcastle Rivers, Kentucky
INSECTS					
Butterfly, Lotis blue	Lycaeides argyrognomon lotis	Females are brown with orange band on wings; males have deep violet blue color; three-fourths inch wingspan	Coastal peat and sphognum bogs and freshwater fens 1 to 1½ miles from coast	Exclusively dependent for habitat	California

GLOSSARY

Alluvium, Alluvial Soil: Soil composed primarily of eroded material such as sand, silt, or clay, that has been deposited on land or on the bottom of water bodies by rivers and streams overflowing their banks.

Aquifer: A body or rack or soil that contains sufficient saturated permeable material to conduct groundwater and to yield economically significant quantities of groundwater to wells and springs.

Aquatic Plant: An organism adapted to or requiring a wetland habitat to complete all or part of its life cycle.

Barrier Island: A detached portion of a barrier bar, usually formed through wave deposits, lying offshore, and usually parallel to the shore whose crest rises above high water.

Beach: The shore zone of a lake, river or the ocean washed by waves.

Biennial: A plant with a life cycle requiring two growing seasons before completion of flowering and fruiting.

Biochemical Oxygen Demand (BOD): The demand for dissolved oxygen needed for decomposition of organic matter in water. If the amount of oxygen dissolved in water is high and the organic matter present is low, the BOD is low, and vice versa.

Bog: A term commonly applied to forested wetlands formed in deep, steep-sided lakes with small watershed areas and poor drainage. High acidity is typical. Decomposition rates are characteristically slow, resulting in extensive deposits of peat. Floating mats of Sphagnum moss, sedge, and heath shrubs such as leatherleaf and cranberry are common along with black spruce, northern white cedar, Atlantic white cedar, or larch.

Bottomland: Flat-lying areas often with high groundwater conditions adjacent to rivers and some lakes. These areas are often floodplain deposits, outwash plains, or glacial lake deposits.

Brackish: A mixture of fresh and saltwater typically found in estuarine areas but also characteristic of some inland lakes and wetlands subject to high rates of evaporation and sluggish drainage.

Breakwater: A structure, usually constructed of rock or concrete to protect a shore area, harbor, anchorage, or basin from waves.

Bulkhead: A structure or partition, usually running parallel to the shoreline of a river, stream, or lake to protect adjacent lands from erosion due to current or wave action and to protect channels from upland sedimentation.

Calcareous: A substrate containing a high concentration of calcium salts.

Competition: Conflict between individuals or populations that are attempting to make use of a common resource.

Deciduous: A descriptive term for woody plants that shed their green leaves or needles during the cold or dry season.

Detritus: Partially decomposed organic material forming the basis for a complex and important food web in many wetland ecosystems.

Dike: A wall or mound built around a low-lying area to prevent flooding. Sometimes called a berm.

Ditch: A long, narrow, man-made channel to expedite natural drainage.

Drainage Basin or Watershed: The area within which all surface water runoff will normally gather in a single tributary, stream, river, conduit or other water course. This area is determined by topography that forms drainage divides between watersheds.

Ecology: The study of interrelationships between plants and animals and their environment.

Ecosystem: The system of interrelationships within and between a biological community and its physical environment.

Emergent: An erect, rooted herbaceous hydrophyte that may be temporarily or permanently flooded at the base but is nearly always exposed at the upper portion.

Enabling Statute: A statute delegating power to local units of government or a State agency to adopt and administer ordinances and administrative regulations or issue special permits for development consistent with more general goals and procedures set out in the statute. It "enables" the local unit or agency to adopt more specific regulations.

Endangered: Nearing extinction; existence of the organism and its environment are in immediate jeopardy; distribution is usually restricted to highly specific habitats.

Energy Cycle: The pathway of energy flow from photosynthesis in green plants, through various herbivores and carnivores and eventually to decomposition and loss as heat.

Ephemeral: Short-lived or temporary, as in ephemeral pool.

Estuary: The mouth of a river entering the sea where the current of the river meets the tide and where salt and fresh waters mix.

Eutrophication: An increase in concentration of nutrients in rivers, estuaries, and other bodies of water. This increase may be due to natural causes, man's influence, or a combination of both.

Evergreen: A descriptive term for woody plants that retain their green leaves or needles throughout the year.

Extinct: No longer known to exist after repeated search of localities where the organism(s) once existed or could be expected to exist.

Floodplain: An area adjacent to a lake, stream, ocean or other body of water lying outside of the ordinary banks of the water body and periodically inundated by flood flows.

Flyways: Routes followed by migrating birds. In North America, ornithologists distinguish between the Atlantic, Mississippi, Central, and Pacific flyways.

Food chain: The means by which energy and material are transferred from a producer (a green plant) to one herbivore and to one or more carnivores. A typical example of a food chain is a green plant, plant-eating insect, and insect-eating bird.

Food web: Complex food chain relationships. Food chain relationships are characteristically complex and more accurately described as food webs since few animals are dependent upon a single source of food.

161

Glacial Drift: Sediment accumulated as a result of glaciation, under a glacier, at its margins or beyond, as glaciofluvial and glacial marine deposits.

Glacial Till: A "boulder clay" — an unsorted and unstratified sediment deposited directly by a glacier in moraines or drumlins and not reworked by meltwater.

Groin: A shore protection structure built (usually perpendicular to the shoreline (to trap sand and other material moving along the shoreline and thus retard erosion of the shore.

Groundwater: Water that penetrates the earth's surface from precipitation and from infiltration by streams, ponds, and lakes.

Habitat: The range of environmental factors at a particular location supporting specific plant and animal communities.

Hammock: Mature broad-leaved evergreen forest typical of parts of Florida.

Herbaceous: Plant material characterized by the absence of wood.

Humus: A soil with a high concentration of organic matter.

Hydrologic Cycle: The cycle of the movement of water from the atmosphere by precipitation to the earth, and its return to the atmosphere by interception or evaporation.

Hydrophyte: Any plant growing in a soil that is at least periodically deficient in oxygen as a result of excessive water content.

Imperiled: Status of an organism as endangered or threatened.

Jetty: On open seacoasts, a structure extending into a body of water designed to prevent shoaling of a channel by sand or other materials. Usually placed alongside channels at entrances.

Kettle-hole Lakes: Lakes formed in depressions left by the melting of large blocks of glacial ice which remained after a glacier receded.

Land Use Regulation: Statutes, rules, ordinances, or guidelines with the force of law controlling the type, mode, design or other aspect of a use of land. Land use regulations are local legislative acts ("ordinances") or State legislative acts ("statutes"). However, they also include formally adopted orders and rules of administrative agencies ("administrative rules and regulations").

Marsh: A common term applied to describe treeless wetlands characterized by shallow water and abundant emergent, floating, and submergent wetland flora. Typically found in shallow basins, on lake margins, along low gradient rivers, and in low energy tidal areas. Waters may be fresh, brackish, or saline.

Meadow: A low, level, moist wetland composed of mostly grasses and sedges.

Mean High Water: The average height of high waters over a defined period.

Mesophyte: Any plant growing where moisture and aeration conditions lie well within both extremes.

Monoculture: The existence of many individuals of one plant or animal species without other species interspersed as under natural conditions, e.g., corn field or a white-pine plantation.

Mudflat: Bare, flat bottoms of lakes, rivers, and ponds, largely filled with organic deposits, freshly exposed by a lowering of the water level.

Ordinance: Locally adopted regulation.

Organic Soil: A "histosol" as defined by the U.S. Soil Conservation Service. In general, a soil is a histosol either if more than 50% of the upper 80 cm of soil is organic material or if organic material of any thickness rests on rock or on fragmented material having interstices filled with organic materials.

Peat: Organic soil which has undergone very little decomposition so that plant remains can be identified.

Perennial: Living for more than two growing seasons or years.

Permeability: The property of soil or rock to transmit water or air.

Pool: A very small body of water, usually naturally occurring.

Predator: An animal that attacks and eats other animals.

Resolution (Data): The observable or represented detail on a map, aerial photo or other data or information product. Resolution depends upon the minimum distance between features, the contrast between features, the data product (aerial photograph vs. a map), and the specificity of characteristics observable or represented by those features.

Rill: A rivulet or small stream.

Riprap: A bulkhead, groin, or other material or structure constructed of selected rock or concrete and placed so as to dissipate wave energy (bulkhead) or collect sand (groin) along a shoreline.

River: A broad, deep inland body of water with a steady, directional current.

Sandy: Substrate composed mostly of sand, very friable, well aerated, and rapidly drained.

Savannah: Wet grassland with scattered trees typical along the Atlantic coastal states.

Scale: (map) The relationship between a measurable distance on a map, aerial photo or other data or information product and the corresponding distance on the earth. Scale is expressed as an equivalence such as 1 inch = 1 mile or as a numerical fraction or ratio (1:24,000 or 1:64,000). Larger scale data or information products are those with features represented at a size corresponding more closely to their actual size than the same features represented on smaller scale data or products. Small-scale maps or products are those with ratios of 1:125,000 to 1:500,000, intermediate scale includes ratios of 1:50,000 to 1:125,000, and large-scale includes ratios of 1:2000 to 1:50,000. Data or products at very large scales are generally referred to as "very detailed" or at "very large scale." These scales appear to be rarely practical for regional or statewide mapping but are essential for local efforts.

Sedge: A grasslike plant in appearance, of the family cyperaceae, often with a triangular base.

Seep: Forested wetland with standing water derived from an underground source.

Shrub: A woody plant that at maturity is less than 6 m (20 feet) tall, usually exhibiting several erect, spreading, or prostrate stems and a generally bushy appearance.

Slough: Small body of stagnant water, or a small marshy or swampy tract of land.

162

Special Permit Uses: Uses neither prohibited nor permitted as of right by regulations but instead permitted only upon issuance of a special permit by a regulatory board or agency after fact-finding to determine the particular natural values and hazards at a site, the impact of the specific proposed use, and the compliance of the use with general or special standards contained in the regulations. The regulatory board or agency often exercises considerable discretion in evaluating the proposed use in light of general regulatory goals and standards and may attach conditions to permit to minimize impact upon critical areas.

Spoil: The material removed from a channel bottom or other body of water during a dredging operation.

Statute: A legislative act adopted by Congress or a State legislature.

Stream: A narrow, shallow body of water with a steady, directional current.

Submergent: An herbaceous or non-vascular hydrophyte, either rooted or nonrooted, which lies entirely beneath the water surface, except for flowering parts in some species.

Submersed: Totally within water.

Substrate: The bottom surface on which plants grow; ground.

Swamp: A forested wetland with a shallow water table.

Threatened: Nearing or endangered status; existence of organism and its environment in potential jeopardy; distribution of the organism is local in a few areas.

Tree: A woody plant which at maturity is 6 m (20 ft.) or more in height, usually with a single trunk, unbranched for at least several feet above the ground, and having a more or less definite crown.

Turbidity: The cloudy condition of a body of water that contains suspended material, such as clay or silt particles, dead organisms, or small living plants or animals.

Watershed: The region drained by or contributing water to a stream, lake, or other body of water.

Water Table: The upper surface of the free groundwater in a zone of saturation except when separated by an underlying of groundwater by unsaturated material.

Wetland: Land where an excess of water is the dominant factor determining the nature of soil development and the types of plant and animal communities living at the soil surface. It spans a continuum of environments where terrestrial and aquatic systems intergrade.

Xerophyte: Any plant growing in a habitat in which an appreciable portion of the rooting medium dries to the wilting point.

BIBLIOGRAPHY

American Littoral Society. Protecting Wetlands: What You Should Know. American Littoral Society, Highlands, New Jersey. A brief booklet on wetland biology, values, losses and protection programs.

Bedford, B., E. Zimmerman, and J. Zimmerman, 1974. Wetlands of Dane County, Wisconsin. Dane County Regional Planning Commission. 581 pp. A comprehensive survey of the wetlands of a particular locality. Of broader interest because of a rating system, diagrams, and narrative describing values and threats. Introductory material contains discussion of wetland hydrology and ecology.

Bellrose, F. C., 1976. Ducks, Geese, and Swans of North America. Stackpole Books, Harrisburg, Pa. Classic work on waterfowl.

Brenneman, R. L., 1976. Local Regulation of "Inland Wetlands" in Connecticut: a Prototype "Management Program" under the Coastal Zone Management Act of 1972. Coastal Area Management Program, Department of Environmental Protection, State of Connecticut. 76 pp. + Appendices. Survey and evaluation of fifteen local wetland programs in Connecticut. Programs are evaluated as models for the Coastal Zone Management Program. Good discussion.

Brinson, M., et. al., 1981. Riparian Ecosystems: The Ecology and Status. U.S. Fish and Wildlife Service, Kearneysville, West Virginia. This report describes the functions, values and management of riverine floodplain and streambank ecosystems. Chapters address inventories and losses nationwide; functions and values; and institutional and methodological considerations.

Council on Environmental Quality, 1979. Our Wetland Heritage. U.S. Government Printing Office, Washington, D.C. This excellent and profusely illustrated report discusses wetland values and threats to wetlands.

Cowardin, L.M., V. Carter, F.C. Golet, and E.T. LaRoe, 1979. Classification of Wetlands and Deepwater Habitats of the United States. USDI. Fish and Wildlife Service Publication. FWS/OBS-79/31, 103 pp. Washington, D.C. This excellent guidebook describes wetland types and sets forth the new wetland classification system which is used as the basis of the National Wetland Inventory.

Darnell, R. M., 1976. Impacts of Construction Activities in Wetlands of the U.S. U.S. Environmental Protection Agency, Office of Research and Development, Corvallis Environmental Research Laboratory, Corvallis, Oregon. EPA-600/3-76-045. Available from NTIS. 393 pp. Most comprehensive work available considering the impact of various types of construction upon wetlands. Good discussion of ecological concepts as they relate to aquatic systems. Extensive bibliography covering wetland ecology and environmental impacts.

Fassett, N.C., 1959. A Manual of Aquatic Plants. McGraw-Hill Book Co. New York, N.Y. 382 pp. Excellent guide to submergent, floating leaved, and emergent wetland flora. Well illustrated with key.

Flood Loss Reduction Associates, 1981. Floodplain Management Handbook. Prepared for the U.S. Water Resources Council. This handbook provides step-by-step guidance for development of a local floodplain management program including protection techniques. U.S. Government Printing Office. Washington, D.C. WR18745467.

Gates, A., 1975. Seasons of the Salt Marsh. Murray Printing Co. 128 pp. Interesting narrative illustrated with drawings describing the changes in salt marsh flora and fauna with change in season. Discusses current threats to coastal ecosystems.

Good, R. E., D. F. Whighans and R. L. Simpson, editors. 1979. Freshwater Wetlands: Ecological Processes and Management Potential. Academic Press, New York, N.Y., 363 pages. This book contains the proceedings of a conference. It includes 19 papers by prominent scientists evaluating leading wetland types including bogs, sedge wetlands, riverine marshes, prairie marshes, lakeshore marshes, and freshwater tidal wetlands. Common topics covered are primary productivity, decomposition and nutrient dynamics of the various wetland types.

Goodwin, R. H., and W. A. Niering, 1971. Inland Wetlands of the United States Evaluated as Potential Registered Natural Landmarks. U.S. Dept. of Interior. National Park Service. Contract No. 14-10-9-900-114. 550 pp. State by state survey of wetlands which may warrant protection as registered natural landmarks. Includes maps, discussion of existing and potential threats to wetlands, and references to publications.

Gosselink, J. G., E. P. Odum, and R. M. Pope, 1973. The Value of the Tidal Marsh. Center for Wetland Resources, Louisiana State University. Evaluation of natural tidal marshes in monetary terms based upon by-product production, aquaculture, waste treatment, and life-support as a function of energy flow. Income capitalized social values are found to be $50,000 to $80,000 per acre.

Greeson, H., J. Clark and J. Clark, editors, 1978. Wetland Functions and Values: The State of Our Understanding. Proceedings of the National Symposium on Wetlands, Lake Buena Vista, Florida, November 7-10, 1978. American Water Resources Association. Minneapolis, Minnesota. 670 pp. A compendium of papers covering the full spectrum of wetlands-related issues including wetlands conservation and science, management and evaluation of wetlands, wetland food chains, wetland habitat, wetland hydrology, wetland water quality, wetland heritage and wetland harvest.

Helfgott, T., M. W. Lefor, and W. C. Kennard, editors, 1973. Proceedings: First Wetlands Conference, June 20, 1973. Institute of Water Resources.

University of Connecticut. 199 pp. Good symposium discussing subjects such as wetland geology, hydrology, soils, water chemistry, floristic and faunistic biology, and management implications and recommendations.

Hoose, P., 1981. Building An Ark: Tools for Preservation of Natural Diversity Through Land Protection. Island Press. Box 38, Star Route 1, Cevelo, California. This report discusses 14 options to land purchase now being used in programs to protect ecological diversity. Much of the book's insight comes from the author's work at the Nature Conservancy and its State Natural Heritage Programs.

Hunt, C. B., 1972. Geology of Soils: Their Evolution, Classification, and Uses. W. H. Freeman, San Francisco. 344 pp. Discusses soils in terms of geologic history, structure, and engineering qualities. Describes relationships of vegetative cover to soil type, groundwater, and climate. Good discussion of "histosols" — wetland soils.

Johnson, P. L., 1969. Wetland Preservation. Open Space Institute, New York, N.Y. 33 pp. Somewhat dated but good discussion of wetland function and values with cost/benefit considerations. Brief history of wetland losses and contemporary methods for regulation and preservation. Model ordinance included.

Johnson, R. and J. McCormack, 1979. Strategies for Protection and Management of Floodplain Wetlands and Other Riparian Ecosystems. Proceedings of a symposium held December 11-13, 1978. Callaway Gardens, Georgia. U.S. Dept. of Agriculture, Forest Service. Washington, D.C.

Klein, S., 1980. Select State Inland Wetland Protection Laws: A Review of State Programs and Their Natural Resource Data Requirements. National Conference of State Legislatures. Washington, D.C. This report briefly summarizes state wetland regulation laws in the states and profiles in more detail the laws in nine selected states.

Kusler, J., 1979. Strengthening State Wetland Regulations. The U.S. Fish and Wildlife Service. Washington, D.C. A description and analysis of state wetland programs with recommendations for improvement and a model statute.

Kusler, J., 1980. Regulating Sensitive Lands. Ballinger, Cambridge, MA. Extensive discussion of state sensitive land programs including guidelines for implementing such programs.

Kusler, J. and J. Montanari, editors, 1979. Proceedings of the National Wetland Protection Symposium. U.S. Fish and Wildlife Service, Office of Biological Services. Washington, D.C. Discussion of wetland values and hazards, protection approaches, and federal, state and local programs.

Kusler, J., and T. M. Lee, 1972. Regulations for Flood Plains. American Society of Planning Officials. Chicago, Illinois. 60 pp. Step-by-step approach to flood plain zoning. Many tables and illustrations. Model ordinances included.

Ladd, E., M. Post, and P. Swatek, 1975. Wetlands and

The Water Cycle. Massachusetts Audubon Society, Lincoln, MA. 22 pp. Concise, well-written, illustrated booklet describing the hydrology of wetlands in the Northeast.

Larson, J. S., editor, 1973. A Guide to Important Characteristics and Values of Freshwater Wetlands in the Northeast. Water Resources Research Center. Publ. No. 31, Univ. of Mass. 35 pp. Good discussion of important values including groundwater, visual-cultural values, wildlife, flood control, and water supply economics. Includes wetlands and surficial geology maps of Massachusetts.

Larson, J. S., editor, 1976. Models for Assessment of Freshwater Wetlands. Water Research Center, Univ. of Mass. Publ. No. 32, 91 pp. Four submodels (wildlife, visual-cultural, groundwater, and economics) are described for assessment of wetlands within a single, three-phase elimination model for relative and economic evaluation of freshwater wetlands. Intended for use by local, regional, and state officials.

Lavine, D., C. Dauchy, D. McCluskey, L. Perty, and S. W. Richards, 1974. Evaluation of Inland Wetland and Water Course Functions: The Connecticut Inland Wetlands Project, Middletown, Conn. 166 pp. Good discussion of wetland functions including physical, biological, and cultural. Contains resource information for Connecticut wetland programs but is of broader interest.

Leopold, L., 1974. Water: a Primer. W. H. Freeman and Company, San Francisco, Calif. Excellent paperback on basic hydrology. Topics discussed include groundwater, stream dynamics, and status of water resources in the U.S.

Magee, D.W., 1981. Freshwater Wetlands. University of Massachusetts Press. Amherst, MA. This manual describes 182 species of indicator wetland plants including the vast majority of genera encountered in freshwater wetlands in the northeast.

Nature Conservancy, 1975. The Preservation of Natural Diversity: A Survey and Recommendations. U.S. Dept. of the Interior. 212 pp. + app. Excellent discussion of the importance of maintaining both species and habitat diversity for ecosystem health. Documents current state and federal regulations which in some way address the issue and makes recommendations for more effective programs.

Niering, W. A., 1966. The Life of the Marsh. McGraw-Hill Book Co., New York. 232 pp. Profusely illustrated and simply written text describing the diversity of wetland types and wetland flora and fauna found in the U.S.

Odum, E. P., 1971. Fundamentals of Ecology. W. B. Saunders Co., Philadelphia. 544 pp. Widely used college ecology text with a wealth of information concerning wetland ecosystems.

Pomeroy and R.G. Wiegert, 1981. Ecology of a Salt Marsh. Springer-Verlag New York, Inc. Secaucus, New Jersey. This book synthesizes 20 years of multidisciplinary study of coastal marsh of Sapelo Island, Georgia to provide a holistic view of the entire salt marsh ecosystem.

Prescott, G. W., 1969. How to Know the Aquatic

Plants. Wm. C. Brown Co., Dubuque, Iowa. 171 pp. Good field guide with well-illustrated dichotomus key to wetland flora.

Ralph M. Field Associates, Inc, 1981. State and Local Acquisition of Floodplains and Wetlands. Prepared for the U.S. Water Resources Council. Washington, D.C. This excellent guidebook addresses approaches for acquiring floodplains and wetlands and sources of technical and financial assistance. It includes 10 case studies of wetland programs from around the nation.

Reid, G. K., 1967. Pond Life, a Guide to Common Plants and Animals of North American Ponds and Lakes. Western Publishing Company, Inc. Racine, Wisconsin. 160 pp. Well illustrated pocket field guide to common wetland plants and animals.

Richardson, J., editor, 1981. Pocosin Wetlands: An Integrated Analysis of Coastal Plain Freshwater Bays in North Carolina. Hutchinson Ross Publishing Company. Stroudsburg, Penn. This contains the proceedings of a conference on pocosins addressing resource ecology, industrial and non-industrial values, resource economies and policy and law.

Richardson, B., editor, 1981. Selected Proceedings of the Midwest Conference on Wetland Values and Management. June 17-19, 1981, Freshwater Society, Navarre, Minnesota. Excellent proceedings; addresses wetland values, hydrology and water quality, wastewater treatment, impacts of wetland losses and perturbations; evaluation methodologies and economies; local protection programs, state and federal protection programs and legal issues. Most papers address wetlands of the midwest although a few consider national issues and research from other states.

Sather, H. J., editor, 1976. Proceedings of the National Wetland Classification and Inventory Workshop, July 20-23, 1975. U.S. Fish and Wildlife Service, Washington, D.C. 248 pp. + addendum. Papers discuss wetland classification needs and existing classification efforts. Interim Wetland Classification System and explanatory material contained in addendum.

Segrest, R. T., and Associates, 1975. Handbook: Building in the Coastal Environment. Resource Planning Section. Office of Planning and Research. Georgia Dept. of Natural Resources. Atlanta, Ga. 119 pp. Description of the coastal ecosystem and resources with illustrated examples of both proper and destructive development practices and their effect on the coastal environment.

Shaw, P. S. and C. G. Fredine, 1956. Wetlands of the United States. Fish and Wildlife Service, Cir. No. 39. Washington, D.C. 67 pp. Classic report discussing the status and distribution of the wetlands of the United States as determined by the 1956 survey by the Fish and Wildlife Service. Uses the wetland classification system developed by Martin et. al. which recognized twenty basic wetland classes. Waterfowl values and wetland losses are considered.

Silberhorn, G. M., G. M. Dawes, and T. Bernard Jr., 1974. Coastal Wetlands of Virginia: Interim Report No. 3. Virginia Institute of Marine Science. Gloucester Pt., VA. 52 pp. Good, brief discussion of Virginia coastal wetlands. Guidelines for the evaluation of wetlands by type. Twelve community types are recognized and described. Management decision criteria are presented for specific uses. Material also contained in: "Wetland Guidelines" issued by the Marine Resources Commission, 2401 West Ave., Newport News, VA.

Tabachnik, J., 1980. The Protection of Inland Wetlands. The Association of New Jersey Environmental Commissions. Mendham, New Jersey. 97 pages. This useful guidebook was prepared for New Jersey communities although it draws from experience of other states. It contains a model ordinance derived in part from draft Our National Wetland Heritage: A Protection Guidebook.

Teal, J. and M. Teal, 1969. Life and Death of the Salt Marsh. Audubon Ballantine Books, New York. 274 pp. Well written history of an Atlantic coast salt marsh from the time of the last glaciation to its eventual destruction by contemporary man. Includes chapters on the ecology of the salt marsh.

Thompson, B. B., 1970. Preserving Our Freshwater Wetlands. Bull. Conn. Arb. 17. 52 pp. Concise discussion by various authors concerning wetland values and preservation techniques. Includes model ordinance.

Thurow, C., W. Toner and D. Erley, 1975. Performance Controls for Sensitive Lands. American Society of Planning Officials. Report No. 307, 308. 156 pp. Considers techniques used by local governments for the protection and regulation of streams and creeks, aquifers, wetlands, woodlands, and hillsides. Cites existing performance standards and ordinances.

U.S. Department of Agriculture, Forest Service, Rocky Mountain Forest and Range Experiment Station, 1979. Mitigation Symposium: A Natural Workshop of Mitigating Loss of Fish and Wildlife Habitats. July 16-20, 1979, Colorado State Univ., Fort Collins, Colorado. U.S. Government Printing Office. Washington, D.C.

United States Water Resources Council, 1971. Regulation of Flood Hazard Areas to Reduce Flood Losses. Vols. 1 & 2. Washington, D.C. 967 pp. Extensive discussion of floodplain regulations. Includes draft statutes and model zoning and subdivision control ordinances for both coastal and inland areas. Analysis of existing legislation, constitutional issues.

Weller, M., 1981. Freshwater Marshes: Ecology and Wildlife Management. University of Minnesota Press. A description of the components of prairie potholes and other freshwater wetlands in terms of their physical structure and biota with extensive discussion of management considerations and strategies.

Wharton, G. W., 1970. The Southern River Swamp - A Multiple Use Environment. School of Business Administration. Georgia State Univ. 48 pp. Good ecological and economic analysis of the southern river swamp. Educational, recreational, water quality, water quantity, and productivity values are discussed along with threats to swamp.

ABOUT THE AUTHOR

Jon A. Kusler, an independent lawyer/lecturer and writer in environmental law, has specialized in legal-scientific issues in the management of water resources for 17 years. In addition to his law degree, he has a master's degree in water resources management and an interdisciplinary Ph.D. in water and land use planning. He has served on the staffs of the University of Wisconsin, University of Massachusetts and Harvard and has direct experience with wetland and floodplain management at all levels of government. He spent four years in Washington as an Institute Fellow at the Environmental Law Institute and has served as a consultant to the U.S. Water Resources Council, EPA, the U.S. Fish and Wildlife Service, and the Federal Emergency Management Agency. He assisted state agencies in Wisconsin, Minnesota, Maryland, Maine, Illinois and most recently, Alaska, in formulating wetland and floodplain programs. Most recently, he conducted training institutes on wetland and floodplain legal issues with the American Bar Association.

Among his many publications are <u>Strengthening State Wetland Regulations</u>, U.S. Fish and Wildlife Service, <u>Proceedings, First National Wetland Symposium</u>, U.S. Fish and Wildlife Service; <u>Vols. 1,2,3, Regulation of Flood Hazard Areas</u>, The U.S. Water Resources Council; <u>Emerging Issues in Wetland and Floodplain Management</u>, The U.S. Water Resources Council; <u>Innovations in Local Floodplain Management</u>, University of Colorado; and <u>Regulating Floodplains</u>, American Society of Planning Officials.

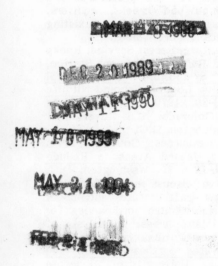